THE CHILD CASES

The Child Cases

HOW AMERICA'S
RELIGIOUS EXEMPTION LAWS
HARM CHILDREN

Alan Rogers

University of Massachusetts Press
Amherst & Boston

ISBN 978-1-62534-072-6 (paper); 071-9 (hardcover)

Designed by Jack Harrison
Set in Adobe Minion Pro
Printed and bound by the Maple-Vail Book Manufacturing Group

Library of Congress Cataloging-in-Publication Data
Rogers, Alan, 1936– author.
The child cases : how America's religious exemption laws harm children / Alan Rogers.
    pages cm
Includes bibliographical references and index.
ISBN 978-1-62534-072-6 (pbk. : alk. paper) — ISBN 978-1-62534-071-9 (hardcover : alk. paper)
1. Child abuse—Law and legislation—United States—Cases. 2. Corporations, Religious—
Law and legislation—United States—Cases. 3. Parent and child (Law)—United States—Cases.
4. Religious institutions—United States—Cases. 5. Children—Legal status, laws, etc.—
United States—Cases. 6. Freedom of religion—United States—Case. I. Title.
KF9323.R64 2014
342.7308'52131—dc23
                        2013050948

British Library Cataloguing-in-Publication Data
A catalogue record for this book is available from the British Library.

For Lisa and Nora

Contents

Acknowledgments

My interest in this project began several months after I completed a book about the death penalty and was on the lookout for the "happier" project I had promised my family. With apologies to my wife and daughter, my foray eventually led me to questions about the intersection of law and religion. Specifically, I became interested in exploring the legal and political consequences of religious parents' reliance solely on prayer when their child fell seriously ill and ultimately died.

I'm glad to have the opportunity to thank in print those people who have helped me bring this book to fruition. I am very grateful to Dean David Quigley of the College of Arts and Sciences at Boston College, who generously funded my conference travel as well as providing me with stipends for four wonderful, enthusiastic, and unbelievably hardworking undergraduate research fellows. At an early stage of my research Rachel Shapiro located and arranged interviews with several of the principal subjects in this story. Rachel Craft, aka the human dynamo, tracked down court cases, law review articles, and missing attorney's files and kept track of every single detail as this project unfolded. Mike Keating watched videos of the Massachusetts legislature in action, and Grace West helped me follow this story all the way to the defeat of the Religious Freedom Restoration Act.

I wish to sincerely thank Ken Casanova, an unpaid lobbyist for Children's Healthcare Is a Legal Duty, who shared with me his knowledge of Massachusetts politics and very generously allowed me to copy his files, an indispensable source for tracking the repeal of Massachusetts's religious exemption statute. I also would like to acknowledge Attorney John A. Kiernan for sharing his insights into David and Ginger Twitchell's trial.

Two scholars read and commented on draft versions of two chapters of this book. I am grateful to Lynne Curry for her constructive comments on a paper I delivered at a conference titled "Constitutional Rights" at San Francisco State University in the fall of 2009 and to Randall J. Stephens and the scholars who regularly attend the Boston Religious History Seminar for their insights into Christian Science and American religion. I owe a deep debt of scholarly gratitude to the anonymous readers who read this manuscript. They read carefully, saved me from errors, and made invaluable suggestions about how to clarify the themes that run through this book. I am entirely responsible for any errors of fact or interpretation.

I thank my colleagues in the History Department at Boston College for their continued interest in this work, especially James Cronin and James O'Toole for their friendship and for cleverly diverting our lunchtime conversation away from my research and toward other topics.

I also would like to thank the students who enrolled in my course "Church and State." They asked incisive questions, and Jim O'Toole, with whom I taught the course, showed me how best to answer them.

In their usual efficient and gracious way Clark Dougan, Senior Editor, and Carol Betsch, Managing Editor, at University of Massachusetts Press saw this book through to completion. Thank you.

Finally, and most important, I am deeply appreciative of my wife, Lisa, and our daughter, Nora, for their patience, support, editing and technological skills, and, above all, their love.

THE CHILD CASES

Introduction

DURING THE LAST TWO DECADES of the twentieth century news media across the United States reported the deaths of seven children and the resultant prosecution of their parents, who belonged to the Church of Christ, Scientist. The parents believed their "enlarged understanding of God," which Christian Science prayer made possible, would heal their children without medical intervention. Charged with violating state child abuse and manslaughter laws for recklessly and willfully withholding medical care from their seriously ill children, the parents claimed their actions were protected generally by the First Amendment's free exercise clause and specifically by religious exemption provisions written into state child abuse and neglect statutes. Prosecutors, on the other hand, argued that the free exercise clause protected belief but the state could regulate harmful religious behavior. Specifically, the state contended that it had a compelling interest in safeguarding the welfare of children and that religious accommodation statutes amended to child abuse laws did not extend to manslaughter.[1]

The 1980s and 1990s were not the first time Christian Science practitioners and parents stood trial for a child's death. In the early twentieth century, at a time when the church experienced meteoric growth, the historian Rennie B. Schoepflin tells us, loose coalitions of professionals—physicians, child welfare reformers, and lawyers schooled in juvenile justice—coalesced to support state laws to protect children from abuse and neglect. The fledging American Medical Association was especially eager to expose fraudulent health care, including Christian Science's spiritual healing. In 1899 the *Journal of the American Medical Association* branded those who practiced spiritual healing "Molochs to infants and pestilential perils to communities in spreading contagious disease" and urged state prosecutors to bring criminal charges against Christian Science practitioners, the men and women employed to help in the healing process, and parents when a child died. The *New York Times* joined the chorus of criticism. One editorial labeled the church a "grotesque cult," and others highlighted the failures of spiritual healing. Similarly, the Roman Catholic Church and mainstream Protestants rejected the claim made by Christian Science to have discovered a fail-safe connection between prayer and painless healing. At trial, however, many jurors held to the popular belief that a child's illness was no more likely to be cured by medicine than by prayer and patience. The church fueled this perception by creating and publicizing a self-reported database of alleged healings and by lobbying state legislatures to enact religious exemption laws that would protect Christian Science parents from charges of child abuse and neglect.[2]

American society had changed dramatically by the late twentieth century, when the medically untreated deaths of Christian Science children seized public attention once again. Medical knowledge and care were vastly improved in the decades surrounding the Second World War. With one exception, the parents whose stories I write about here were born in the 1950s, the first generation of Christian Scientists to come of age in an era when antibiotics, vaccines, and modern surgery routinely saved lives and led to a sharp increase in life expectancy. These developments made it far more difficult for the church to compare its record of healing favorably with that of professional medical care and also evidently caused a steep decline in membership while creating a schism within the church. Some Christian Scientists routinely sought conventional medical attention while others, paradoxically, including the parents of the children who suffered death without medical intervention, embraced "radical reliance," a total disavowal of medical care as a way of treating illness. Confronted with a dramatically changed medical culture, these young parents doubled down.[3]

The first generation of post–Second World War Christian Science parents married in the 1970s, and their children were born in the early 1980s into a society splintered by the civil rights revolution, the Vietnam War, and youthful challenges to authority of every kind. Only one-third of the children who were members of the Christian Science Church at the age of sixteen remained members as adults. The flight of young people from the church and the era's social instability encouraged some parents to cling more tightly to radical reliance as a demonstration of their commitment to tradition and truth. They expressed confidence that this strategy provided them with an infallible guide to good parenting, especially in tumultuous times. Notably, however, a contemporary textbook for child protective workers highlighted as one cause of child abuse parents' "lack of capacity for coping with the pressures and tensions of modern life."[4]

As war, social turmoil, and personal problems increased the levels of parental stress, a voluntary data collection system attached to the U.S. Children's Bureau counted more than four hundred thousand reports of child abuse and neglect. At the same time, a survey conducted by the longtime children's advocate Vincent DeFrancis, the director of the Children's Division of the American Humane Society, showed that in the decades after the Great Depression nongovernmental child protective agencies had all but disappeared. Moreover, not a single state had developed an adequate child protection program to match the needs of all the reported cases of child neglect and abuse. By the 1980s the founder of the National Center on Child Abuse and Neglect estimated that one thousand children died each year as a result of abuse and neglect by their parents. The rapidly increasing number of maltreatment reports together with horrific individual cases of child abuse and death were given extensive media coverage. A cluster of national magazines, including *Time, Life, Newsweek, Good Housekeeping,* and *Parents Magazine,* published lengthy articles about the epidemic in the 1960s and 1970s.[5]

Leaders of the Christian Science Church worked hard to differentiate the behavior of parents in the grip of radical reliance from that of non–Christian Science parents whose purposeful neglect also led to the death of their child. Church spokespersons emphasized that the child abuse and manslaughter charges brought against Christian Science parents were legally mitigated by their faith, and, as they had for a century, church officials made a scientifically undocumented, invidious comparison between the numbers of children who died under medical care and those who had been unsuccessfully treated with spiritual healing. But to prosecutors, jurors, and many Americans, the tragic results of spiritual healing were indistinguishable from the thousands of other cases of child abuse, neglect, and death.

This is not to say that state courts across the country or even within a single state uniformly interpreted the question of whether religious exemption provisions protected Christian Science parents from misdemeanor negligence and criminal prosecution when their child died without medical care. For example, courts at every level in California held that the state's religious exemption for spiritual healing did not protect a Christian Science parent whose child died without medical care from prosecution for manslaughter. In Minnesota, by contrast, both the trial court and the state Supreme

Court, using somewhat different reasoning, determined that child neglect and manslaughter laws had a common purpose and must be read and applied together. Therefore, the religious exemption provision attached to child neglect also protected a parent who chose prayer to treat an ill child from a manslaughter charge. Diverse interpretations of the protection afforded by a religious exemption provision also clouded public understanding within particular states. A jury in Florida found a Christian Science couple guilty of felony child abuse and third-degree murder. An appeals court in the state ruled that parents' right to hold religious beliefs did not permit them to withhold medical care from their child. But the state Supreme Court overruled both the jury's verdict and that of the appeal court, holding that confusion about the protection afforded the parents by the spiritual healing provision was evidence of vagueness that violated the parents' right to due process. While within their legal right, the parents' tactics of delay and appeal, likely with the approval and funding of the church, meant that a meaningful final decision in the courts came long after the wrenching shock of a child's unnecessary death largely had been forgotten and kept the door open to similar and perhaps successful arguments in other states where Christian Science parents practiced radical reliance. At the same time, the church mounted an intense nationwide lobbying effort to retain spiritual exemptions in all states. Lacking funds and an effective national organization, children's advocates working to repeal religious exemption laws focused on those states where parents' prayers had failed to save children's lives. This strategy led to repeal in Massachusetts, South Dakota, Colorado, and Oregon.[6]

Beginning in the 1970s medical professionals, especially pediatricians, a handful of child advocacy activists, national legislators, and state prosecutors, launched a campaign to eradicate the scourge of child abuse. The Christian Science Church supported the Child Abuse Prevention and Treatment Act, but its interest centered on carving out a statutory exemption that would make possible its continued use of spiritual healing. Child advocates fought to repeal the exemptions, to treat Christian Scientists the same as any parent who violated the law prohibiting child abuse and neglect. It was tough going. The battle to repeal religious exemption laws had to be waged state by state and often, as noted above, against a state court ruling favorable to the church's interpretation of the exemption statute reformers sought to repeal. The church also had wealth and power that supported lobbyists, lawyers, and lavish media campaigns. Opponents of religious exemptions relied on small contributions and volunteers. State legislators were reluctant to act, fearful of trespassing on their constituents' perception of religious freedom. In addition, the church cloaked its self-interest in an expansion of its defense to include two ecumenical concerns that drew support from the Roman Catholic Church and many Protestant denominations: state encroachment on the right to pray and parents' right to raise their child as they saw fit. The Christian Science Church distanced itself from other, smaller religious groups that, like Christian Scientists, had unsuccessfully used prayer to heal children. Such a self-interested stance made good political sense, but the church's strategy turned a blind eye to the child victims of its spiritual healing practice and alienated a large, diffuse segment of the American public. Public opinion helped make repeal possible, but it was the emergence of a handful of dedicated leaders that won repeal of religious exemption statutes in a half dozen states.[7]

This book is about a legal and constitutional struggle over whether a religious belief may trump a generally applicable and neutral law prohibiting child abuse and neglect. A close analysis of this tragic story will shed light on the political practices and power of the Christian Science Church as well as on the limitations placed on the First Amendment's free exercise clause by the Supreme Court. The church proffered, and well-educated, middle-class parents accepted, a belief and a practice that invited harm to their own children. At trial, parents offered a religious defense, although the state had been committed to protecting the health and welfare of children for centuries. Yet not only parent-members of the Christian Science Church but also state legislators throughout the nation enabled child abuse and neglect by passing religious exemption laws. Consequently, innocent, seriously ill children died unnecessarily without medical care. In brief, the Christian Science Church, like other churches, is not an example of unalloyed good.

I argue that a child's death rationalized by a potentially harmful religious practice erodes commitment to the rule of law. In a well-ordered society the law must protect all persons. When the law permits a child to die at the hand of another, that act undermines the public good and strips the child of the right to equal treatment before the law. Christian Scientists would have the public believe that a generally applicable, neutral law to protect children should not regulate their spiritual healing conduct—regardless of its outcome.

The Constitution's guarantee of religious freedom cannot reasonably be read to permit a child to be harmed by a religious practice, nor does it allow religion to be a permissible legal defense when a person harms a child.

Similarly, more than a century's experience shows that the effect of a religious exemption from state child abuse laws has been to limit the government's commitment to protecting children from abuse and death. The stories that follow show clearly that the basic moral principle of justice requires that children be protected uniformly by law. A religious belief that permits a child's death cannot trump the law or Americans' moral responsibility to protect defenseless children.

The battle to win the public's approval of these legal and moral imperatives and of the specific charges brought against the Christian Science parents whose practice of radical reliance led to the deaths of their children was waged primarily by three protagonists: Rita Swan, the president of Children's Healthcare Is a Legal Duty (CHILD), spoke out against spiritual healing and religious exemption laws in courthouses and legislatures across the country; Nathan Talbot, the chief spokesperson for the Christian Science Church, was present at every trial of Christian Science parents to explain the church's beliefs and defend the parents' practice of spiritual healing; Mary Baker Eddy (1821–1910), the discoverer and founder of Christian Science, spoke to the issues being debated in her century-old book *Science and Health*.

In a hallway adjacent to a Florida courtroom where, in 1989, Christian Science parents were on trial for the death of their child, Rita Swan, a former Christian Scientist, spoke passionately to reporters about why parents should not rely on prayer alone when a child is seriously ill. She began by telling her personal story. Raised in the Christian Science Church, Rita and her husband, Doug, were taught that prayer was the only answer to illness. When their fifteen-month-old son Matthew developed weakness in his left leg that slowly robbed him of his ability to walk and suffered recurring bouts of high fever, the young couple called a Christian Science practitioner—a person whose spiritual understanding of God reaches the consciousness of the patient and eradicates the belief in disease—and asked her to pray for their son's recovery. The practitioner told Rita that Matthew's illness stemmed from her fear and that she should not interfere with his recovery. "You can't be sick," the practitioner whispered to Matthew. "God is your life. There is no disease in the kingdom of God." But during the next several weeks Matthew grew weaker and suffered excruciating pain. Pushing back against the only truth they knew, the Swans took Matthew to a hospital, but emergency surgery came too late. After being held a week in intensive care, Matthew died of spinal meningitis on July 7, 1977. A doctor later told the Swans that with early detection and antibiotics the cure rate for bacterial meningitis is about 90 percent.[8]

After Matthew's death the Swans withdrew from the Christian Science Church. In 1980 they brought a wrongful death suit against Matthew's practitioners and the church. A Michigan trial court dismissed the suit on First Amendment grounds and the state Supreme Court affirmed, ruling it could not untangle permissible belief and impermissible conduct. Three years later Rita and Doug founded CHILD, an organization they view as a legacy to their son. Having roughly four hundred members across the country and operating on a shoestring budget, the Swans' organization works to repeal state laws that give parents a legal right to withhold medical care from their children based on religious belief. According to its website, CHILD disseminates information about child abuse and neglect, opposes all religious exemptions to child health and safety laws, lobbies in support of the right of children to equal protection, and files amicus briefs in support of those rights. CHILD is the only organization in the United States focused on the problem of religiously based medical neglect of children. Its primary adversary is the Christian Science Church.[9]

Nathan Talbot, the soft-spoken director of the Christian Science Church's well-financed public relations operation in the 1980s, also talked to courthouse reporters. He began his talking points by emphasizing the love Christian Science parents have for their children and by explaining that the choice between medical care and Christian Science treatment is always left to the individual. He added that parents freely choose to treat their child's illness only with prayer. As used by Talbot and other Christian Scientists the word *prayer* is neither a request directed to a personal God, asking him to restore a sick person's health, nor a manifestation of faith. To Christian Scientists, prayer is a demonstration denying the illusory thought of material reality and affirming the truth that "Spirit is immortal Truth; matter [disease] is mortal error." In support of this belief, the church compiles "empirical evidence that disease and injuries of all types can be healed through prayer." Talbot acknowledges that not all children are successfully healed through prayer, though he quickly adds that many children die in hospitals without anyone calling the "medical model into question." His comparison implies that the effectiveness of prayer and that of medical care are similar. Therefore, health care decisions "belong morally and should belong legally, in the hands of parents." Talbot's well-rehearsed comments blended popular values: personal and religious autonomy, a parent's right to raise her child as she sees fit, and the power of prayer. He avoided specifics.[10]

Mary Baker Eddy, the self-proclaimed discoverer and founder of Christian Science, first articulated the "divine Principle of healing" in 1875. Four years later, at a time when Protestant orthodoxy had bowed to countless secular and religious challenges, she established the Church of Christ, Scientist, in Boston. Born into a stern Congregational household in rural New Hampshire, Eddy experienced ill health as a child that persisted into adulthood, and, not coincidentally, she struggled with the question of God's responsibility for human suffering. In 1862 she became a patient of Phineas Parkhurst Quimby, who held the view that a patient's illness and thoughts were linked. Under his care, Eddy's health improved dramatically. Shortly after Quimby's death in 1866 Eddy hurt her back, an injury from which, according to her account, she immediately recovered after reading biblical passages about Jesus's healing powers. This experience prompted her to establish a new religion, or, as Eddy later wrote in *Science and Health, with Key to the Scriptures,* to recover the "lost element of healing" that is Christian Science. Eddy's discovery of this spiritual principle led her to conclude that healing could occur when a person's prayer demonstrated that he or she understood that God had created a perfect spiritual world in which sin, sickness, disease, and death did not exist. This promise of good health and a pain-free life spurred the church's rapid growth in the late nineteenth and early twentieth centuries at a time when medical science was still in its infancy and the church could favorably compare its self-proclaimed success rate in spiritual healing with that of medical care.[11]

The church's triumphs, however, brought problems. Internal dissent and charges of practicing medicine without a license threatened its stability and continued growth. In 1881 nearly one-third of Eddy's followers abandoned her. To counter these centrifugal forces, Eddy tightened her intellectual control over the church's theology and created a centralized power structure. She decreed in 1892 that the only books permitted at a Christian Science service were the Bible and *Science and Health.* She also reorganized the government of the church, establishing at the Mother Church in Boston a self-perpetuating board of directors with full and final authority over all matters. Moreover, Eddy stipulated that the structure and rules she had laid out were to remain the permanent, unchallenged authority in the church.[12]

About the same time Eddy restructured the church, many state legislatures tightened requirements for medical licensure and, prompted by English common law and parliamentary statutes, embraced the idea that the state had a responsibility to protect children from, among other things, harmful religious practices. Eddy opposed licensure reforms as contrary to spiritual healing and religious liberty. When, in 1898, at the urging of the Harvard

University professor and philosopher William James, the Massachusetts legislature rejected a medical licensure bill, Eddy celebrated by inserting into *Science and Health* a paean to the popular idea of constitutionally protected religious liberty and individual autonomy. "Massachusetts put her foot on a proposed tyrannical law, restricting the practice of medicine," she wrote. "If her sister States follow this example in harmony with our Constitution and Bill of Rights, they will do less violence to that immortal sentiment of the Declaration, 'Man is endowed by his Maker with certain inalienable rights, among which are life, liberty, and the pursuit of happiness.'"[13]

Framed by this constitutional perspective and driven by a dichotomous religious scheme that shunned compromise with medicine, Eddy insisted that the only acceptable manifestation of belief had to be all or nothing. "The scientific government of the body," Eddy wrote in *Science and Health*, "must be attained through the Divine Mind. It is impossible to gain control over the body in any other way. On this fundamental point, timid conservatism is absolutely inadmissible. Only through radical reliance on Truth can scientific healing power be realized." This command embroiled parents and the church in high-profile confrontations with the state over the failure to protect children.[14]

Between 1887 and 1915 more than thirty practitioners and parents who administered spiritual treatment that led to a child's death were criminally charged, the practitioners for practicing medicine without a license and the parents for manslaughter. At trial, the practitioners and parents raised a similar defense: Prayer treatment was a safe, proven system of healing, and a constitutional right to religious freedom shielded them from prosecution. State prosecutors countered by arguing that an adult was free to treat illness however they chose, but the state could regulate harmful religious behavior to protect children even when the law infringed on a citizen's First Amendment right to religious freedom. Only a handful of convictions were upheld on appeal.[15]

The state's interest in protecting children was rooted in English common law, codified in English and U.S. law and upheld by the U.S. Supreme Court. The question of whether a parent had a legal duty to provide medical care for a seriously ill child if that law contradicted their religious faith first came before an English court in the mid-nineteenth century. At common law it was a misdemeanor for a parent to neglect to furnish a child with meat, drink, clothing, or "physic." If a jury found that a parent's neglect to bestow these necessities caused the child's death, under the common law formula the parent was liable to a charge of involuntary manslaughter.[16]

A religious group centered in Essex County in England, the Peculiar People, rejected physicians' care. (The name derived from 1 Peter 2:9, where Christians are labeled "a royal priesthood, a holy nation, a peculiar people.") In 1868 Thomas and Mary Ann Wagstaff's daughter Lois became seriously ill. The couple relied largely on the prayers of the church's elders to treat their child. Brought to trial when Lois died, Thomas, a laborer, and Mary Ann testified that they sincerely believed in God's healing power and that they had done all they could to save their daughter's life. The trial judge's instructions posed two questions to be answered by the jury in reaching their verdict: Did the parents' refusal to seek medical assistance for their child result from a sincere belief that God would heal the infant or from an intention to avoid their parental duty to provide medical care? And did the defendants do all they could to care for their child? The jury returned a verdict of not guilty.[17]

Although correctly based on the existing law, the jury's verdict stimulated widespread public criticism and led Parliament to amend the Poor Law, clarifying parents' responsibility to their children, and in 1894 to enact the Prevention of Cruelty to Children Act. Three years later Thomas Senior, a member of the Peculiar People, was convicted of manslaughter in the death of his fourteen-month-old son Amos. An appeals court affirmed Senior's conviction. Within days of the appeals court's ruling Senior was back in court, charged with the death of his eight-month-old son, the seventh of Senior's twelve children to die without medical aid. The trial judge's charge to the jury emphasized four points: (1) they must be satisfied that the child's death was caused or accelerated by the want of medical assistance; (2) that under the circumstances a reasonable parent would have provided medical care; (3) that the defendant had the economic means to provide medical aid; (4) that if the defendant had done anything expressly forbidden by the statute to cause or accelerate the death of the child he should be found guilty of manslaughter, regardless of his motive or state of mind. On this charge, the jury convicted Senior.[18]

On appeal, Lord Chief Justice Charles Russell held the trial judge's charge to the jury to be correct. The phrase "medical aid" does not appear in the law, Russell acknowledged, but a clear inference could be drawn from the statutes on the subject that the legislature's intent was "to provide for the protection of children." Senior had willfully neglected to give medical care to his infant son, and therefore the manslaughter conviction stood.[19]

Comparable statutes stipulating a parental duty to provide a child with medical care were enacted in many U.S. jurisdictions in the late nineteenth century. A law passed in New York in 1881 established a parental duty to provide a child with "food, lodging, clothes, medical attendance and education." J. Luther Pierson, a railroad worker and a believer in the Christian Catholic Church's healing ministry, refused to allow a physician to attend his sixteen-month-old daughter, who had contracted whooping cough in the winter of 1901. After a six-week-long struggle the child died of catarrhal pneumonia. The state charged Pierson with willfully failing to provide his child with medical care, and a jury convicted him of criminal neglect. Three years later before the Court of Appeals of New York, Pierson argued that the law requiring a parent to furnish medical care for a child violated his constitutional right to the "free exercise and enjoyment of religious profession and worship."[20]

Writing for a unanimous court, Judge Albert Haight rejected Pierson's argument and concluded with an encomium to the separation of church and state. The judge began by paraphrasing *Reynolds v. U.S.* (1879) in which the Supreme Court struck down the Mormon practice of polygamy. Liberty of conscience, the "full and free enjoyment of religious profession and worship is guaranteed," Haight declared, "but acts which are not worship are not." Pierson could believe whatever he wanted, but his acts were subject to state regulation. Because the "peace and safety of the state" include the "protection of the lives and health of its children," the state legislature is empowered to enact laws for that purpose. Therefore, Haight found that the state's role as *parens patriae* (parent of the country) could constitutionally infringe on Pierson's right to "liberty of conscience." Other religious groups, Haight added, referring to Christian Science, believe "science and Divine power may be invoked together to restore diseased and suffering humanity. We place no limits upon the power of the mind over the body or the power of faith to dispel disease. We merely declare the law as given us by the legislature." With that, the court affirmed Pierson's misdemeanor conviction for "willfully, maliciously, and unlawfully" neglecting to provide medical care for his infant daughter. The decision marked the first time a U.S. court of last resort declared that a parent's religious belief was not a defense against a charge of failing to seek medical care for his child's serious illness.[21]

The New York court's decision made it clear the state could legally protect children from faith healing, but it had little immediate impact. In the decades after 1903 the Christian Science Church and the state initiated changes that made it more difficult to prosecute religiously motivated denial of medical care to children. First, to create the appearance of professionalism the church established its own licensing standards and created a standardized training regime for its practitioners. Second, it decreed that practitioners were independent contractors, making it very difficult to extend responsibility to the church when a practitioner's behavior could be said to have accelerated or caused a child's death. These changes led prosecutors to charge parents rather than practitioners, but, as the *New York Times* pointed out in an editorial in 1920, drawing a legal line as to precisely when a parent relying on prayer should call a physician "is hard to say—so hard that Judges and jurors refuse" to convict. Third, church lobbyists convinced legislators to add religious exemptions to child neglect and abuse statutes, giving parents a statutory defense. Fourth, on the national level the U.S. Children's Bureau, founded in 1912, launched a broad child welfare agenda, but it did not include a program aimed at child abuse. In addition, social workers, those closest to potential problems, operated via a strategy aimed at achieving an in-home solution to suspected abuse rather than bringing it to the authorities' attention. Finally, New Deal legislation shifted the focus away from child abuse to concentrate on child neglect among impoverished families. Together, these social and legal changes caused state courts to struggle to balance the state's responsibility to protect children against parents' right to treat their child only with prayer according to their sincerely held religious belief.[22]

For these reasons, among others, when the issue of child abuse resurfaced in the early 1960s, it was framed as a medical rather than a social welfare problem. The link between medical care and child protection had several important dimensions. First, by the 1950s pediatrics was firmly established as a prominent medical specialty, and pediatricians were well positioned to replace social reformers as spokespeople for children's well-being. Second, the publication in 1962 of "The Battered Child Syndrome" in the *Journal of the American Medical Association* defined child abuse as a clinical condition caused generally by a parent. This medical "discovery" spurred the production of hundreds of sensational stories and scholarly articles about brutal acts of child abuse and led eventually to the requirement of mandatory reporting of suspected child abuse. The American Academy of Pediatrics took up the cause, and state and national legislation quickly followed. Between 1963 and 1967 all fifty states passed a mandatory reporting law. To support state programs Congress passed the Child Abuse Prevention and Treatment Act (CAPTA) in 1974. The act included two major concessions to Christian Scientists. The regulations accompanying the act included an exemption for a parent accused of child abuse who was "legitimately practicing his religious beliefs" and, in order to be eligible for federal child abuse prevention and treatment funds, states were required to add a prayer treatment exemption to their child neglect and abuse laws.[23]

The exemption statutes written into state civil and criminal codes took a variety of forms. The majority of states used language similar to CAPTA's regulations, stating that a parent may not be charged with abusing a child "for the sole reason that" the child is treated by spiritual means. Some states used stronger language, stipulating that spiritual treatment shall constitute health care and that spiritual treatment could be a defense to prosecution. A handful of states specifically named Christian Science as the religion exempted. More than a dozen states implied the same preference by exempting parents who treat their child according to the "tenets" of a "well-recognized church" by a "duly accredited practitioner thereof." Only Oklahoma stated that the prayer exemption in its child neglect statute does not extend to those cases "where permanent physical damage could result to such a child."[24]

That Christian Scientists were able to write into CAPTA an exemption for spiritual healing and win state approval for similar laws highlights the church's political clout, particularly since medical advances and the failure to recruit new young members caused the number of Christian Scientists to decline precipitously after the 1940s. To push its legislative agenda, the church uses a formidable lobbying apparatus, including at least one salaried person in each state and up to a dozen local, church-appointed legislative assistants. Lobbyists routinely speak with state legislators and county district attorneys and rally rank-and-file church members to attend legislative hearings and contact their legislators. The church also employs a dozen lobbyists in Washington. This entire lobbying network is directed by the manager of the committees of publication headquartered at the Mother Church in Boston. In short, the church is highly organized and well prepared to advocate the constitutionality of its practice of spiritual healing for children.[25]

In the same year Eddy founded the Christian Science Church the Supreme Court interpreted the free exercise clause for the first time. In *Reynolds v. U.S.* (1879) the court upheld federal antipolygamy laws and articulated a free exercise of religion doctrine that remained substantially unchanged for more than eight decades. Congress could pass no law restricting religious belief, but religious conduct could be limited if it threatened public order or safety. The court's ruling quoted Thomas Jefferson: "The legislative powers of the government reach actions only, and not opinions." The fact that a person's conduct was linked to a religious belief did not protect the believer from the law. A unanimous court declared that religious practices that undermined the public interest did not come under the protection of the First Amendment.[26]

The court's argument rested on the premise that in a republican society individual rights, including a robust right of conscience, were vital, but they could not jeopardize the well-being of others or of "ordered liberty." Jefferson's intellectual mentor, the seventeenth-century English political philosopher John Locke, articulated the harm principle as follows: Individuals could not "take away, or impair the life, or what tends to the preservation of the life, the liberty, health, limb, or goods of another." Using the Lockean–Jeffersonian formulation of the dynamic relationship between religion and government, the *Reynolds* court concluded that "Congress was deprived of all legislative power over mere opinion, but was left free to reach actions which were in violation of social duties or subversive of good order."[27]

The court added a measure of flexibility to the *Reynolds* formula in 1940 when it confirmed that the freedom to believe was absolutely protected, and that unless the state had a compelling reason to limit conduct, believers were free to act. This subjective formula guided the court's decision in *Prince v. Massachusetts.* The court held that the state could impinge on constitutionally protected religious belief because it had a compelling interest to protect the well-being of children.[28]

Between 1963 and 1990 the court deviated from its dominant free exercise jurisprudence, allowing religious groups to argue that their actions should be immune to criminal prosecution. In *Sherbert v. Verner,* Justice William Brennan initiated a new approach mandating that neutral and generally applicable laws could be subject to strict scrutiny, a test requiring the state to establish that it has a compelling interest justifying the law's impingement on a fundamental right. The court's *Sherbert* ruling was extended to compulsory school laws in *Wisconsin v. Yoder* (1972), in which Amish parents successfully claimed that the state's generally applicable, neutral school attendance law was a threat to their religious way of life, which required them to be "aloof from the world." Before state appeals courts and in public forums Christian Scientists made use of *Sherbert* and the "way of life" argument to justify exemption from state laws requiring parents to provide medical care to seriously ill children.[29]

Christian Scientists saw *Wisconsin v. Yoder* (1972) as a decision likely to help the church realize its goal of constitutionalizing protection for spiritual healing. The Supreme Court rejected Wisconsin's claim that only religious beliefs, not actions, came within the First Amendment's protection and recognized the right of Old Order Amish parents to withdraw their children from school after they had completed the eighth grade, contrary to a neutral, generally applicable state law. According to Christian Scientists, the court's ruling signaled recognition of the "special needs of certain religious groups" and opened the way to approving spiritual healing. The unique and fundamental role played by spiritual healing mirrored the Amish tradition of agricultural work and its relationship to their belief. In dissent, Justice William O. Douglas argued that children's constitutionally protected religious rights could be different from those of their parents. Christian Scientists ignored that argument.[30]

Nearly a century after Eddy embraced America's sacred secular documents to buttress the popular notion that restrictions on religious practice violated the First Amendment as well as the individual liberty promised by the Declaration of Independence, David N. Williams, a church lobbyist and constitutional law commentator, argued that *Sherbert* and *Yoder* had all but ended the *Reynolds* distinction between religious belief and practice. That distinction was applied to religious practices that were harmful. But "serious spiritual healing," Williams wrote in 1989, doesn't belong in that category. Rather, the benefits "for turning consistently to this way of healing might be real and significant." Therefore, *Sherbert* and subsequent cases put the burden on the state to prove "a truly compelling interest in restricting any religious practice," and a showing that "no less restrictive means 'are available to achieve' that interest." In other words, "First Amendment rights are so basic to society that free exercise must be guarded up to the very point at which overriding state interest compels us to place these limits." Opponents of the practice of spiritual healing must prove that the state has a compelling interest to restrict Christian Science healing for children. To do so, Williams argued, the state cannot simply rely on the "a priori assumption" that medical care is superior to spiritual healing. Christian Science parents convicted for the death of their child repeated Williams's argument before appellate courts.[31]

In 1990 the court abandoned the notion that all generally applicable, neutral laws were presumptively unconstitutional when applied to religious groups. Writing for the majority in *Employment Division v. Smith* (1990), Justice Antonin Scalia declared, "[The] government's ability to enforce generally applicable prohibitions of socially harmful conduct 'cannot depend on measuring the effects of a government action on a religious objector's spiritual development.'" Neutral and generally applicable laws with the "incidental effect" of burdening religious conduct did not offend the First Amendment.

Religious exemptions to general laws, Scalia added, were impracticable in a pluralistic society and would make each citizen "a law unto himself."[32]

Abundant evidence shows that, like the court, many Americans have concluded that a line must be imposed between religious belief and actions. In 1988 a survey of four hundred jury-eligible residents of Maricopa County, Arizona, found widespread tolerance for the religious beliefs of others but virtually no tolerance for religious practices perceived as endangering children. While 98 percent agreed with the statement "People have the Constitutional right to believe in and practice the religion of their choice," nearly as many, 92 percent, agreed with the statement "Spiritual healing may have its place, but medical care should be required by law." Major newspapers across the country adopted a position similar to that of the would-be jurors. The *San Francisco Chronicle* praised the California Supreme Court's ruling that parents "have no right to the free exercise of religion at the price of a child's life, regardless of the prohibitive or compulsive nature of the governmental infringement." Writing in the *Washington Post,* the columnist Nat Hentoff, one of the foremost popular authorities on the First Amendment, noted that according to the Christian Science Church parents may choose to provide medical care for themselves and their children. Therefore, Hentoff concluded, juries should bear in mind that "the free-exercise-of-religion defense by the parents is not based on an absolute religious command but on the exercise of an option. All the more reason for state intrusion to save the life of a child." Grand juries in five states handed down manslaughter indictments against Christian Science parents who denied their child possible lifesaving medical care, and trial juries in Florida, California, and Massachusetts returned guilty verdicts on that charge. However, as suggested above, not all state appellate courts followed the people's lead but instead struggled to draw a bright line between permissible religious belief and impermissible conduct.[33]

The competing demands that existed in the 1980s between the popular understanding that the law must protect children regardless of their parents' religious beliefs and the constitutional mandate that Congress shall make no law impinging on religious freedom drew Christian Scientists, the courts, and children's advocates into debate about the meaning of religious freedom. Christian Scientists argued that an exemption from a generally applicable, neutral law prohibiting child abuse was the answer, while children's advocates argued that nothing short of repeal of such laws would save children's lives without oppressing a religious minority.

The question posed to the courts by the deaths of children of Christian Science parents is not, does prayer cure illness? but, should the law protect a parent whose religious conduct endangers or causes the death of a child? Christian Scientists claim its "system of prayer" is a successful alternative method of heath care, but that claim is buttressed only with anecdotal evidence collected by and for the church and indelibly stained by the deaths of children who, had they been medically treated, would have in all likelihood survived their illness. When pressed on this score, the church's stock response is to attack the medical profession, equating the failure of spiritual healing practices with the fact that some children die when under professional medical care.[34]

Christian Scientists are free to advocate and to use prayer as a remedy for illness. But courts have repeatedly ruled that that right does not extend to parents whose conduct jeopardizes the life of a child. Yet forty-four states and the District of Columbia have enacted religious exemptions to child abuse and neglect laws that may be interpreted as allowing parents to use spiritual healing without fear of prosecution. And if prayer proves unsuccessful and a child dies, Christian Scientists argue that statutory exemption from criminal prosecution for child abuse, together with the constitutional right to the free exercise of religion, bars a parent from being prosecuted for manslaughter, a position adopted by twenty states. To date, children's advocates have not been able to convince more than a handful of states to repeal religious exemptions protecting parental conduct that is harmful to a child.

Although both CHILD and the Christian Science Church emphasized care and the avoidance of harm to children, each defined the terms *care* and *harm* differently and each insisted on a different way of realizing that goal. CHILD insisted on the repeal of religious exemptions in order to protect children from their religious parents, whereas the church regarded children's care as a moral interest, an outgrowth of religious belief and family values that must be protected from state intervention. Talbot rejected laws substituting state power for religion-based parental authority, while Swan championed rights and duty, the language of the law.

The cases I discuss in this book are arranged chronologically by the accused parents' trial dates and tell the story of the prosecutors' efforts to bring the parents to justice. Each chapter is named for the child victim or victims and carries forward the case against the accused parents from indictment through the appeals process, if applicable. The legal process in each case followed a roughly similar pattern. After an indictment had been handed down by a grand jury, the defense filed a motion to dismiss the charge, arguing that the state's religious exemption law allowed spiritual healing as an alternative method of care. In some cases the defense strategy was to exploit the ambivalently worded exemption statute to make a full-blown religious defense, namely, that denial of such a defense violated the defendant's First Amendment right to the free exercise of religion. Before the trial court the state countered that the exemption amended to the state's child abuse and neglect statute did not extend to manslaughter, a charge leveled against a parent who willfully and recklessly neglected to provide medical care for a seriously ill child. Appeals from both sides followed the trial court's rulings on these issues. The appeals courts' decisions were mixed.

There were important divergences in the several cases. First, the facts of each case varied: the cause of the child's death; the care extended to the child by the parent and the Christian Science practitioner; the medical testimony as to the severity of the illnesses and the likelihood the child could have survived with timely medical intervention; at what point a reasonable person would have recognized the child's symptoms as life-threatening. Second, the trial attorneys' skill, strategy, and degree of aggressiveness they brought to the case coupled with the trial court judge's rulings on motions made by the defense and the state largely shaped the outcome. Third, the several appeals courts came to widely disparate conclusions.

Despite the guilty verdicts in every case that went to trial and three state appeals court decisions upholding the parents' convictions, the repeal of state religious exemption laws proved extraordinarily difficult. Legislative hearings on repeal bills were held in three states that had experienced the death of a child, but the transition from law to legislation succeeded only in Massachusetts. There, in the home state of the Christian Science Church, experienced, skilled leaders—a former prosecutor, a children's advocate, and a passionate legislator—led the way to repeal.

Chapter 1, "Amy Hermanson," introduces the basic tenets of the Christian Science Church, especially Eddy's instructions about how to care for ill children. It also looks at the passage of CAPTA, including a religious exemption for spiritual healing, and explores the Hermansons' conviction in 1986 for the death of their child from medically untreated diabetes and their successful appeal.

Chapter 2, "Shauntay Walker, Seth Glaser, and Natalie Rippberger," describes the deaths of three California children from medically untreated bacterial meningitis, a judge's pretrial ruling that the legislature did not intend the spiritual healing amendment to be a defense against a criminal prosecution, and Walker's several appeals until the California Supreme Court ruled in 1992 that parents have "no right to free exercise of religion at the price of a child's life."

Chapter 3, "Ian Lundman," examines a young boy's death from medically untreated diabetes and the trial court's dismissal of the state's criminal charge brought against the boy's mother for failing to seek medical care for him. I discuss in addition the subsequent successful wrongful death suit brought by the boy's father—the parents had divorced—against his son's mother, a Christian Science practitioner, and the Christian Science Church.

Chapter 4, "Ashley King," describes the lengthy, often duplicitous, but unsuccessful effort of a mother to heal her eleven-year-old daughter's cancerous tumor with prayer, her resistance to hospital care, and her attorney's aggressive attack on Arizona's criminal justice system, concluding in the parents' pleading no contest to a misdemeanor.

Chapter 5, "Robyn Twitchell," looks at a boy's painful decline and death, the carefully prepared and masterful prosecution of his parents by the Massachusetts special prosecutor John A. Kiernan, and the Supreme Judicial Court's affirmation of a parent's common law duty to provide medical care to her or his child. However, the court set aside the Twitchells' conviction on due process grounds.

Chapter 6, "Repeal of Religious Exemptions," elucidates the Massachusetts legislature's repeal of the state's religious exemption law in 1993. This development was spurred by the successful Twitchell prosecution, the Supreme Judicial Court's decision, and the creation of a children's advocacy group led by Kiernan, now a private attorney, Jetta Bernier, the executive director of the Massachusetts Committee for Children, and state senator Shannon O'Brien. Although the hoped-for spontaneous chain reaction did not occur, five other states also repealed their religious exemption laws.

The conclusion, "Religious Freedom and the Public Good," brings the repeal of religious exemption laws up to 2001 and traces the rise and fall of the Religious Freedom Restoration Act (1993), an attempt by conservatives and a wide spectrum of religious groups, including the Christian Science Church, to win back what they lost as a result of the Supreme Court's decision in *Employment Division v. Smith* (1990).

An analysis of this story will help us understand that the broad strokes in which proponents and opponents alike characterize spiritual healing are somewhat misleading. The history of the effort to protect children from harm cannot fully be captured within a simple church versus state frame-work. Rather, it is about the intersection of private lives driven by faith and public events dominated by law and policy. There was a spectrum of opinion within the church about the degree to which radical reliance or spiritual heal-ing generally should be the rule for seriously ill children. There are hints that some within the church's leadership circle thought imposing radical reliance on children could threaten the existence of the church. The problem was that the effort by Christian Science leaders to buttress the practice of spiritual healing with religious exemption laws and to work to extend constitutional protection for religious conduct put them in harmony with other religious groups, but it also gave license to those who embraced radical reliance for their seriously ill children. Church leaders were eager to mask the differences within the church, and that left secular opponents of the practice of imposing radical reliance on children with no choice but to advocate repeal of laws that allowed children to be harmed.

1

Amy Hermanson

T WO DAYS AFTER THE DEATH of their seven-year-old daughter Amy from untreated juvenile diabetes on September 30, 1986, Chris and Bill Hermanson stood before Chris's employees and friends at the Sarasota Fine Arts Academy. Everything is going to be okay, Chris told the group. Later she told a friend, "Amy made a conscious decision to pass on. It was her choice, Amy's choice." Bill seemed equally untroubled by self-doubt about Amy's death when, during his talk to the group, he stressed the positive aspects of the couple's faith and offered Christian Science literature to anyone who wanted to understand the church's beliefs. The Hermansons also called a family meeting. Mark Morton, Amy's uncle, was one of the attendees. Bill explained that he and Chris hadn't deprived their daughter of treatment but had relied on spiritual healing, a nonmedical form of treatment recognized by the state of Florida. Recalling the event three years later, Morton's anger at Bill's apparent lack of remorse over his daughter's death and his emphasis on the couple's legal defense if the state brought a criminal charge bubbled to the surface. Amy's father, Morton said, "sat there with an itemized list of all their procedures, saying how they did everything according to the law." Morton added, "It was all I could do to keep myself from getting up and walking out." Over the next six years Bill Hermanson's assertion about the law was contested in the Florida courts, and in newspapers across the country Amy's name headed the list of children of Christian Science parents whose deaths fueled a nationwide debate about the limits of religious freedom and the need to protect children from abuse and death.[1]

Teachers at the Julie Rohr Academy, where Amy Hermanson was a third grader, described her as a "sunny 7-year-old with blond hair and bubbly ways" who loved to sing. But beginning in early September 1986 Nancy

Strand and Laura Kingsley, two teachers at the academy, grew increasingly concerned about Amy's health. They noticed a change in her looks, behavior, and energy level. The music teacher at the school, Gail Whitmore, thought she had a "sadder, depressed look," and another teacher found the little girl "nearly incoherent," unable to sing her favorite song, "It's a Small World." Amy's mother brushed away these concerns. When told that Amy cried at school, Chris blamed it on the emotional stress created by the new school environment. When Amy lay down on the floor at midday, her mother said a growth spurt had sapped her energy. Still, Amy's rapid weight loss and the dark circles under her eyes alarmed teachers, friends, and relatives. "I had to kind of look at her twice to even recognize her," Suzanne Perino, Amy's babysitter, told investigators.[2]

On September 22, eight days before Amy's death, her parents noted something "particularly wrong." Bill telephoned Thomas Keller, a Christian Science practitioner in Indiana. Like all church-certified practitioners stretching back to Mary Baker Eddy's first students in the late nineteenth century, Keller began his career as a full-time healer after fulfilling a simple set of criteria: he belonged to a Christian Science Church; he vowed to follow Eddy's teachings; he completed two weeks of instruction from a Christian Science teacher; and he submitted letters to the church hierarchy attesting to his spiritual character and his ability to heal others. A healer did not ask a patient or the parents of a sick child to describe the illness or its symptoms because to do so, practitioners believed, would undercut the belief that pain and illness were not real. Practitioners did not heal others directly. Their silent prayer affirming the truth that disease is a mortal error helped a patient overcome the illusion that was causing the suffering. Healing would occur when the patient became convinced of the unreality of the material world. Practitioners emphasized that treatment could not fail, "except in the sense that a patient had not yet gained a complete understanding of the true goodness of reality."[3]

According to Eddy's instructions, the spiritual treatment of children's illness should focus on the parents. "If the case is that of a young child or infant," she told the Christian Science men and women who were employed to help in healing, "it needs to be met mainly through the parent's thought." Through prayer they need to be convinced that "sickness is a dream from which the patient needs to be awakened." In this way a parent's belief in the reality of illness may be overcome and the child healed. Eddy warned, however, that the full potential of spiritual healing had not yet been realized.

Therefore, Christian Scientists cannot claim a perfect record, but occasional failure must not undermine a Christian Scientist's fundamental belief that "the divine Mind has all power."[4]

Keller prayed for Amy long distance. There was no noticeable improvement in her health, but Chris and Bill nevertheless left Sarasota to attend a Christian Science conference on spiritual healing in Indianapolis. Amy and her nine-year-old brother, Eric, were left in the care of twenty-four-year-old Beth Ackerman, a part-time employee of the Christian Science Church and Chris's Fine Arts Academy who lived with the Hermansons. During an outing to an amusement park, Amy couldn't complete a round of miniature golf. One of Beth's friends said the little girl looked "like a zombie." By the time her parents arrived home from their conference in the Midwest at 2 a.m. on Monday, September 29, Amy was pale and immobile. She had been vomiting. About 9 a.m. the Hermansons called Frederick Hillier, a local Christian Science practitioner, who prayed for Amy, following a healing system spelled out more than one hundred years earlier by Eddy.[5]

Eddy's commitment to health and healing had its origins in the so-called American mind cure phenomenon and in bouts of illness she suffered during childhood and as an adult, leading her to search for a remedy to illness. For more than three decades beginning in the 1830s Eddy, like many other Americans, experimented with a variety of health reforms, including Sylvester Graham's vegetarianism, the therapeutic effects of rechanneling the body's invisible magnetic force, which Franz Anton Mesmer called animal magnetism, and homeopathy, an alternative medical practice in which practitioners used highly diluted preparations coupled with an analysis of the patient's physical and psychological state in order to prescribe a remedy. Eddy concluded that the patient's faith in the medicine, not the medicine itself, caused their recovery. Beginning in 1862 Eddy studied and later became a partner of Phineas Parkhurst Quimby, an itinerant mental healer from Maine who relied on mesmerism. She received treatment and lessons from Quimby before leaving to begin a practice of her own.[6]

In the winter of 1866, about a month after Quimby's death, Eddy allegedly suffered serious injuries after falling on an icy sidewalk in Lynn, Massachusetts. Physicians were unable to help. However, while bedridden, Eddy read an account of Jesus's healing of the sick (Matthew 9:2–7) and reported being restored to health instantly. From that moment forward her approach to Christianity included salvation not only from sin but from sickness as well. Realizing the power and appeal of her discovery, she published *Science and*

Health, with Key to the Scriptures in 1875 and four years later launched the Christian Science Church. *Science and Health* proclaims there is no evil in the world, no sin, no disease, no death. At its most basic, Eddy's argument is simple: God is perfect, humankind is God's creation, and therefore, appearances to the contrary, humankind is perfect. "Man is not matter," Eddy declared. "He is not made of brain, blood, bones, and other material elements." The spiritual world is real, free of imperfections, and attainable on earth by humans who understand God.[7]

Eddy contends that Jesus left a blueprint in the scriptures describing how humans may yield to God and how Christ demonstrated the power that results from this practice, which she called "Christ-power," in countless healings during his three-year public ministry on earth. Eddy's teachings held that the same Christ-power is attainable by anyone who follows the scientific principles revealed in the Bible and explained in *Science and Health.* Christian Science's method of healing—that is, its spiritual treatment of disease and prayer as a demonstration that life is spiritual and eternal—flows from the religion's two basic premises: first, the material world and all its living inhabitants and innate elements are not reality; second, all disease is rooted in the human mind's blindness to God's presence and is the cause of disease. Drugs do not heal "but only relieve suffering temporarily, exchanging one disease for another." According to Christian Science, God creates the true reality. It is perfect and outside the material world, which is a product of human senses and therefore imperfect. The alleged science of Christian Science is embodied in the process of seeking communion with the God-Mind and with God's perfect reality through prayer and spiritual awakening. When this state is achieved, God's reality and power become so real they eclipse the temporal reality of disease and pain. These experiences are rooted not in blind faith, say Christian Scientists, but in successful, verified personal experience. Christian Science thereby lays claim to being a form of Christianity whose truths are substantiated by empirical evidence.[8]

At about the same time as Hillier, the local Christian Science practitioner contacted by the Hermansons, began to pray for Amy, her aunt, Chris's sister Leslie Morton, did some research. She knew Amy's grandfather had had diabetes, and, after consulting several health books, her family doctor, and a diabetes foundation, Leslie concluded that Amy too suffered from that disease. She convinced Chris's father, Jack Morton, to confront the Hermansons about Amy's health. Brushing aside Morton's plea for medical intervention, Bill told him the family had performed a healing early that morning, with

Hillier guiding them through prayer by telephone, and as a result Amy had improved dramatically. Leslie Morton didn't believe it and called the Department of Health and Rehabilitative Services, telling a social worker that something was terribly wrong with Amy and that her parents refused to call a doctor. On Tuesday morning, September 30, Willy Torres, a counselor with the state agency, called Bill to inform him that the agency had received a complaint alleging child abuse of his daughter and that a hearing had been set for that afternoon before the Juvenile Court. Torres also told Bill the purpose of the hearing was to determine if the court should order medical treatment for Amy.[9]

At 9:30 a.m. on Tuesday Hillier arrived at the Hermansons' home to continue prayer treatment. He suggested calling Mary Jane Sellers, a Christian Science nurse who soon arrived on the scene and was standing by Amy's bedside thirty minutes later. Because Sellers had no medical training, she sought simply to make Amy comfortable. She gave Amy a few drops of water and put Vaseline on her lips. The girl didn't move. Her complexion was sallow, and a brown fluid ran from her mouth and nose. About two hours later she began vomiting, and her condition worsened. Sellers recommended calling an ambulance, while Hillier insisted that church headquarters in Boston should be contacted first. When that call was completed, Sellers called paramedics. At 1:27 p.m. Chris called her husband at the County Courthouse, saying, "Amy [has] taken a turn for the worse." By the time the paramedics arrived at the Hermansons' home Amy lay dead on her parents' bed. By her side were Eddy's *Science and Health* and a King James Bible.[10]

The Hermansons were arrested on November 5 and released without bail after a five-week investigation by the Sarasota County sheriff's office. Bill, thirty-nine years of age, and Christine, thirty-six, were arraigned on Monday, November 24, 1986, and charged with child abuse and third-degree murder (child abuse plus death) and manslaughter. The couple had moved to Sarasota three years after their marriage in 1970, and their two children, Eric and Amy, were born in that affluent community. Bill held a graduate degree in business from Grand Valley State University and had served as comptroller at Principia College, a college for Christian Scientists located in Illinois. Chris had completed a bachelor's degree in music and a master's degree in education at the University of Michigan. Until he was arrested for Amy's death, at which time he took a leave of absence from his job, Bill was senior vice president of United First Federal Savings and Loan in Sarasota, and Christine owned and managed the Sarasota Fine Arts Academy. Shortly after they arrived in Paradise, a popular nickname for Sarasota, the couple joined the First Church of Christ, Scientist. A Christian Scientist since childhood, Bill was elected first reader, the highest and most important position within a local church, and Chris, who converted to Christian Science just prior to her marriage to Bill, played the organ at Sunday service.[11]

In the days before the Hermansons' arraignment, the defense and the state attorney for Sarasota County made public statements outlining their basic arguments in broad strokes. Dan Dannheisser, a personal injury lawyer with a practice based in Sarasota, represented the Hermansons and told the *Sarasota Herald Tribune* the Hermansons "did everything possible under the circumstances," describing the couple as "fully loving and caring parents." The attorney Joseph Whitelock, a self-identified Christian Scientist and a consultant in the case, said Florida law "forbids prosecution for child abuse and neglect when parental action is based on religious belief." But Mark Futch, chief assistant state attorney for Sarasota County, countered that assertion, saying, "[The] prosecution exemption does not apply when great harm or death occurs." The legislative intent of the exemption was aimed at removing a child from parental custody, Futch maintained, going on to say, "I don't think the intent of the Legislature was a defense in a case where death occurs." The Hermansons, Futch concluded, "certainly should have gotten some kind of qualified medical attention for the child."[12]

The spotlight placed on Christian Science parents charged with felony child abuse was an unanticipated outcome of what Barbara J. Nelson labels "the rediscovery of child abuse." A surge in professional research, coupled with intense media coverage of abused children, led nearly every state to pass some form of child abuse reporting law between 1963 and 1967. Initially perceived by legislators as a no-cost, noncontroversial response to public concern over child abuse, reporting laws soon generated a demand for services. Rep. Mario Biaggi (D–NY), a former Manhattan police officer who had observed incidents of child abuse, was the first member of Congress to tackle the problem. His legislative work set the stage for Sen. Walter Mondale, who picked up the issue of child abuse in 1972. The next year Mondale's subcommittee held hearings designed to show the "human side of child abuse." A bill followed. The Child Abuse Prevention and Treatment Act (CAPTA) sailed through Congress in December 1973, and President Richard M. Nixon signed it into law on January 31, 1974.[13]

The act authorized Secretary of Health, Education and Welfare (HEW) Caspar Weinberger, perhaps with encouragement from John Ehrlichman and H. R. Haldeman, who were Christian Scientists and aides of President Nixon, to write into the law's regulations a "religious immunity" provision: "A parent or guardian legitimately practicing his religious beliefs who thereby does not provide specified medical treatment for a child, for that reason alone shall not be considered a negligent parent or guardian; however, such an exception shall not preclude a court from ordering that medical services be provided to the child where his health requires it." In order to qualify for federal child abuse funds CAPTA required states to enact a religious exemption law that was the "same in substance" as that promulgated by HEW. While this provision was dropped in 1983, by then every state had added a religious exemption statute, and the Christian Science Church successfully lobbied states to retain the provision.[14]

Because the Hermansons rejected a plea bargain of fifteen years' probation for guilty or no contest pleas, in April 1988 Judge Stephen Dakan heard arguments as to whether they should stand trial or could legally claim their actions were protected under a Florida law of 1975 that seemed to allow religious parents to withhold medical treatment from their child. Florida's religious exemption statute was virtually the same as that appended to CAPTA. The pivotal section of the law's "spiritual treatment proviso" states, "A parent legitimately practicing his religious beliefs, who does not provide specified medical treatment for a child, may not be considered abusive or neglectful for that reason alone." Thomas H. Dart, a local corporate attorney, argued that the charges against the Hermansons should be dismissed because their actions were specifically protected under the 1975 law. He also made a constitutional argument. Referring to the Supreme Court's decision in *Wisconsin v. Yoder* (1972), in which the court decided that enforcement of the state's compulsory high school attendance law would seriously endanger Amish religious beliefs, Dart contended that "the very existence of the Christian Science Church would be threatened by the removal" of the spiritual treatment proviso. The First Amendment's mandate that Congress shall make no law prohibiting the free exercise of religion justified Florida's proviso.[15]

Assistant State Attorney Pat Whitaker rebutted Dart's argument, insisting that the spiritual treatment proviso is not a defense to a criminal prosecution of a parent who "willfully or by culpable negligence" deprives a child of medical treatment and in so doing causes great bodily harm to the child. Such a parent "shall be guilty of a felony of the third degree," he said. In addition, the spiritual treatment proviso violates the First Amendment's prohibition against the establishment of religion by advancing one faith over another in what is essentially a special provision for Christian Scientists. The law violated Amy's rights because she was denied the benefit of health care the state requires for children of other faiths. Judge Dakan took the motions under consideration.[16]

In June, Judge Dakan ruled on the pretrial motions made by the defense and the state and cleared the way for a jury to answer at least some of the questions raised by Amy's death. Dakan denied the Hermansons' motion to dismiss all charges. He did grant their motion to dismiss the charge of manslaughter but ruled a jury should hear evidence on the counts alleging violations of felony child abuse and third-degree murder. Dakan also ruled that the Hermansons could use the spiritual treatment proviso as a statutory defense. Finally, he rejected the state's contention that the spiritual treatment proviso was an unconstitutional violation of the First Amendment's establishment clause. The lawyers for both sides expressed satisfaction with the judge's orders. "We've got two charges remaining that we think can be prosecuted," Assistant State Attorney Whitaker said. The defense attorney Dart disagreed, saying, "We don't believe the elements are there" to prove the couple guilty of child abuse or murder.[17]

The Hermansons appealed Judge Dakan's ruling denying their motion to dismiss all charges. As they had before the trial court, the couple insisted the spiritual treatment proviso exempted them from culpability in Amy's death. They filed a petition with the Supreme Court of Florida for a writ of prohibition and a writ of certiorari, which if granted would have stopped the trial court's ruling and transferred jurisdiction of the case to the Supreme Court of Florida. On November 30, 1988, the motion was denied. The Hermansons made the same argument before the Court of Appeal of Florida, with the same result, and four days later U.S. Supreme Court Justice Arthur M. Kennedy denied without comment the Hermansons' emergency request to block their trial on grounds of religious freedom. Trial was scheduled for Monday, April 10, 1989.[18]

Jury selection in the Hermansons' trial began on Monday in the Sarasota County Court, located just two blocks from the First Church of Christ, Scientist. Both buildings are cream-colored stucco, and each is about sixty years old. Inside the courtroom the Hermansons sat impassively at the defense table while jury selection took place. When lawyers questioned a group of prospective jurors about whether their ideas concerning religion and child rearing would affect their ability to be objective, Donald Benbow, one of the interviewees, raised his hand and, when recognized, said, "I have an opinion. I think it was bad judgment" for the couple to withhold medical care. Dart asked the prospective jurors whether they could accept the spiritual treatment proviso as a legal defense even if they didn't accept the Christian Science belief in spiritual healing. None of the potential jurors were Christian Scientists, but all of them were parents. Some said they thought children deserved medical care but promised to put aside their personal views during the trial. By Tuesday afternoon a jury of three women and three men had been empaneled.[19]

Lawyers made their opening statements Wednesday morning, highlighting the central issue of the Hermanson case: Did Florida law shield parents who unsuccessfully substitute spiritual healing for medical care? Futch spoke graphically and bluntly. Seven-year-old Amy Hermanson, he told the jury, died in her parents' bed, surrounded by unhelpful adults and choking on her vomit. Her parents could have saved her from death by diabetes simply by calling a doctor, who would have given the girl a lifesaving injection of insulin. But they chose to protect their belief in spiritual healing instead of their child. "This case is not about the religion of these defendants," he said, "it's about the abuse that was inflicted on this child." Amy died an awful death, the lead defense attorney, Edward M. Booth, said, but it wasn't because her parents didn't try to save her. The Hermansons relied on spiritual healing, a method of treatment embraced by the Christian Science Church and authorized by Florida law. "Religion is the issue in this case," he said. "These are good people, good parents, loving parents, who took care of their child the best they knew how." As late as the morning before her death, Booth concluded, "they firmly believed that God was healing their child."[20]

Outside the courtroom Patricia Ensign, a spokesperson for the Christian Science Church in Florida, explained more fully the church's belief in spiritual healing, quoting Eddy: "Man is never sick. Sickness is not real and Truth [Eddy's synonym for Christ] can destroy its seeming reality." Ensign added, "We study what we understand to be God's rules for healing. We don't always demonstrate them perfectly, but we do the best we can. We are taught to have faith completely in God because his power is greater than any other power." Illness and pain are conditions that "claim to be" in the mind of the apparently sick person, explained Ensign. "We don't ignore when something is claiming to be," she continued. "We know it has to be handled. If we can see clearly enough that it is not of God, we can dispel it." Ensign concluded her brief explanation of the central ideas of Christian Science by making an argument for self-serving toleration: "We want people to have what they feel will do them the most good. But by the same token, we want the privilege to go to what we feel is the best source of health. So did the Hermansons."[21]

Three medical experts weighed in on the issues that would be before the Hermanson jury. Dr. Philip Pennell, the director of health and human values programs at the University of Miami School of Medicine, spoke to the question of what, if anything, children understand about Christian Science's beliefs about death. Specifically, Pennell was asked if Amy could make a "conscious decision to pass on," as her mother told a family friend she had. "We have no idea what Amy's feelings were about this," Pennell answered. A seven-year-old has "no cognitive grasp of the meaning of death," he continued, avoiding use of the euphemism "pass on" favored by Christian Scientists. "The fact of the matter is," he explained, "medical technology has come to the point where the child need not have died from diabetes. Routine therapy would have been sufficient to keep her from dying." Her parents withheld that therapy. "She certainly didn't make the decision," Pennell said. Sherman Holvey, the president of the American Diabetes Association, explained the nature of the illness. In the case of insulin-dependent diabetes the body becomes unable to convert food into energy and bodybuilding tissue. Without insulin, which regulates glucose levels in the blood, Holvey said, unused sugar builds up in the blood, and the body's energy sources are soon depleted. Fat cells break down, and the blood becomes more acidic. Finally, the body enters a diabetic coma. Dr. Ronald Goldberg, the director of the Diabetes Research Institute at the University of Miami, added, "There is still a 20 to 40 percent death rate, even in people treated with insulin, but it's 100 percent, sooner or later, in children who don't receive insulin."[22]

During a break in the trial, reporters clustered around Rita Swan, the co-founder and president of CHILD, and Nathan Talbot, the national spokesman for the Christian Science Church. Swan was asked to retell the story of why she left the church and to describe her work in attempting to convince state legislators that all parents, regardless of their religious beliefs, have a duty to provide their children with medical care. Talbot was asked why Christian Scientists allow children to die.

Rita told her story this way: She and Doug Swan were teenagers from Christian Science families when they met at a Christian Science study group at Kansas State Teachers College in 1960. Three years later they married and during the next twelve years completed their graduate work, Doug earning a doctoral degree in mathematics and Rita a doctorate in English literature. The Swans moved to a Detroit suburb when Doug accepted a teaching position at the Detroit Institute of Technology. When their first child, Cathy, was born in 1969, she suffered from ear infections, and Rita and Doug prayed, repeating an argument they had learned as children: "God is good; God created man as His perfect spiritual image. God didn't make disease, and therefore disease is unreal." At the time, Rita recalled, spiritual healing seemed to work, though years later she attributed Cathy's relief to "dumb luck." Matthew, the couple's second child, was born in 1975. At the age of fifteen months he became ill with a persistent high fever that came and went over a period of weeks. When their prayers failed to effect a healing, Rita continued, she turned to Jeanne Laitner, a friend and a prominent Christian Science practitioner. Laitner claimed Matthew's fever was caused by Rita's fear and warned that unless she overcame it Matthew could not be healed. "We had no conception that the fever was a sign of infection," Rita said, "that the fever could come and go, but the disease would go on." By Father's Day, June 19, 1977, Matthew couldn't walk or sit up. The next morning he lay immobile and expressionless. When Laitner made a house call later that day, Rita asked why healing hadn't taken place. "You don't give up on the arithmetic book just because you can't work out all the problems," Laitner responded. Rita recalled that she nodded, "willing to comply and submit" to the belief that Laitner's prayers would heal Matthew.

But during the night Matthew began screaming, gnashing his teeth, moaning incoherently, and convulsing as his life appeared to be slipping away. At this point, Rita said, she called a new practitioner, June Ahern, who exuded confidence. She could "do the work of healing Matthew" she told the Swans, if they would stop hovering over their child and put out of their minds any thought of resorting to *materia medica*. That prescription fit the Swans' lifelong beliefs, and Doug even said he was "afraid of what medical science would do to" their son. But a day later Matthew appeared to be paralyzed, and Ahern suggested he had a broken bone in his neck, a signal that he could be taken to a hospital without violating Christian Science guidelines. "Don't tell them about the fever," Rita recalled Ahern telling her. "Just say he fell off the bed and you'd like him checked out for a broken bone." At the hospital a doctor diagnosed Matthew's illness as bacterial meningitis, and with the Swans' consent he underwent emergency brain surgery.

Immediately after learning that Matthew had undergone surgery and lay in intensive care breathing with the aid of a respirator, the two practitioners who had once prayed for the child's healing refused to pray for him any longer because he, that is, his parents, had voluntarily accepted medical care.

Desperate for spiritual help, Rita reached out to a United Church of Christ, and without hesitation the entire congregation prayed for Matthew. When Doug spoke to Dean Joki, the sole member of the Detroit Christian Science Committee of Publication, and told him how repentant he was for allowing Matthew to suffer under Christian Science treatment, Joki fired back, "Oh, come now, that kind of resentment isn't going to heal anything." Matthew died about 1 a.m. on July 7, 1977, from a disease that Doug and Rita learned could have been treated with antibiotics easily and successfully in its early stage.

Angry and feeling betrayed, the Swans officially left the Christian Science Church. Some Christian Scientists called, urging the Swans not to leave the church. Bill Laitner, Jeanne's brother-in-law, told the couple, "Just grit your teeth and forget about this." Others called to share their stories about Christian Scientists who had lost children and stayed in the church. According to Rita, not one caller from the church offered sympathy, and they all rejected the idea that parents owed their child a duty to provide the proper and necessary care for the child's health and well-being. One caller even spoke of a parent's obligation to a child "as a false belief [the Swans] had to abandon."

Christian Scientists missed the point, Rita concluded. "We had lost our son. That fact was more important to us than whether the church criticized or forgave us, whether hundreds of medical patients died of meningitis, or whether Christian Science was a foolproof panacea or littered with tragedies."[23]

The Swans left Detroit in 1978, moving first to North Dakota, where Doug and Rita taught at Jamestown College, and then, in 1982, to Bronson, Iowa, population 209, where they lived in a farmhouse and taught at nearby Morningside College. In 1980 the Swans brought a wrongful death suit against the Christian Science Church. The Wayne County Circuit Court in Michigan dismissed the suit, ruling that the two practitioners who prayed for Matthew as well as the Christian Science Church were protected by the First Amendment's guarantee of religious freedom. The U.S. Supreme Court declined to hear an appeal. Three years later Rita and Doug created CHILD, an organization dedicated to combating "inhumane religious practices that affect children."[24]

When Swan appeared in Sarasota in 1989 to attend the Hermansons' trial, she was a slim woman in her midforties with short gray and black hair. She had told the story of Matthew's death many times over the intervening years. She had also accumulated a mass of information about the unnecessary deaths of children whose parents relied on spiritual healing, testified before state legislative committees considering repeal of religious exemption laws, and advised prosecutors preparing to bring parents to trial for not providing their ill children with medical care. The trial in Sarasota, Swan told the *Miami Herald,* "signals to the nation that society does not approve of this behavior, and Christian Scientists had better wake up and listen."[25]

Christian Science Church officials had a long-standing policy of not talking to the press except to explain official policy. Talbot, a good-looking man with a full face, hazel eyes, and an unctuous manner that many found irritating, bent that rule only slightly. Before he came to the Mother Church as the editor of religious periodicals, Talbot earned a bachelor of arts degree from the University of Idaho and a law degree from Willamette College of Law in Oregon. He left his law practice, he told the *New England Monthly,* because he decided the "healing ministry was really where my heart was." Standing in a hallway of the Sarasota County Court, Talbot admitted that the most controversial aspect of Christian Science is its application to children. "We agree with everyone else that the child comes first. The question is," he said in a soft voice, "what method of treatment is best?" In Sarasota and at each of his other stops where Christian Scientists were on trial for a child's death, Talbot's answer was the same. Hundreds of children die in hospitals every year, he argued, but no one pays attention to that. Not a single doctor is charged with murder, unlike Christian Science parents who use an alternate method of treatment with a long history of success. "The real issue," he said during a recess at the Hermansons' trial, "is that the prosecution wants the state to sanction one method of healing." Radiating reasonableness, Talbot asked, "Why shouldn't Christian Science parents be allowed to choose the care they want for their children?" The church must "do a fuller job of helping society understand that it has a wonderful gift in spiritual healing," he told the *Miami Herald.* "It would be a loss for all of us to prosecute out of existence spiritual healing."[26]

On Thursday, April 13, the jurors heard a succession of witnesses summoned by the prosecutors, beginning with Dr. James C. Wilson, the associate medical examiner for Sarasota. He testified that an autopsy showed the cause of Amy's death to be diabetic ketoacidosis due to juvenile onset diabetes mellitus. Dehydration and weight loss were consistent with the disease process, he said. In addition to her skeletal appearance, Amy's vertebrae and shoulder blades were prominent and her abdomen distended, as if she had been undernourished. Her eyes were quite sunken because of her dehydration. According to Wilson, a physician could have diagnosed the disease at any point up to a few hours prior to Amy's death and, within the bounds of medical probability, she would have survived with the proper medical treatment.[27]

Three additional witnesses testified that they had seen Amy's health failing in the weeks before her death. Victoria Neuhaus, an adult piano student of Chris Hermanson, told the court that six days before Amy died, Chris had brought her child to Neuhaus's piano lesson. Normally a cheerful little girl, Amy complained throughout the lesson and was so weak she was unable to walk, Neuhaus recalled. "Chris, she obviously is sick; you should take her to a doctor," Neuhaus said. "No, she'll be all right," Hermanson replied. Amy's former homeroom teacher, Laura Kingsley, described Amy as bright and creative but said she became progressively thinner, weaker, and lethargic during the month of September. Helen Falb, an employee at Hermanson's music academy, testified that Amy looked skeletal and that the child told her she had been vomiting and was unable to sleep. Falb said she did not tell Amy's parents about the conversation. "I knew about their religion and I knew they wrote my paycheck and I didn't want to create a stir," Falb testified.[28]

Mary Christman, a family friend of the Hermansons, was slated to be the state's star witness. Prosecutors believed her testimony would show the Hermansons to be selfishly and callously duplicitous because they had told Christman they had used medical treatment for their own physical problems but argued at trial that their religious beliefs caused them to deny medical care to Amy. Such behavior, prosecutors were prepared to assert, constituted culpable negligence, grounds for conviction of third-degree murder.

Late Thursday afternoon the state prosecutor Deno Economou called Christman to testify. Acting on Chris's warning as to what Christman would probably say, Dart objected, calling her testimony potentially "inflammatory" and likely to prejudice the case against Bill Hermanson, who was not present during a conversation she had had with Chris after Amy's death. Judge Dakan ordered the jury out of the courtroom so he could listen to Christman's testimony and decide whether to allow the jury to hear what she said.[29]

Christman said she visited Chris three days after Amy's death and during their conversation Chris told her of times when she and Bill sought medical treatment for themselves despite their religious beliefs. Bill had taken Novocain while having dental work, and she had delivered two children by Caesarean section. "I said, 'God, Chris, if Bill had Novocain and you had two Caesarean sections, which I've had myself, how could you have done that without any anesthetic?'" Chris replied, "Well that was a different situation."

Amy Hermanson   35

"And I said, 'Well, I'm sorry, but when it comes to the death of a child, I think anything that can possibly be tried should be done.'"

"I was frustrated and baffled," Christman told Judge Dakan, "when a simple shot of insulin would have saved the child's life. She looked like a refugee from a death camp." Chris insisted, "Amy felt no pain, there was no illness. It was 'negative transfers' that she was picking up from other people." She also contended that Amy's body would have rejected the insulin because her husband's body rejected Novocain. Christman stated further that Chris ended their conversation by saying, "Amy fully knew that the choice was hers, whether to live or die. Amy glimpsed something from the other world, and she wanted that more than she wanted this world."[30]

After hearing Christman's remarks, Judge Dakan decided to allow the jury to hear her testimony the next day. On Friday, however, the prosecution announced it had completed its case without presenting Christman's testimony. Economou had blundered by failing to notify the defense that Christman would testify, and that mistake violated the state's discovery rule. Dakan, who on Thursday had said the jury could hear the testimony, reversed himself Friday and ruled it inadmissible. Outside the court, Economou said Christman's taped interview had been "inadvertently withheld" from the defense. Henry Lee, chief assistant state attorney for Sarasota County, said he still hoped to introduce Christman's evidence by questioning the Hermansons under oath during rebuttal.[31]

That plan collapsed. When court convened on Monday the defense rested without presenting any witnesses. "Your honor, if it please the court, the defense rests," said Booth. Those ten words made it clear that the prosecutors, jurors, and the public were not going to hear the Hermansons tell how they tried to heal their seven-year-old daughter through prayer alone or why they chose not to seek medical care as Amy slipped into a diabetic coma. Outside the courtroom lawyers were divided about the defense strategy. On one hand, the move prevented prosecutors from questioning the couple on the stand. But the attorney Patrick Doherty, who was not involved in the Hermanson case, said that while defendants have the right not to testify and that jurors are instructed by the court not to hold that against them, "it raises the inference that these people are not taking the stand because they have something to hide." On the other hand, the tactic allows the defense to have the final word. Studies show, said Doherty, "that helps win cases." Judge Dakan expected the jury to begin deliberations on Tuesday after closing arguments were made and his instructions were given.[32]

Lawyers for the prosecution and the defense asked the three women and three men of the jury to choose between starkly different views of Amy's death. His voice rising and falling in a preacher-like rhythmic cadence, the silver-haired Booth, a generation older than Economou, asked the jurors to put aside their personal beliefs about Christian Science and its reliance on spiritual healing and to acknowledge that a 1975 Florida law protected the Hermansons' right to use the healing methods endorsed by their church. "Is it fair under our system of justice to brand this mother and father as murderers because they put their faith in God instead of a doctor?" Booth demanded. "You may not like it; you may not approve of it, but it was their way of caring for their daughter."

Economou, a thin, boyish-looking man, countered by saying the case was about Amy's right to live, not about the religious rights of the parents. Standing directly in front of the jurors and speaking in a soft voice, he showed the jurors color photographs of Amy's corpse and begged them to remember her suffering. "If they wish to become martyrs for that religion for themselves, they have that right," he said. "They do not have the right to make a martyr of that seven-year-old child." Besides, Economou added, extrapolating incorrectly from the decision made by the Christian Science nurse Sellers to call an ambulance when it became apparent spiritual healing was not working for Amy, "Christian Science believes in the sanctity of the life of a child and the use of medical treatment, but the Hermansons turned their back on both and that is not a legitimate practice of religion."[33]

Judge Dakan instructed the jury not to judge the defendants' religious beliefs: "You are not to decide if the defendants correctly interpreted their religion, only whether the defendants held a sincere belief that the teachings of their religion authorized them to take a particular course of action." He also carefully defined culpable negligence, a legal charge that allowed jurors to decide if the Hermansons had acted reasonably and with the safety of others in mind:

Each of us has a duty to act reasonably toward others. If there is a violation of that duty, without any conscious intention to harm, that violation is negligence. But culpable negligence is more than failure to use ordinary care for others. For negligence to be called culpable negligence must be gross and flagrant. The negligence must be committed with an utter disregard for the safety of others. Culpable negligence is consciously doing an act or following a course of conduct that the defendant must have known, or reasonably should have known, was likely to cause death or great bodily injury.[34]

The six jurors filed out of the courtroom around noon. One hour into their deliberations they sent out a note asking if the Hermansons could ask for medical help and, if so, whether they would need permission from the church. Dakan replied he could not answer those questions and instructed the jurors to rely on trial testimony. Two hours later, as Chris and Bill Hermanson watched intently, the jury returned to the courtroom and announced they had found both defendants guilty of third-degree murder and felony child abuse in the death of their seven-year-old daughter Amy. One of the Hermansons' lawyers announced plans to appeal, and Judge Dakan postponed sentencing and released the couple pending that appeal. Flanked by their lawyers, the couple pushed their way through a crowd of reporters and well-wishers and without a word to anyone left the courtroom. According to church records, the Hermansons were the first Christian Scientists in twenty years to be prosecuted in the United States for denying a child medical care for religious reasons.[35]

The juror Matthew J. Welsh and another juror said they were struck by the testimony showing that the Hermansons ignored repeated warnings from friends and teachers about Amy's failing health. The jury foreman, Clyde W. Pierce, characterized the Hermansons' behavior as "a seeming lack of care, a coldness. It's hard for anybody to believe they could let it get that far."[36]

Amy's death and the couple's murder conviction did not seem to give rise to ambiguity or regret on the part of the parents. Bill Hermanson told Hillier, the practitioner who had prayed for Amy as she died, that his arrest and trial occurred "not because we failed, but because we had been so successful that we expected that success to continue." Three days after he and his wife were found guilty Hermanson told a group of approximately fifty Christian Scientists that his confidence in spiritual healing was unshaken. "They don't know they made the wrong decision," he said of the jury. He ended his talk on a note of self-pity, saying without a trace of irony, "It isn't always easy being a Christian Scientist. I know."[37]

In the wake of the Hermansons' conviction, newspaper editorials and state politicians who had been instrumental in enacting the spiritual healing proviso in 1975 that Christian Science parents believed to be a shield protecting them from criminal prosecution if prayer failed called for the law to be repealed. An article in the *Miami Herald* read, "Whatever their religion, parents must understand—and clearly—that they are obligated to seek medical care for an immature child who is seriously ill. To leave the religious exemption law on the books is to work an injustice to both the child and any parent who would rely on it." "Freedom of religion was not on trial with Chris and Bill Hermanson," the *St. Petersburg Times* pointed out. "In this country people can believe whatever they want. But a line always has been drawn where the lives of children are involved. The right of a child to receive lifesaving medical care ought to be subject to no ambiguity." The former state representatives Barry Kutun and Jack Gordon felt betrayed by Christian Science lobbyists who spoke about unwanted school physical exams and religious freedom but never about the tragic consequences that could follow from serious, untreated children's illnesses. Both men now thought the law "never would have passed" if legislators had realized it endangered children.[38]

Nearly three years after Amy's death and two months after the Hermansons' conviction, they stood before Judge Dakan once again to be sentenced for third-degree murder. Chris stood with her head down, her eyes filled with tears. Bill stood at her side, expressionless. Dakan spoke sympathetically, acknowledging they already had suffered greatly by their daughter's death. "I cannot imagine any worse punishment that the court could inflict," he said. Before he sentenced the couple, Dakan listened as each one made a public statement, their first since Amy's death. The Hermansons did not express remorse but said they were confused. "It is almost incomprehensible," Bill said, "that we could be found guilty of killing our child when exactly the opposite is what was going on." He added, "We loved Amy very much and we still do." Standing at the podium located between the defense and prosecution tables, Chris spoke next. In a faint, trembling voice, she said, "I just have a difficult time understanding a justice system that has let us go this far and brought us to the point where we are standing in front of you with a conviction when our family and our children are the absolute center of our activities."

After imposing a four-year jail sentence, Dakan suspended it and placed the Hermansons on fifteen years' probation. He also ordered the couple to get regular medical checkups for their two surviving children, Eric, twelve years old, and Paul, sixteen months. Dart, the Hermansons' attorney, told the court the couple intended to appeal their conviction and sentence. Pending the outcome of their appeal, their lawyer said, the Hermansons would obey the judge's order and take the boys to a doctor. "As firmly as they believe in their religion, they're law-abiding," he added.[39]

On September 28, 1990, the Court of Appeal of Florida, Second District, announced its decision in regard to the Hermansons' appeal of their conviction for felony child abuse and third-degree murder. The fundamental argument underlying each of the Hermansons' contentions was that their prosecution and conviction violated their right to practice their religion. The couple contended the trial court should have granted their motion to dismiss all charges because Florida's child abuse statutes accommodated their use of spiritual healing. The Hermansons also argued that the jury impermissibly decided whether they had acted reasonably in following their religious beliefs. The state claimed the trial court erred in dismissing the manslaughter charge and in allowing the jury to consider the spiritual treatment proviso as a statutory defense.[40]

In a *per curiam* opinion, the appeal court ruled the trial court had erred by allowing the Hermansons to use the spiritual exemption as a statutory defense to the crimes they were charged with committing. That mistake benefited the Hermansons by creating a "legal tangle" that tainted the entire trial and underlay most of the issues raised by the Hermansons on appeal. Despite this initial error, the appeal court concluded, the Hermansons "received an eminently fair trial," and the jury rendered the correct verdict: the Hermansons' right "to hold their religious beliefs did not permit them to exercise that right at the price of Amy's life."[41]

The appeal court bluntly rejected the Hermansons' contention that the spiritual proviso allowed a parent "to permit the death of a child by the failure of the parent to provide readily available medical treatment." Any immunity provided by the statute applies only to the reporting and investigating of allegations of child abuse, but, the court ruled, "if death is involved different responsibilities come into play."[42]

The court also handled the Hermansons' constitutional argument roughly, holding, "There is no constitutional impediment in the First Amendment to the United States Constitution or in article 1, section 3 of the Florida Constitution to a prosecution for felony child abuse, third-degree murder or manslaughter for failure to provide necessary medical care when based on sincerely held religious beliefs." The Florida court's decision followed a long line of U.S. Supreme Court decisions.[43]

The U.S. Supreme Court first defined the free exercise of religion in 1879. George Reynolds, a Mormon, challenged the constitutionality of a federal law prohibiting polygamy, at the time a mainstay of the Church of Jesus Christ of Latter-day Saints. He argued that the First Amendment's free exercise clause protected both religious faith and conduct and that his marriage to two women could not be legislated away by Congress because plural marriage was linked inseparably to his religious belief. In essence, Reynolds sought an exemption for his religious belief from a criminal law that was neutral on its face and applied to all Americans.[44]

The question raised by Reynolds, Chief Justice Morrison R. Waite wrote for a unanimous court, is "whether religious belief can be accepted as a justification of an overt act made criminal by the law of the land." Because religion was not defined by the Constitution, Waite began, the court must look to "the history of the times" when the First Amendment's free exercise clause was adopted. Specifically, the chief justice relied upon Thomas Jefferson's preamble to the Virginia statute establishing religious freedom: "That to suffer the civil magistrate to intrude his powers into the field of opinion, and to restrain the profession or propagation on supposition of their ill tendency, is a dangerous fallacy which at once destroys all religious liberty. It is time enough for the rightful purposes of civil government for its officers to interfere when principles break out into overt acts against peace and good order." These two sentences, Waite explained, distinguish "what properly belongs to the church and what to the State." Using this guideline, the court rejected the claim that personal religious conviction provides an exception to the general obligations of the law. To permit such an excuse would make the individual "superior to the law of the land, and in effect to permit every citizen to become a law unto himself. Government could exist in name only under such circumstances."[45]

In another case involving the Mormon church, *Davis v. Beason* (1889), an Idaho territory court convicted Samuel D. Davis of violating a statute requiring a prospective voter or officeholder to swear under oath that he was neither a polygamist nor a member of a group that counseled or encouraged that crime. The law in effect barred nonpolygamist members of the church from voting or holding office. Although a church member, Davis took the oath. He was subsequently indicted and convicted for conspiracy to pervert administration of the territory's laws. Davis appealed his conviction to the U.S. Supreme Court, claiming the law violated his First Amendment right to the free exercise of religion. "To call the advocacy [of bigamy and polygamy] a tenet of religion," Justice Stephen Field maintained, "is to offend the common sense of mankind." The First Amendment is intended to allow everyone to embrace any religious belief and form of worship they choose as long as they are not "injurious to the equal rights of others." That is why religious freedom must be subordinate to criminal laws. "Probably never before in the history of this country has it seriously been contended that the whole punitive power of the government for acts," Field wrote, "must be suspended in order that the tenets of a religious sect encouraging crime may be carried out without hindrance." The court held the voter registration statute constitutional, bolstering the distinction between religious belief and religious conduct and its corollary that the state could legitimately regulate conduct that harmed others.[46]

In 1944 the Supreme Court specifically extended its distinction between religious belief and conduct to include the protection of children. Sarah Prince appealed her conviction for violating the child labor laws of Massachusetts, claiming the work she and her nine-year-old niece Betty Simmons performed in offering Jehovah's Witnesses' pamphlets for sale was protected by the First Amendment's free exercise clause and by a parental right to authority in her own household and in the rearing of her children. Prince was the aunt and legal guardian of Simmons, and both were ordained ministers in the Jehovah's Witnesses church. On the evening of December 18, 1941, Prince and Simmons stood on a street in Brockton holding up for sale to passersby copies of the *Watchtower*. In the lower court Simmons had testified she believed it was her religious duty to carry out this work.[47]

Writing for the majority, Justice Wiley Rutledge acknowledged the case presented a difficult issue. The right to "freedom of conscience and religious practice" has a prime place in the Constitution, and the "custody, care and nurture" of a child resides first with the parents. Against these "sacred private rights" stands society's interest in safeguarding children's welfare and the state's assertion of authority to achieve that goal. In 1925 the court had held that the Oregon legislature had unreasonably interfered with a constitutional right of parents to direct the education and upbringing of their children, but in *Prince,* Rutledge held, "The family itself is not beyond regulation in the public interest, as against a claim of religious liberty." Neither parenthood nor rights of religion are beyond the reach of the state as *parens patriae.*[48]

The court noted that the state's authority over children was broader than it was over adults. Adults may choose to preach in the streets, but the Massachusetts law prohibiting minors from working on the streets is a reasonable and constitutional means of fulfilling the state's responsibility to protect children's welfare. "Parents may be free to become martyrs themselves," Rutledge concluded in the landmark decision's most often quoted statement, "but it does not follow they are free, in identical circumstances, to make martyrs of their children before they have reached the age of full and legal discretion when they can make that choice for themselves."[49]

The court's decision in *Prince* fit its free exercise jurisprudence dating to *Reynolds*. It rested on the assumption that the legislature, not the courts, was best equipped to assess the public good. If the law identified a harmful act—child labor—and punished everyone who violated the law, the fact that a person acted or failed to act for religious reasons did not challenge the law's legitimacy. "The touchstone throughout the free exercise cases," the law professor Marci Hamilton argues, "has been whether the legislature identified actions that led to unacceptable harm to society."[50]

The court abruptly altered its free exercise jurisprudence in 1963. Writing for the majority in *Sherbert v. Verner*, Justice William Brennan held that when applied to religious groups, neutral and generally applicable laws could be subject to strict scrutiny, a test requiring a state to establish it has a compelling interest justifying a law that impinges on the free exercise of religion. Adell Sherbert, a member of the Seventh-day Adventist Church, was fired from her job in a South Carolina textile mill because she refused to work on Saturday, her faith's Sabbath. She could not find other employment for the same reason, and she applied for unemployment benefits. The state commission denied Sherbert's claim, finding she "failed, without good cause" to accept available work. This ruling forced Sherbert to choose between her religion and receiving benefits. Denying Sherbert unemployment benefits, the court held, imposed an unconstitutional burden on her free exercise of religion because the state had failed to demonstrate a compelling interest. Although the court added that "only the gravest abuses" endangering compelling interests gave "occasion for permissible limitation," the decision seemed to open the door to the argument by religious groups that neutral, generally applicable laws could be challenged as unconstitutional.[51]

In *Wisconsin v. Yoder* (1972) the court extended its *Sherbert* analysis to compulsory school attendance laws. Wallace Miller and Jonas Yoder were members of the Old Older Amish faith, and Adin Yutzy had recently joined a Conservative Amish Mennonite congregation. Obeying their religions' beliefs, they stopped sending their children to school after they completed the eighth grade, a violation of Wisconsin's compulsory education laws, which required children to attend school through the twelfth grade. In court the three men argued that the law violated their constitutional right to the free exercise of religion and their right to raise their children in conformity with their religious beliefs. The state of Wisconsin countered by referring to Supreme Court opinions that upheld the right of states to legislate compulsory school attendance. In 1971 the Wisconsin Supreme Court reversed the trial verdict and ordered the three men to pay a small fine. The state appealed to the U.S. Supreme Court.[52]

Chief Justice Warren Burger affirmed the lower court's decision, holding that applying Wisconsin's compulsory high school attendance law to children of members of the Old Order Amish and Conservative Mennonite Church violated the parents' rights under the First Amendment's free exercise clause and their right to raise their children as they saw fit. Requiring Amish children to attend high school would severely threaten their religion and their way of life. Salvation, according to their fundamental belief, "requires life in a church community, separate and apart from the world and worldly influence." By contrast, Burger wrote, a high school education emphasizes worldliness, competitiveness, and material success, goals at "marked variance with Amish values and the Amish way of life."[53]

The court also determined that the state's interest in universal education was "not absolute" but could be balanced "when it impinges on fundamental rights and interests" such as the free exercise of religion and the right of parents "with respect to the religious upbringing of their children." Therefore, the state's reliance on *Reynolds* and *Prince* was misplaced. Since those two decisions, Burger argued, the court had not supported an absolute divide between religious belief and action. And, contrary to *Prince*, no danger to a child's welfare results from allowing an abbreviated education. For these reasons the court created an exemption from Wisconsin's generally applicable, neutral law solely for the Amish.[54]

Among others, David N. Williams, a Washington lobbyist for the Christian Science Church, embraced the Supreme Court's new doctrine and language. He posed a lawyer's brief-like question: "Should religious healing be prohibited simply because it's religious?" The answer is that under the standard articulated in *Reynolds,* yes, it should be, but *Sherbert v. Verner* changed the test. The state must now show a "compelling reason for restricting religious practice," a difficult challenge for the state, according to Williams, given the Christian Science Church's success with spiritual healing, especially when compared to the number of children "martyred [by] medical technology." In addition, Williams claimed, the *Yoder* court provided constitutional protection for a religious "way of life," a standard that will "prevent the state from forcing families to adhere to secular rules at the expense of religion." Williams's argument led to the conclusion that the state could not convince the Supreme Court it had a compelling interest allowing it to interfere in the Christian Science Church's practice of healing.[55]

To Williams's dismay as well as to that of many other American religious groups, in *Employment Division v. Smith* (1990) the Supreme Court cast aside *Yoder's* expansive religious liberty, holding in favor of a return to the principle that a violation of a criminal law could not be annulled by religious motivation. "We have never held," Justice Antonin Scalia wrote for the majority, "that an individual's religious beliefs excuse him from compliance with an otherwise valid law prohibiting conduct the state is free to regulate. On the contrary, the record of more than a century of our free exercise jurisprudence contradicts that proposition." Neutral and generally applicable laws do not violate the First Amendment's free exercise clause.[56]

The appeal court in Florida also rejected the Hermansons' contention that a parent who relies on spiritual rather than medical treatment will never know beforehand when the line is crossed and they should stop relying on spiritual treatment in favor of seeking medical care. This argument, the court noted, forms the basis for the couple's claim that their due process rights have been violated because the statutes containing the term "culpable negligence" do not give them adequate notice as to what behavior constitutes a criminal act and when that behavior occurs. In response to this argument, the court cited Justice Oliver Wendell Holmes: "The law is full of instances where a man's fate depends on his estimating rightly, that is, as the jury subsequently estimates it, some matter of degree. An act causing death may be murder, manslaughter, or misadventure according to the degree of danger attending it, by common experience in the circumstances known to the actor."[57]

Finally, the Hermansons alleged, the jury's verdict was based on insufficient evidence to find them guilty of culpable negligence, defined as "gross or flagrant conduct evincing a reckless disregard for human life." In response, the appeal court highlighted the testimony of several witnesses who had observed Amy's condition and behavior during the month before her death. The child had lost so much weight she appeared skeletal. There were deep, dark circles under her eyes that had not been there before. She was lethargic and too tired to participate in gym class or stay awake during the day. Despite Amy's evident deteriorating condition, the Hermansons chose to give her spiritual treatment alone rather than conventional medical treatment. In fact, the evidence presented was sufficient for the jury to find the Hermansons "had acted in reckless disregard of Amy's health, and ultimately, her life."[58]

After its review, the appeal court affirmed the judgment of the lower court and held that the Hermansons had been properly convicted of felony child abuse and third-degree murder for failing to provide medical treatment for their daughter, Amy. The Hermansons immediately filed a motion for re-hearing and clarification that the appeal court denied except for the request that it certify a question "of great public importance" to the Florida Supreme Court. The appeal court forwarded the following question: "Is the spiritual treatment proviso contained in section 415.503 (7)(f), Florida Statutes (1985), a statutory defense to a criminal prosecution [for felony child abuse] under section 827.04 (1) Florida Statutes (1985)?"[59]

Nearly six years after Amy's death, on July 2, 1992, the Florida Supreme Court handed down its decision. Justice Ben F. Overton, appointed by the Democratic governor Reubin Askew in 1974, wrote for a unanimous court. He focused exclusively on the Hermansons' claim that the Florida statutes under which they were convicted did not give them fair warning of the consequences of practicing their religious belief and that their conviction was therefore a denial of due process. Overton pointed out that the Court of Appeal had difficulty explaining why the religious accommodation proviso was only part of the civil child abuse statute and not the criminal abuse statute, and the trial court held that the same section protected the Hermansons only to the extent of making it a jury issue. The U.S. Supreme Court, Overton wrote, has ruled, "Confusion in lower courts is evidence of vagueness which violates due process." The Florida Supreme Court also had ruled on this point: "A person of common intelligence must be able to determine what type of activity the statute is seeking to proscribe." Finally, by authorizing spiritual treatment in one statute and declaring that same conduct criminal under another statute, "the State trapped the Hermansons, who had no fair warning that the State would consider their conduct criminal." In short, when read together, the child abuse statute and the spiritual treatment proviso are ambiguous and result in a denial of due process because the statutes fail to give parents fair notice "of the point at which their reliance on spiritual treatment loses statutory approval and become culpably negligent." For these reasons the Florida Supreme Court quashed the appeal court decision and vacated the Hermansons' conviction.[60]

"We are elated over the decision," Victor Westburg, the national spokes-man for the Christian Science Church said. Although it was limited to due process, "we see it as a first step in protecting parental rights." Chris's father, Jack Morton, also was pleased with the court's decision and appeared to have reconciled with his daughter's religious beliefs. "Our faith has been in them

[Chris and Bill] and in God," he said. "It's not a Christian Science problem as much as it's a decision-making process. People that believe in God rely on God for healing. I prefer that [Chris] made her own decision, just like I did when we were raising our children." The Hermansons said nothing publicly. Three years before the Florida Supreme Court's ruling became public, Bill and Chris Hermanson left Sarasota for St. Louis and a fresh start.[61]

The deaths of other Christian Science children did not allow the issue of religious accommodation and child abuse to fade away so quickly and easily.

2

Shauntay Walker, Seth Glaser, and Natalie Rippberger

In 1984 three children raised in Christian Science families in California died from medically untreated bacterial meningitis. Just nineteen days after four-year-old Shauntay Walker became sick and died on March 9, the same disease claimed the life of seventeen-month-old Seth Glaser and, early in December, that of eight-month-old Natalie Rippberger. The state charged each of the Christian Science parents with felony child endangerment and involuntary manslaughter because they failed to provide their children with medical care, choosing instead to rely solely on spiritual healing. For more than a decade the three cases wended their way through the California courts. Prosecutors worked to bring the parents to justice and to protect other children from suffering a similar fate in the name of religious freedom. Despite a decade of unfavorable legal outcomes and negative publicity, the church largely protected the accommodation statutes for which it successfully had lobbied by encouraging expensive, lengthy appellate court battles that blunted the moral impact of the children's deaths at the hand of their religious parents but did not undercut legislative support for spiritual healing.[1]

California was among the many states that changed its child neglect laws in the mid-1970s to conform to HEW's newly established criteria. Enacted in 1872, California's initial effort to protect children stipulated that a parent of a minor child who willfully failed "to furnish necessary food, clothing, shelter, or medical attendance" was guilty of a misdemeanor. An amendment passed in 1925 added, "or other remedial care," a phrase widely understood to signal approval of healing prayer. Those four words were clarified in 1976, when, in order to qualify for federal funds to fight child neglect and abuse, California, like all other states, amended its child neglect and abuse statutes to exempt from misdemeanor punishment a parent who used spiritual healing to treat an ill minor child.[2]

Christian Scientists interpreted each of these three versions of California's child neglect law differently than the legislature intended. Clara and Merrill Reed were tried in 1902 for failure to adhere to the 1872 statute stipulating "medical attendance" for their daughter, who, despite her parents' prayers, died of untreated diphtheria. In his closing argument on behalf of the Reeds, Will A. Harris, an attorney from Los Angeles, encouraged the jury to ignore the law's clear intent to protect children and instead to privilege the Reeds' religious beliefs. He argued, "The world is full of things we don't understand. And the prosecutors would have you convict this father and mother because the prosecutors don't understand Christian Science. You are not to convict these people because you cannot understand their beliefs. Why, that is the reason Christ was nailed to the Cross—because he taught things that were not down in the books of the regular school." The Reeds were acquitted.[3]

Seeking to legitimize similar trial court outcomes, Christian Scientists urged the California legislature in 1925 to add the phrase "or other remedial care" to the state's child neglect law with the understanding that prayer would be an affirmative defense against a manslaughter charge. Similarly, in 1976 church advocates claimed that the spiritual treatment amendment, coupled with "other remedial care," signaled the legislature's intent to shield Christian Scientists from child neglect and abuse charges as well as prosecution for manslaughter. In 1986 the California Court of Appeal brushed aside this argument as based on "defective evidence" and being "flatly erroneous."[4]

The church's legal and legislative efforts spring from its theology. Christian Scientists, as noted earlier, believe the only true reality is God, who is Mind or Spirit. The physical body and the understanding that the body is afflicted with disease or pain are errors of the mortal mind. "Sickness," Eddy wrote in *Science and Health,* "is part of the error which Truth casts out. Error will not expel error. Christian Science is the law of Truth, which heals the sick on the basis of the one Mind or God. It can heal in no other way, since the human, mortal mind so-called is not a healer, but causes the belief in disease." DeWitt John, an editor of the *Christian Science Monitor* and a board member of the church in the 1960s and 1970s, spelled out how this belief shaped Christian Scientists' perception of medicine. "The fundamental assumptions of Christian Science are opposite to those of medical theory," John wrote. "For example, that all disease is essentially a mental condition, and that man, in his true nature, is essentially a spiritual being and not a material organism." For these reasons, Christian Scientists assert, spiritual healing is incompatible with medicine, and the two cannot be mixed. At the same time, John failed to mention, Christian Scientists routinely use medical care for childbirth, setting broken bones, and correcting for defective eyesight and hearing.[5]

The church documents its claim to successful spiritual healings of every category of illness. In the two decades from 1969 to 1989 church publications list more than 7,000 healings, including 2,451 healings involving children, of which 640 were allegedly medically diagnosed. This evidence, the church argues, supports the contention that healing, in Christian Science's experience, has occurred frequently and often is not explainable under ordinary medical rubrics. Many critics have pointed out, however, that because the church does not meet scientific testing standards—it does not conduct double-blind, placebo-controlled trials or participate in medical studies or keep records of the children who die while receiving prayer treatment—an objective analysis of the success and failure rate of spiritual healing is not possible. Still, Christian Scientists rely on this self-generated data to buttress their belief and to convince nonbelievers that spiritual healing is a reasonable alternative to medical care. This rationale was manifest in the legal defense waged by the California parents on trial for child neglect and involuntary manslaughter.[6]

As we have seen, Christian Scientists may enlist the help of a practitioner, a person who has studied the tenets of the religion, is considered a catalyst for healing, and has been certified by the church. A practitioner attempts to detach any sense of illness from her mental image of the patient. This treatment is based on the premise that a person cannot be ill because sickness is illusory, as is the human body and all things material. In addition to confirming Christian Science teachings, practitioners use a demonstration prayer to help clients break the "dream of material senses," as Eddy put it. Often a practitioner employed by an ill client will engage him or her in silent meditation or instruct the sick person to repeat the following passage from *Science and Health*: "There is no life, truth, intelligence, nor substance in matter. All is infinite Mind and its manifestation, for God is All-in-all. Spirit is the real and eternal; matter is the unreal and temporal. Spirit is God, and man His image and likeness. Therefore man is not material, he is spiritual." The client's and the practitioner's mental state is all-important. The thoughts of the sick person and the thoughts of those around him or her can be harmful or helpful to an ill person. Because a practitioner must never think a client suffers from a real health problem, no mention is made of the physical condition being treated by prayer. Healings are accomplished when a practitioner is able to help an ill person "realize the presence of health and the fact of harmonious being until the body corresponds with the normal condition of health and harmony."[7]

It seems reasonable to assume that not all Christian Science parents confronted with a seriously ill child adhered unwaveringly to spiritual healing. A Christian Science family living in Sacramento took steps, although hesitantly, ambivalently, and ultimately in compliance with a juvenile court order, to save the life of their son by making use of advanced medical care. In September 1983 the parents of the three-year-old Eric noticed a problem with one of his eyes. They contacted a Christian Science practitioner, but after several weeks passed without a healing the worried parents took their son to a physician. The initial diagnosis was glaucoma, but further testing revealed Eric had retinal blastoma, cancer of the eye. With the approval of Eric's parents, his left eye was surgically removed in November at a Sacramento hospital. However, tests conducted after the surgery raised the possibility that not all the cancer had been removed. Eric's doctor recommended chemotherapy and radiation, but the child's parents refused to permit any follow-up medical treatment, citing their Christian Science belief in spiritual healing. They preferred to place their son's care in the hands of a practitioner.[8]

Acting on the advice of Eric's physician, the Office of Child Abuse, Sacramento County Department of Social Services, filed a petition with the Juvenile Court of Sacramento County in January 1984 to have Eric declared a dependent ward of the court so the physician's recommended postoperation treatments could be carried out. The court heard evidence that, in the absence of medical treatment, there was a high statistical probability the cancer would return and Eric's life would be endangered. Largely for this reason the court supported the petition, declared Eric a dependent child, and placed him in the custody of his parents, who were ordered to facilitate his treatment "until further order." The parents complied with the order, moving to Contra Costa County when Eric's treatment regime began at an Oakland hospital.[9]

In December, Eric's attending physician recommended to the Contra Costa County Social Services Department that the child's therapy program be continued for two more years but with less frequent treatments. A social services caseworker concurred, explaining it was the agency's standard practice to adopt a physician's recommendation. In addition to the caseworker's testimony, a referee for the Contra County juvenile court heard testimony from a doctor and Eric's father. The child's physician stated that although no new cancer had been detected, Eric would be "at risk" unless the court-ordered "observation phase" were implemented. Eric's father explained that he and his wife opposed any further medical treatment. "The basis is that we are Christian Scientists. Eric is having Christian Science treatment and we believe that he should have only Christian Science treatment." The father's admission that their child was receiving both spiritual and medical treatments was contrary to accepted Christian Science teaching and implies the parents' dilemma about how best to treat Eric. On February 27, 1985, the juvenile court continued Eric's dependency status, ordering his parents to "follow the treatment and medical procedures recommended by the attending physician." The parents appealed the referee's order. They made three arguments: the juvenile court lacks jurisdiction to continue the dependency status; the dependency jurisdiction cannot be continued "in the absence of a clear and present need for treatment"; and California law recognizes the validity of treatment by spiritual means alone.[10]

Reviewing more than two dozen cases, the California Court of Appeal rejected the parents' first claim. Acknowledging that Eric currently was without a showing of cancer, Judge Marc Poché found that "no reason in either law or logic exists to demonstrate why the state, with the substantial interests it is entitled to assert on its behalf as well as for a child, should be compelled to hold its protective power in abeyance until harm to a minor child is not only threatened but actual. The purpose of dependency proceedings is to prevent risk, not ignore it." Actual harm to a child was not necessary to continue the custody of the juvenile court, the unanimous court concluded.[11]

Second, the court found substantial evidence to support the referee's conclusion that Eric's best interests required continuation of his dependency status. His attending physician stated there was a 40 percent chance that Eric's cancer would recur and "he would die if there's nothing monitored and nothing done about it." The court also noted that Eric's father testified that "unless ordered by the court, he would not have Eric monitored but would instead rely exclusively on only Christian Science treatment." When the physician's dark prediction was linked to the father's desire to rely on spiritual healing, Judge Poché concluded that "Eric's best interests would not be served by exposing him to the possible peril" that could result if the family relied solely on prayer.

Third, the court considered the parents' argument—"asserted at all stages of the dependency proceedings"—that California law recognized "the validity of treatment by spiritual means alone." The parents based their argument on the California Welfare and Institution Code, section 300.5, which provided the following: "In any case in which a minor is alleged to come within the provisions of Section 300 on the basis that he or she is in need of medical care, the court in making such a finding, shall give consideration to any treatment being provided to the minor by spiritual means through prayer alone in accordance with the tenets and practices of a recognized church or religious denomination by an accredited practitioner thereof." While acknowledging that section 300.5 allowed the court to consider spiritual treatment, Judge Poché's decision characterized the statute as a thin reed. It does not specify what conclusions shall be drawn from the fact that a minor is receiving treatment by spiritual means instead of conventional medicine or preclude the court from exercising its "very extensive discretion in determining what will be in the best interests of a child." Specifically, the statute does not prohibit the court from concluding that "spiritual treatment alone is not sufficient to arrest a danger" in which "conventional medical treatment is more likely to succeed." The parents' petitions for a rehearing and for review by the California Supreme Court were denied.[12]

Like Eric's parents, Suzanne Shepard realized that her daughter Marilyn was seriously ill. Marilyn complained of stomach pains. Suzanne, a Christian Science practitioner with thirteen years' experience, prayed. But ten days before Christmas in 1986 Marilyn looked up from the couch where she had lain for three days and said, "Mommy, I'm going." The six-year-old had slipped into a coma. As Suzanne later recounted that moment, she asked herself, "Do I want to be a good Christian Scientist and not have a daughter, or be a bad Christian Scientist and have a daughter?" She rushed Marilyn to St. Louis Children's Hospital, where an emergency operation for a ruptured appendix and treatment for peritonitis saved her life. At the hospital, members of Shepard's Christian Science Church attributed Marilyn's illness to Suzanne's lapse from total reliance on God. Suzanne did not leave the church after her daughter's recovery. She continued to attend the Kirkwood Christian Science Church, but she stopped working as a practitioner and publicly advocated that the church abandon its position that spiritual healing and medical treatment were incompatible. While it seems likely that stance irritated church members, it was Suzanne's affiliation with the ex–Christian Scientist Rita Swan that led to her formal expulsion from the church in October 1993.[13]

In these two instances a California court and a Missouri parent found that when a child's life is endangered, reliance on prayer must yield to a course of action that is in the child's best interest. The Christian Science parents of Shauntay Walker, Seth Glaser, and Natalie Rippberger, contemporaries of

Eric and Marilyn, chose radical reliance rather than medical care or a combination of spiritual healing and medical care when their children's life was at risk. The road not taken led to the children's death and to criminal charges against the parents.

When Laurie Walker's four-year-old daughter Shauntay became ill with flu-like symptoms on February 21, 1984, Walker employed Norma Alpert, an accredited Christian Science prayer practitioner. Alpert later testified she "neither noticed, nor looked for, symptoms of fever" and "saw no evidence" of a stiff neck. In fact, over the next seventeen days Shauntay not only had a high fever and a stiff neck but also vomited and lost weight. Walker, a dark-haired, thirty-year-old single mother employed as a financial analyst for the California Department of Health Services in Sacramento, never called a doctor but instead relied completely on Christian Science spiritual healing. A neighbor who saw Shauntay on the fifth day of the girl's illness told her husband, "I never saw a little girl look so sick." Apparently fearful of what other non–Christian Scientists might say or do if they saw Shauntay's deteriorating physical condition, Walker kept her daughter home from preschool, lied about why Shauntay was not at school, and refused to allow her mother and other inquisitive relatives and friends to visit the child. At the same time, Walker, who had converted to Christian Science three years earlier, brought church members into her home to pray for the child's recovery. Nevertheless, Shauntay became increasingly weaker, disoriented, and irritable and experienced difficulty breathing. Walker's sister, Claudia Oswald, who somehow gained access to Shauntay on March 8, said the child was "basically comatose." She begged her sister to take the child to a doctor, and when Walker refused, Oswald, shocked and angry, threatened to inform the authorities of the child's condition. Later that day Walker secretly moved Shauntay to a Christian Science friend's house, where at 1 a.m. on Friday, March 9, the child died. The next day Walker called to tell her sister of Shauntay's death. During that conversation Walker adamantly insisted she would not consult a doctor if another of her children became ill, an admission that prompted Oswald to call the police.[14]

An autopsy found the cause of death to be bacterial meningitis, a disease that can be effectively treated with antibiotics and is rarely fatal if diagnosed. At her death, Shauntay, or Sunny, as her father called her, weighed twenty-nine pounds. A police investigation into Shauntay's death led the district attorney of Sacramento County to file felony child endangerment, involuntary manslaughter, and felony murder charges against Walker. The California penal code defined child endangerment as follows: "Any person . . . having the care or custody of any child, willfully causes or permits the person or health of such child to be injured, or willfully causes or permits such child to be placed in such situation that its person or health is endangered, is punishable by imprisonment in the county jail not exceeding one year, or in the state prison for 2, 4, or 6 years." The specific section of the penal code with which the state charged Walker defined involuntary manslaughter as "the unlawful killing of a human being without malice in the commission of a lawful act which might produce death in an unlawful manner and without due caution and circumspection." Essentially, the information accompanying the charge alleged Walker was criminally negligent because she failed to summon a doctor, and her inaction probably caused Shauntay's death.[15]

Walker wept when Rudolph Loncke, a Sacramento Municipal Court judge, ruled she must stand trial on involuntary manslaughter and felony child endangerment charges in the death of her daughter. Judge Loncke dismissed a murder charge against Walker, saying he did not believe it was an appropriate case for the felony murder rule. Assistant Chief Deputy District Attorney for Sacramento County John O'Mara expressed satisfaction with both rulings, but Walker's lawyer, Thomas A. Volk, an attorney from Sacramento, insisted that the exemption for spiritual healing written into California law protected his client's conduct, that all charges against her should be dropped, and that she should be freed immediately. The court ordered Walker to appear for arraignment in Sacramento Superior Court on October 12. She posted a five-thousand-dollar bail bond and left the building by a side door without speaking to reporters.[16]

Less than three weeks after Shauntay's death, the Christian Science parents of seventeen-month-old Seth Glaser, Eliot and Lise, grew worried about their son's health. Eliot was born in Pasadena to a Christian Science family, and Lise, the daughter of an Episcopalian priest, converted to Christian Science when she and Eliot married in 1977. On Wednesday, March 21, 1984, Seth developed a runny nose, a persistent cough, and a fever, symptoms medical experts later identified as the likely onset of the infection that led to his death. Later in the week Seth had difficulty breathing and a rapid heart rate. Lise telephoned Virginia ("Gina") Scott, a Christian Science practitioner who had prayed for Seth on earlier occasions, and she began the work of healing. About 4:30 p.m. on Tuesday, March 27, when Eliot called to say he was about to bicycle home from work, Lise told him Seth had a "pretty high fever," and she asked Eliot to pray about it on his way home. The next morning Seth's temperature had subsided, and he ate and drank, but he couldn't stand, and his face sometimes turned purple. Eliot was worried enough to stay home from work. Lise called Scott and told her, "It's really gone bad again." Scott disagreed. Her allegedly scientific reasoning supported a "very strong feeling that the prayer was being effective." Eliot and Lise fed Seth twice, and he vomited the food each time. About 11 a.m. they realized Seth's fever had risen and that he had lost muscle control, so they arranged to take Seth to Scott's home at 1 p.m. On the way from their home in Culver City to Scott's residence in a wealthy neighborhood in Santa Monica, Seth vomited a third time and experienced convulsions. Eliot stopped the car, and Lise noticed the boy's limbs were cold, but they did not seriously consider getting medical help.[17]

Eliot carried Seth into Scott's home. Because the house was chilly, Scott turned on the heat and took the infant outside to her sunny patio, where she laid him on a mattress. After about ten minutes she brought Seth back into the house, but she asked the Glasers to remain outside. Scott telephoned Al Carnesciali, an official of the Christian Science Church in southern California. Scott knew "the church wants to be kept informed of any cases in which the church may be criticized as a result of their method of taking care of illnesses through prayer, especially when a child is involved." She was aware Seth was near death and that Shauntay Walker's death was under police investigation. When the frightened Lise came inside the house, Scott said, "Honey, God is right here taking care of him." She added, "Maybe it would be better for you [two] to take a walk right now."

Scott laid Seth on a blanket on her office floor and began to pray. His breathing became slow and shallow, a change Scott interpreted as a sign her prayers were healing Seth. At the same moment, about 2:45 p.m., he stopped breathing, and Scott felt "he had passed on." She called Carnesciali again, and he told her to call the House of Hall Mortuary to make arrangements for the body. She picked up the infant, put him on the couch, and began mouth-to-mouth resuscitation, later telling a police officer she "had seen it performed on television." When the Glasers returned from their walk, they too tried desperately to resuscitate their baby. No one suggested calling paramedics or taking the boy to a hospital.

Rather, Scott and the Glasers continued to pray. Resurrection remained a hope and promise of their faith. Scott claimed she had once revived an old woman who had stopped breathing. About 4 p.m. Lise phoned Beverly DeWindt, another practitioner, who told her she "had revived a seven-year-old boy and there's proof of that." Buoyed by DeWindt's "demonstration" that death was nothing more than a "mortal dream," "we [all] stuck with it," Lise said later. "We just prayed and we prayed." In response to Scott's earlier call, a hearse came for the infant's body about 4:30 p.m., but the Glasers asked if they could have more time to pray. At some point Scott gave up, but for the next seven hours—until the hearse returned to Scott's home close to midnight—DeWindt and the Glasers continued to pray for Seth's revival. In compliance with the law, the funeral director reported the death to the coroner's office, and a police investigation followed.[18]

On June 20 a grand jury returned a sealed indictment to Deputy District Attorney David Wells, who two days later charged the Glasers and Scott with felony child endangerment and involuntary manslaughter. "We're not charging them with praying," Wells said. "We're charging them with failure to seek conventional medical practices when it became apparent they should." Speaking for the Christian Science Church, Carnesciali issued a statement articulating the church's customary invidious comparison between medical and spiritual care: "I couldn't help feeling a deep compassion for the families of children who have died quite suddenly of meningitis in hospitals. Surely, there is no justice in such deaths. Neither is there apparent justice in arbitrarily singling out parents because of their religious beliefs. . . . The parents of hundreds of children suffering from meningitis who receive up to the minute medical care—and yet pass on—are not similarly the objects of criminal proceedings." Freed on their own recognizance, the Glasers and Scott entered not guilty pleas on July 23.[19]

Seven months later Judge Laurence D. Rubin of the Santa Monica Municipal Court ordered Eliot Glaser, twenty-seven, and his wife, Lise Glaser, twenty-six, to stand trial on child endangerment and involuntary manslaughter charges brought by District Attorney Wells. Judge Rubin dismissed the same charges against Scott, noting the baby was so ill by the time she saw him that medical treatment after her intervention probably would not have saved the infant's life. Yet Rubin told Scott he did not condone her conduct and advised her to mention the death of Seth Glaser whenever she touted the power of prayer. Wells vehemently disagreed with Rubin's decision to dismiss the charges against Scott. "What [Scott] was doing was engaging in human sacrifice," the district attorney said. "She was sacrificing a child for religious principles."[20]

The Glasers were arraigned on March 13, 1985. Outside the court, the defense attorney Douglas Dalton said the speed with which Seth's illness happened meant Eliot and Lise "had no idea of the seriousness of the illness until about an hour before the child died." The prosecutor disagreed, saying "it was their duty to know" the boy was seriously ill. "Ignorance is no defense and Christian Science ignorance is no defense." Dalton signaled he intended to file a motion claiming the prosecution had insufficient evidence to prove the charges. There the matter stood while the prosecution and defense waited for the Walker case to work its way through the appeals process.[21]

About three months before the Glasers were arraigned, eight-month-old Natalie Rippberger struggled with an illness her Christian Science parents sought to heal with prayer. Natalie had been feverish and sick for a week despite the prayers of her parents, Mark Rippberger, a thirty-two-year-old environmental engineer at a cleanup firm, and Susan Middleton, thirty-six, and two Christian Science practitioners. Alarmed, the Rippbergers summoned Therese Miller, a Christian Science visiting nurse, to their home in Healdsburg, a barnlike structure without a bathroom or cooking facilities on property owned by Susan's parents, near Santa Rosa, California. Miller noted that Natalie "was very warm to the touch" and "somewhat responsive" but that "her eyes tended to roll back in her head" and "she cried when her position was changed." After staying with the baby for an hour, Miller advised the parents to keep Natalie warm and to keep trying to give her nourishment. She also recommended they notify the Santa Rosa Christian Science Committee on Publication (the so-called committee is composed of a single Christian Scientist who oversees legal and public relations matters) because Natalie did not appear to be responding favorably to prayer treatment. During her daily visits Miller observed that Natalie's eyes were "rolling or jerking," her legs were "very rigid," and she was unable to bend her legs at the knees. On December 6, the twelfth day of the child's illness, Miller noted that Natalie's condition had deteriorated: she was experiencing "heavy convulsions" and was "unresponsive." Miller told the Rippbergers the "situation was serious," but she did not recommend medical care. She bathed Natalie, changed her sweat-soaked clothing, and silently read some verses from the Bible and passages from *Science and Health.* After a restless night during which Miller prayed and "voiced the truth to the baby," Natalie "awakened to heavy convulsions." During the remainder of December 7 and all the next day Miller was busy with other cases and returned to the Rippbergers' home on the ninth. That day, Natalie died. Miller told the parents to call the coroner.[22]

Aware of the Walker and Glaser cases then pending and the complex legal issues and constitutional questions likely to be raised if he charged the Rippbergers, Sonoma County District Attorney Gene Tunney moved cautiously. He deliberated for three months before bringing charges of felony child endangerment and involuntary manslaughter against the Rippbergers. On May 30, 1985, Tunney presented evidence to substantiate these charges at a preliminary hearing before Judge Frank Passalacqua of the Sonoma County Municipal Court.[23]

Dr. A. Jay Chapman, an expert in the field of forensic pathology, had performed an autopsy on Natalie's body the day after her death and determined the cause of death to have been acute purulent meningitis of the brain and spinal cord. Chapman also reported to the district attorney's office that his analysis revealed medical care had been withheld from the child. He testified that the condition of the child's brain indicated she underwent considerable pain before she died. Complementing Chapman's autopsy report, Miller and Dr. Michael W. Witmer, a specialist in infectious diseases and a clinical professor at the University of California San Francisco Medical School, testified for the prosecution.[24]

The prosecutor Peter Bumerts guided Miller through the chronology of events leading to Natalie's death. When the infant experienced convulsions on December 6, Miller told the court, she and the Rippbergers knew Natalie was in "serious condition," but no one thought of calling a doctor. "We all believed and expected a healing through prayer," she said. In fact, Witmer subsequently testified, Natalie had "[one] of the most serious afflictions" a child can get, but, he added, "This child was curable or treatable with any of a half-dozen drugs. Had she received any of them, she would be alive today." Even in a worst-case scenario in which antibiotics were not given until a child presented symptoms such as rolling eyes, rigidity, and convulsions, he said, a baby would have an 85 to 90 percent chance of survival. A deeply comatose infant who had been deprived of antibiotic treatment for more than a week would probably have a 50 percent chance of survival. On the other hand, Witmer testified, without medical treatment "virtually all eight-month-old infants with bacterial meningitis would die." On cross-examination, the defense attorney David E. Mackenroth, a Christian Scientist, asked Witmer about the relationship of prayer and medical treatment. "I pray every day for all my patients," the doctor said. "But prayer alone would not do it in this case. I also feel that the gift of penicillin is a gift from God." Satisfied that the district attorney had presented sufficient evidence to sustain the charges against the Rippbergers, Judge Passalacqua ordered the couple to stand trial for felony child endangerment and involuntary manslaughter.[25]

The same week Natalie Rippberger died, Laurie Walker filed pretrial motions in Sacramento County Superior Court, Judge James C. Long presiding.

As he would for the next thirteen years, Thomas Volk represented Walker. Outside the courthouse Volk and O'Mara publicly outlined their trial strategies. Volk insisted the 1976 amendment to California's child neglect statute "protects the conduct that Laurie engaged in. It supports our position 100 percent." O'Mara, a tall, barrel-chested man in his midthirties, countered, "It doesn't matter" if Shauntay's death "was because of religion or because [Walker] had been shopping." The child died unnecessarily because Walker's conduct was criminally negligent. At the motion hearing Volk elaborated on his off-the-cuff remarks. He argued that the charges against Walker should be dismissed because the spiritual healing amendment to the child neglect statute constituted a complete defense to any prosecution based on her treatment of Shauntay's illness with prayer rather than with medical care and because the statutes under which she had been charged failed to give fair notice that her conduct was criminal.[26]

Judge Long's analysis of Walker's motion to dismiss began with a close reading of the spiritual healing amendment to section 270 on which Walker's statutory defense rested: "If a parent provides a minor with treatment by spiritual means through prayer alone in accordance with the tenets and practices of a recognized church or religious denomination, by a duly accredited practitioner thereof, such treatment shall constitute 'other remedial care' *as used in this section*." First, Long ruled, the legislature did not intend the spiritual treatment provision contained in the last paragraph of section 270 to bar prosecution for child endangerment and involuntary manslaughter. Legislative history made it clear the exemption was a defense only against a misdemeanor charge of a parent's failure to fulfill a duty to provide a child's basic necessities, but it was not intended to afford a defense against criminal negligence. Second, contrary to Walker's argument, the legislature did not enact the exemption in response to Christian Scientists' demand for a defense against a criminal prosecution. It was true, Judge Long acknowledged, Christian Scientists lobbied for the amendments of 1925 and 1976. However, a bill's sponsor "is not determinative of the intent of the legislature as a whole in passing it," and, more important, in *People v. Arnold* (1967) the California Supreme Court rejected the argument made by a mother who treated her sick daughter by spiritual means that providing "other remedial care" was a defense to a manslaughter prosecution. "'Other remedial care,' the *Arnold* court ruled, "does not sanction unorthodox substitutes for 'medical attendance.'" Third, Judge Long continued, other parts of the legislative history of section 270 support a conclusion that the legislature did not intend to extend the religious exemption to life-threatening situations. The most persuasive evidence of the legislature's intent was found in section 270 itself: the phrase "as used in this section" underscored the fact that the statute's spiritual treatment accommodation was confined to the misdemeanor failure to provide food, clothing, shelter, or medical care, not to criminal negligence. Finally, Walker's argument that her due process rights were violated because none of the statutes defining criminal child endangerment gave her fair warning of criminal liability failed to take notice of the laws dealing with the welfare of children. Child welfare provisions did not give prayer treatment "blanket approval when the health or life of the child is endangered." From this point, Judge Long concluded, it was easy to reach the conclusion that a parent who provided spiritual treatment when medical treatment was necessary may be liable for criminal negligence. Walker had fair notice that the state did not condone treatment by prayer when a child's life is in danger. On the basis of this analysis Judge Long denied Walker's motion to dismiss the charges against her.[27]

Walker petitioned the Court of Appeal for a writ prohibiting the Superior Court from carrying out its ruling that she stand trial as charged. The appeals court summarily denied her petition, whereupon Walker renewed her objections in the California Supreme Court. The state's highest court granted her petition for a writ prohibiting the lower court from enforcing its ruling denying her motion to dismiss the charges of child endangerment and involuntary manslaughter against her and transferred the matter back to the Court of Appeal.[28]

Briefs were filed with the court in the summer of 1985, giving the attorneys involved in the case an opportunity to build public opinion in their favor as well as to influence the court. Defense attorney Volk used sound bites and a topic sentence from his brief to reach his intended audiences: "No public offense has been committed" by Laurie Walker, he said and she is being "made a sacrificial example." Example of what, Volk didn't say, but his statement implied that Walker was being punished for her faith. He hinted at the existence of an unholy alliance between prosecutors who trivialized religion and activist judges. "Prosecutors are uncomfortable with the [spiritual healing] law," he said, "and they are trying to rewrite the law in the courtroom rather than through the legislature." An argument drawn from Walker's brief touched more lightly on a related issue: Did parents have a legal right to use prayer to heal their sick child or did the state determine when parents must turn to conventional medical care? Citizens were told "the treatment of illness by spiritual means through prayer is recognized," Volk said, but "nowhere in the state or federal statutory scheme is a citizen told at what point such treatment becomes unlawful." That opens the door to the arbitrary, unconstitutional enforcement of the law.[29]

Speaking carefully, Deputy Attorney General James Ching outlined the state's argument. The Walker case, he said, presents an opportunity to reexamine the common understanding of the "roles of parents and the state when the lives of children are endangered." The legislature did not intend the child neglect law to apply to life-threatening situations, Ching said, and other statutes empower the state to intervene to save the life of a child. The laws Walker has been charged with violating have nothing to do with church–state relations. Any parent who fails to provide a child with medical care is liable for prosecution. The law is neutral and general. Plus, Christian Science does not compel its members to choose spiritual healing over medical treatment. Walker acted voluntarily and therefore she cannot claim religious cover for her conduct.[30]

Before the Court of Appeal in October, Volk argued that the legislature amended the child neglect law in 1976 specifically to remove criminal sanctions for parents who engage in spiritual healing according to their religious beliefs and fail to provide medical care for their children. Judge Hugh Arthur Evans, who was nominated to the Court of Appeal in 1974 by Gov. Jerry Brown, asked if that interpretation applied if the child died. Volk replied that unfortunately neither spiritual healing nor medical care had a perfect record. Attorney General Ching argued that Walker should be tried as charged because the state is obligated to protect children.[31]

In its published opinion of January 10, 1986, the Court of Appeal refused to bar Walker's trial. The court rejected Walker's contention that the faith healing exemption amended to the state's child neglect statute established a complete defense against the criminal charges of child endangerment and involuntary manslaughter. Failure to provide medical care could place a child in danger and, regardless of Walker's religious belief, constituted the proper basis for a charge of involuntary manslaughter. The court also rebuffed Walker's alternative argument that she was denied due process of law because section 270 and other related provisions "create a confused state of law with regard to liability for injury to a child resulting from treatment by prayer."[32]

Writing for the unanimous three-judge panel, sixty-four-year-old Judge Evans denied Walker's motion to dismiss the charges against her. His opinion was straightforward and blunt. The "plain language" of the child neglect statute "precludes any inference that a parent who provides spiritual treatment would be insulated against charges of involuntary manslaughter or child endangerment should the lack of medical attendance result in the death of the child." Section 270, Evans wrote, "contains nothing ambiguous to interpret." Likewise, Walker's argument about legislative intent is "unsupportable." Had the legislature wanted to allow spiritual treatment as a defense beyond section 270 "language to that effect could have easily been included in the 1976 amendment." Judge Evans added that no amount of legislative history, certainly not self-serving letters written by Christian Science lobbyists, "can fill a void in statutory language." And Walker may not rely on a common law defense either. California has long recognized the failure to "exercise due care in the treatment to another" as sufficient basis for a manslaughter charge. Therefore, failure to provide medical care, "regardless of the parent's religious beliefs," may constitute the "lack of due caution" that would allow a parent to be convicted of involuntary manslaughter.[33]

Finally, Walker argued, as noted above, that because section 270 failed to indicate at what point spiritual treatment as an alternative to medical care becomes criminal conduct she was not given fair notice as to when her conduct became unlawful. Evans addressed this issue by saying the point at which parents may be subject to criminal charges of endangerment and involuntary manslaughter "is clear—when the lack of medical attention places the child in a situation endangering its person or health." Without regard to religious belief, he concluded, a jury will determine if Walker's conduct had reached that point.[34]

Less than three months later, on March 27, 1986, five of the seven members of the California Supreme Court voted to hear appeals from Walker and Rippberger. Coincidentally, the court's step into the conflict between criminal laws and religious rights was followed within months by a wave of political turbulence that swept three of the judges who had voted to hear Walker off the court. During his tenure as governor, from 1974 to 1982, Brown made four appointments to the California Supreme Court, including the first female chief justice, Rose Bird, and the first Hispanic, Cruz Reynosa, as well as Stanley Mosk, a former attorney general, and Joseph Grodin, a former professor at the Hastings College of Law. According to a statute from 1934, a governor's appointments to the California Supreme Court and the courts of appeal are confirmed by a three-member Commission on Judicial Appointments and are subject to a retention vote by the people at the next gubernatorial election. During their tenure on the court, Chief Justice Bird and Justices Reynosa and Grodin joined a number of controversial rulings, but none was more out of step with public opinion than their opposition to the death pen-

alty. Brown's successor, Gov. George Deukmejian, was outspoken in his opposition to the liberal trio, and his denunciations of them led to their ouster
by voters in 1986, allowing Deukmejian to make three new appointments to
the court. The court that heard Walker's appeal in the spring of 1988 was thus
very different from the one that had voted in 1986 to hear the case.[35]

Volk, Attorney General John Van de Kamp, and Warren Christopher, who
held high office under Presidents Lyndon Johnson and Jimmy Carter and was
a senior partner at O'Melveny and Meyers, a firm in Los Angeles representing the Christian Science Church, submitted briefs to the court. Volk focused
on legislative intent, arguing that the spiritual healing amendment to Penal
Code section 270 provided a complete defense to any prosecution based on
Walker's treatment of her daughter with prayer rather than medical care. He
also claimed that, when read together, the spiritual healing provision and
the felony child endangerment and involuntary manslaughter statutes violated Walker's right to due process because the child neglect statute did not
make clear at what point "lawful prayer treatment becomes unlawful, thus
requiring her to speculate as to the meaning of penal statutes." Van de Kamp
rejected Walker's argument that section 270 of the penal code—the child neglect statute with its spiritual healing amendment—should be read to create a "parallel exemption" from prosecution for felony child endangerment
and involuntary manslaughter. He argued that section 270 should be read
in conjunction with the several provisions of the state's child dependency
laws. Those provisions, he pointed out, allowed the state to assume custody
of a child "for the express purpose of assuring medical care for a child whose
parent is furnishing spiritual treatment." Speaking for the Christian Science
Church, Christopher argued at length for a pivotal constitutional distinction
between the governmental compulsion of a religiously objectionable act and
the governmental prohibition of a religiously motivated act. Essentially, he
sought to distinguish the Supreme Court's decision in *Prince v. Massachusetts* (1944) prohibiting a parent from violating child labor laws in the name
of religion from the California lower court's decision compelling parents on
pain of imprisonment to use medical care at the point at which a reasonable
person would conclude spiritual healing had proved ineffective and the child
could be seriously harmed or die without medical intervention.[36]

The court, led by Chief Justice Malcolm M. Lucas, Governor Deukmejian's
former law partner and a man touted as being far more cautious than his liberal predecessor, heard hour-long oral arguments from the state and the defense in the closely watched Walker case on March 8, 1988. Deputy Attorney

General Clifford K. Thompson defended the charges brought against Walker, articulating both statutory and constitutional arguments to support the state's position. While the 1976 law gave limited recognition to spiritual healing, he told the court, it was not a substitute for medical care for a sick child. "The only question is whether a reasonable person would know this child was dying," he said. "If the answer is 'yes,' then there is criminal liability." The 1976 law, Thompson added, also seemed to grant unconstitutional religious preference to Christian Scientists. "The law openly discriminates," he said, "by pinning a badge of inferiority on other religions." Volk countered by arguing that the child neglect statute did bar Walker's prosecution and if enforced it would violate her First Amendment right to the free exercise of religion. Justice Mosk sharply questioned Volk, asking whether the 1976 statute violated the First Amendment's establishment clause by giving preference to a particular religion. The statute recognized spiritual healing only by an "accredited practitioner," a thinly veiled reference to Christian Science, and in effect excluded prayer by Catholic priests or Jewish rabbis or "others who are not 'accredited' healers." Volk conceded Mosk's point but argued that the court could construe the statute to include other religions and avoid the constitutional problem. As a "friend of the court" representing the church, Christopher asked the court to take judicial notice of the "fact" that "society has recognized the practice of Christian Science as a reasonable and acceptable alternative to conventional care." In closing, he pleaded with the court "not to put [parents] through the additional trauma of a trial." Court watchers speculated that a ruling would be forthcoming in the fall.[37]

Later that same day, after oral argument, the court met in conference to discuss the case. As the most senior member of the court in terms of service, Mosk led off the discussion, outlining his views on the key statutory and constitutional issues of the case. According to custom, Chief Justice Lucas spoke last and assigned Mosk to write the court's opinion. Working within a mandated ninety-day window for completing the process, Mosk's draft—with the exception of the establishment clause issue—won quick approval from his brethren on the statutory issues.[38]

While Mosk worked to complete the court's opinion, the *Sacramento Bee*, the state capital's paper of record, acknowledged the complexity, ambiguity, and venality enmeshed in Walker's case. The primary issue, the associate editor Peter Schrag wrote, cannot be framed as a simple conflict between an individual's religious right and the state's power to impose its laws. At the same time, it is not so complicated that the only sensible answer is elusive. "There is no way that a reasonable society," Schrag wrote, "can place a parent's right to choose a religious healer above its duty to protect the life and welfare of a child." The question is not will prayer help, but whether the state can allow prayer to substitute for a penicillin shot to combat meningitis. There are indeed incompetent physicians and caring religious healers, but the sanctioning of spiritual treatment entangles the state in religious beliefs that have no connection to reasonable medical treatment.

Walker may be correct, Schrag wrote, when she highlights the ambiguity seemingly built into the law under which she was charged. Maybe the legislature did intend the spiritual healing amendment to the child neglect provision to block criminal charges of child endangerment and involuntary manslaughter. But the legislative record was not entirely clear on that point. In fact, Schrag continued, the legislature may have been deliberately ambiguous, masking the fact that it succumbed to the Christian Scientists' pressure for legal recognition of spiritual healing while at the same time creating a loophole that allowed the state to prosecute in case of a child's death.

The way out of this dilemma, the *Bee* suggested, was for the state's highest court to declare that section 270 violates the establishment clause and to recognize that because Walker "conscientiously relied on ambiguous language she cannot be prosecuted." Even if this solution were adopted, however, it wouldn't cure the "venality of the political process." The state must be very careful how and when it imposes its judgment about the care of a child over that of a child's parents. But in circumstances in which medical care is needed to protect the life of a child, society "must not leave the slightest doubt where it stands."[39]

Under the headline "Children Are Suffering as Faith Healers Hide Behind Religious-Exemption Shield," the *Los Angeles Times* published an op-ed piece by Anthony Shaw, a pediatric surgeon and member of the American Academy of Pediatrics, that was sharply critical of the religious exemption clause in the state's child abuse and neglect statute. Labeling it "unfair and harmful" as well as vague, he blasted the law because it provided immunity from prosecution for medical neglect only to parents belonging to a "recognized religion." That exclusionary phrasing denied legal protection to the "larger number of negligent parents whose spiritual credentials are unrecognized or whose denial of medical care to their children is not supported by any religious philosophy." Although the chief purpose of child abuse laws is to protect children, Shaw wrote, "to the extent that it excuses a class of parents from legal accountability for an otherwise prosecutable offense, puts children

of such parents at increased risk." The American Academy of Pediatrics opposed religious exemption clauses, he went on, noting that "it may protect
severe (even fatal) physical discipline, failure to seek needed medical care, or
refusal of a proven efficacious treatment of a critically ill child." The fact is,
Shaw argued, "no statute should exist that permits or implies that denial of
medical care necessary to prevent death or serious impairment to children
can be supported on religious grounds." The academy recognizes the positive
role religion plays in the lives of families, he concluded, but "nothing short of
total expungement" of the clause "which permits harm to children under the
shield of religious exemption will do."[40]

A cluster of letters to the *Times* followed Shaw's op-ed piece. Some southern Californians expressed support for spiritual healing, and others doubted
its efficacy. A letter writer from Malibu highlighted the fact that the four-
year-old Shauntay "died for a belief she could not understand or decide
on," adding, "Nothing rational about that. Nothing even human." A woman
who had been raised in a Christian Science family remembered "crying and
screaming because of severe earaches and suffering for weeks with awful sore
throats." She still believed prayer "has a place in our lives," but as an adult
she now knew "God also gave us the gift of knowledge, medical knowledge
included, which should be used especially with children." A self-identified
second-generation Christian Scientist shared her experience, boasting about
the good health her four young sons enjoyed thanks to spiritual healing. Another letter writer tackled head-on the issue of Shauntay's death, claiming
there was "absolutely no certainty [she] would be alive had she been under
medical care." Besides, the writer pointed out, "the Constitution guarantees
freedom of religion."[41]

On November 10, 1988, Justice Mosk wrote for a unanimous court on the
manslaughter charge. Mosk spent most of his legal career on the bench. The
oldest son of a nonobservant Reform Jewish couple, Mosk attended public
schools in Rockford, Illinois, and graduated from the University of Chicago
in 1933, at the outset of the Great Depression. His father's small business collapsed the same year, and the family moved to southern California. Just seven
years after receiving his law degree, Mosk, at the age of thirty-one, was appointed by Gov. Culbert Olson to the Los Angeles Superior Court, where he
served uninterruptedly (except for time spent in the U.S. Army during the
Second World War) until elected attorney general in 1959. Gov. Edmund G.
"Pat" Brown appointed Mosk to the California Supreme Court in 1964, where
he remained until his death in 2001.[42]

In a forty-nine-page ruling the California Supreme Court became the first state high court to rule that a Christian Scientist could be tried for manslaughter for failing to provide medical care to a seriously ill child. It affirmed the Court of Appeal's judgment, holding that Walker's prosecution for child endangerment and involuntary manslaughter violated neither statutory law nor the California or U.S. constitution. Section 270 of the Penal Code required parents to provide their children with certain basic necessities so the state did not have to assume that obligation. The child neglect statute permitted treatment by spiritual means, but it could not be read to exempt parents from felony child endangerment or involuntary manslaughter statutes. A jury using an objective standard could find Walker's failure to provide Shauntay with medical care criminally negligent. The court also rejected Walker's constitutional arguments. The First Amendment's free exercise clause did not absolutely protect her conduct, and she had sufficient notice that prayer in lieu of medical care would be accommodated only to that point when the child's life was threatened with serious harm or death.[43]

Mosk's opinion rested on three related propositions. First, the misdemeanor child neglect law (section 270) exempted parents who utilized prayer treatment from the statutory requirement to furnish medical care, a conclusion that reversed the court's decision in *People v. Arnold* (1967). Second, the purpose of the requirement in section 270 that parents furnish certain routine necessities for their children was to relieve the state from assuming that obligation and was not linked to the specific purpose of the involuntary manslaughter and felony child endangerment statutes. In addition, there was no evidence the legislature intended the spiritual healing provision to affect the manslaughter statute. The "ineluctable conclusion," Mosk wrote, is that legislators "were fully conscious of the potential liability" remaining under the child endangerment and involuntary manslaughter statutes for conduct they had made legal in section 270 "but simply chose to leave the matter unaddressed." The legislature's "considered silence" cannot be used to infer that by amending a misdemeanor support provision it "actually exempted from felony liability all parents who offer prayer alone to a dying child." Third, by relying solely on prayer to treat her seriously ill child Walker's conduct departed so far from what an "ordinarily prudent or careful man under the same circumstances [would do] as to be incompatible with a proper regard for human life" and was therefore criminally negligent. Walker manifested her sincerity and good faith in treating Shauntay with prayer, but the charge of criminally negligent involuntary manslaughter doesn't turn on her "subjective intent to heal her daughter but on the objective reasonableness of her course of conduct." In sum, Mosk concluded, using prayer alone to treat a seriously ill child constitutes criminal negligence as a matter of law. Whether Walker's behavior was sufficiently culpable to justify conviction for involuntary manslaughter and child endangerment is a question for a jury.[44]

Having rejected Walker's statutory arguments for dismissing the charges against her, Mosk focused on her constitutional claims. Walker and the Christian Science Church contended that the First Amendment protected her conduct from criminal liability. Without doubt, the First Amendment barred government from "prohibiting the free exercise" of religious belief, but religiously motivated conduct was "subject to regulation for the protection of society." To determine whether the state's regulation of religious conduct violates the First Amendment, Mosk relied on *Wisconsin v. Yoder* (1972), namely, the significance of the state's interest must be balanced against the seriousness of the religious imposition. The government's compelling interest in protecting the well-being and lives of children is an "interest of unparalleled significance." Balanced against the state's interest was a law requiring Walker to provide medical care to a seriously ill child that significantly encroached on her reliance on prayer treatment as a manifestation of genuine faith. Two points led Mosk to the conclusion that the state's compelling interest justified its restrictions on Walker's religious conduct: First, resorting to medicine does not constitute a sin for Christian Scientists, subject a church member to stigmatization, or result in divine retribution; second, in *Prince v. Massachusetts* (1944) the U.S. Supreme Court ruled that "parents may be free to become martyrs themselves. But it does not follow they are free, in identical circumstances, to make martyrs of their children before they have reached the age of full legal discretion when they can make that choice for themselves." *Prince,* Mosk explained, dealt with a free exercise claim asserted by parents whose religious beliefs required that children sell religious tracts in violation of child labor laws. "If parents are not at liberty to martyr children by taking their labor," Mosk reasoned, "it follows that they are not at liberty to martyr children by taking their lives." The "right to practice religion," the Supreme Court stated, "does not include the liberty to expose the community or child to communicable disease or the latter to ill health or death."[45]

"In an attempt to avoid this inexorable conclusion," Mosk wrote, the church argued the significance of a "purportedly pivotal distinction" between state compulsion of a religiously objectionable act and state prohibition of a religiously motivated act. Accepting for the sake of argument the force of this distinction, "we find that it has no relevance in a case involving an interest of this magnitude." Parents have "no right to free exercise of religion at the price of a child's life."[46]

The final piece in Mosk's unanimous opinion for the court focused on Walker's due process claim, namely, that the child endangerment and involuntary manslaughter statutes and section 270, if read together, led to the conclusion that Walker did not receive fair notice that her unsuccessful use of spiritual healing could lead to felony criminal charges. Framing her argument in the form of a rhetorical question, Walker asked, "Is it lawful for a parent to rely solely on treatment by spiritual means through prayer for the care of his/her ill child during the first few days of sickness but not on the fourth or fifth day?" Just as the Florida appeal court in the Hermanson case had, Mosk quoted Justice Oliver Wendell Holmes: "[The] law is full of instances where a man's fate depends on his estimating rightly, that is, as the jury subsequently estimates it, some matter of degree. An act causing death may be murder, manslaughter, or misadventure, according to the degree of danger attending it by common experience in the circumstances known to the actor." A reasonable person acting with caution would realize when additional or alternative steps were necessary to save a child's life. Further, the statutes at issue were not conflicting and were easily distinguished. Section 270 outlined the routine provision of child support at parental expense, while the child endangerment and involuntary manslaughter statutes protected against grievous physical harm. The objectives of the statutes could be clearly distinguished. "It cannot be said," Mosk concluded, "that the legality of [Walker's] conduct under section 270" constitutes an "inexplicably contradictory command" with respect to felony child endangerment and involuntary manslaughter.[47]

In addition to his opinion for the court Mosk wrote a concurring opinion in which he argued that the spiritual healing amendment to section 270 violated the establishment clause of the California and U.S. constitutions admonishing the legislature "to make no law respecting an establishment of religion." Two broad categories of legislation were prohibited by this constitutional command: laws that uniformly benefitted all religions, and laws that discriminated among religions. In regard to the second category, Mosk wrote, "the First Amendment mandates governmental neutrality between religion and religion and between religion and non-religion." Article I, section 4 of the California constitution makes this value explicit when it assures that "free exercise and enjoyment of religion without discrimination or preference are guaranteed."[48]

The Christian Science Church tailored the language of section 270 so that its protection for spiritual healing applies selectively to Christian Scientists. The statute excludes from criminal liability only those parents who provide a child with "treatment by spiritual means through prayer alone in accordance with the tenets and practices of a recognized church or religious denomination, by a duly accredited practitioner thereof." The provision does not protect parents "not affiliated with a 'recognized' church, or a church that does not 'accredit' prayer 'practitioners.'" The one group of parents "squarely protected by the terms of the statute are Christian Scientists." If the legislature wants to accommodate prayer treatment, Mosk warned, it must do so in a nonpreferential manner to avoid fatal constitutional defects.[49]

The *Sacramento Bee* summarized the California high court's lengthy opinion and four years of litigation in an eight-word headline: "Trial Ok'd for Mom in Prayer-Cure Death." The *San Francisco Chronicle* praised as a "landmark ruling on religious freedom" the Walker court's decision that "society's interest in protecting the health of children outweighs the First Amendment's guarantee of the free exercise of religion." Citing the Walker case, among others, the American Academy of Pediatrics echoed that contention by stating, "The constitutional guarantees of freedom of religion do not sanction harming another person in the practice of one's religion." The *Los Angeles Times* editorial page noted, "Most Californians who instinctively trust doctors and medicines rather than prayer, will have no trouble with the balancing test the high court set forth." But, the paper warned, whether Walker "genuinely believed that a Christian Science practitioner would heal her daughter and whether that faith was reasonable" are very difficult questions of fact for jurors to answer. Volk brushed aside questions about complexity, saying only that the ruling "tears the theological heart out of the Christian Science religion." He vowed to appeal the California court's ruling to the U.S. Supreme Court.[50]

On June 19, 1990, the U.S. Supreme Court denied Walker's appeal (cert. den.), letting stand the California Supreme Court's unanimous ruling and clearing the way to bring Walker, the Rippbergers, and the Glasers to trial for felony child endangerment and involuntary manslaughter charges. That same day, four and a half years after Natalie Rippberger died of meningitis, her parents Mark Rippberger and Susan Middleton, third-generation Christian Scientists, were brought to trial in Santa Rosa, California. Sonoma County Deputy District Attorney David Dunn and the defense attorney David Mackenroth, a member of the Church of Christ, Scientist, exchanged sharp rhetoric on the eve of the Rippbergers' trial. "They're putting Christ

Jesus on trial for quackery," Mackenroth said. "Would we feel sympathetic to [the Rippbergers] if they had beaten this child to death?" Dunn asked. "Child abuse can take various forms." Nathan Talbot, the church's spokesperson, contributed a strangely misguided argument. "The government does have a right—an obligation—to protect children," he said. "On the other hand, the government can't arbitrarily pick one method of healing just because some people prefer it."[51]

The Rippbergers' appeals delayed the beginning of their trial until July 1989, when Sonoma County Superior Court Judge Lloyd von der Mehden and a Santa Rosa jury heard opening statements from the prosecutor Dunn and the defense attorney Mackenroth. "This is a case of child abuse," Dunn said. Natalie "was not beaten to death or starved, but she's dead just as if she were beaten and starved." He went on to describe how day by day Natalie's condition became more serious and more painful. She vomited and suffered convulsions, and her body was rigid. She could easily have been treated and her life saved if her parents had sought medical help, Dunn said. Mackenroth described the Rippbergers as devout parents who "dearly loved" their child and called the family's ordeal "heart-rending and said the couple prayed day and night until the little girl died in her father's arms." Mackenroth concluded by arguing that the law protected the Rippbergers' religious beliefs.[52]

District Attorney Dunn called only the same three witnesses who had testified at the preliminary hearing: the Christian Science nurse Therese Miller, who left the church after Natalie's death; the forensic pathologist A. Jay Chapman; and the physician and medical school professor Michael Witmer. Miller described in detail Natalie's deteriorating condition. Although she was concerned about Natalie, she told the court, she did not call a doctor because "that wasn't within the scope of my job. I was a Christian Science nurse."[53]

Mackenroth grilled Miller about her working relationship with the Rippbergers during Natalie's illness. His purpose was to show that Miller had acted as an accomplice to the crimes charged against the Rippbergers. If his strategy was successful, Mackenroth could then urge the court to strike her testimony as an uncorroborated accomplice, thus depriving the prosecution of its only witness who had seen Natalie during her illness. An abbreviated, paraphrased version of Mackenroth's questions and Miller's answers reveals the lawyer's strategy:

Q: Did you ever administer medications?
A: No.
Q: Did you know the Rippbergers "were using Christian Science care"?
A: Yes.

Q: Did you "look away from the disease and turn to the higher power"?
A: Yes.
Q: Did you assist the parents "not to see the reality of the physical
  symptoms"?
A: Yes.

Chapman testified that his autopsy showed Natalie had died from meningitis, and he estimated the infection had been present in the infant's body for
a week and a half to two weeks. During that time, he told the court, the baby's
brain became swollen and softened by the bacterial infection. Witmer testified that the presence of fever and lethargy in an eight-month-old infant were
serious symptoms of infection, "calling for medical intervention, the use of
antibiotics, and close monitoring for further symptoms." He emphasized that
without antibiotics a child had virtually no chance of surviving.[54]

At the conclusion of the prosecution's presentation of evidence, Mackenroth moved for an acquittal. Judge Von der Mehden denied the motion.
He also ruled that Miller was not an accomplice because she did not advise the Rippbergers as to Natalie's treatment and did not "aid and abet the
alleged crimes." Therefore, her testimony was admissible. The Rippbergers
objected.[55]

In their defense, the Rippbergers called Dr. Russell W. Steele, an expert in
infectious diseases, Dr. Cyril H. Wecht, a pathologist, and Samuel S. Hill, a
professor of religion. Steele testified that there was insufficient evidence in
the autopsy report to make a judgment as to whether Natalie would have
survived had her illness received "conventional medical care." He stated that
the swelling of the brain would have caused less pain in baby Natalie than in
an adult. Wecht criticized the autopsy report as being incomplete. Hill told
the court that spiritual healing is the "hallmark" of Christian Science, and for
a Christian Scientist to reject spiritual healing "would be to betray [the] faith,
to cut the heart out of Christian Science."[56]

Mark Rippberger was the final witness for the defense. When he joined the
church as a youngster, he told the court, he made a commitment to rely solely
on Christian Science, and he "had always found Christian Science methods
of healing to be sufficient and successful." For that reason he had "never taken
his children to a doctor or a dentist, and did not own a thermometer for
measuring fever." Then, in a voice choked with emotion and with tears in
his eyes, Rippberger told a hushed courtroom and the subdued jury of nine
women and three men how he and his wife prayed for their daughter in the
early stages of her illness. When her fever worsened and she "clenched her

tiny fists," he contacted church officials and hired an accredited practitioner. When she failed to show improvement, he said, Susan and he took turns "holding the baby, praying and singing hymns" through the night. About 3 a.m. on Natalie's last day of life, Rippberger said, straining to hold his emotions in check, he lay down to sleep with Natalie in the bed. Two hours later she was "making gulping sounds, like she wanted to swallow. She was cradled in my arms. She stopped breathing." With prompting from Mackenroth, Rippberger added that he didn't know why his daughter had died. It never occurred to him to consider medical care. "In 30 years of Christian Science," he said, "prayer and its application to illness had always proven to be extremely reliable."[57]

The next day Dunn asked Rippberger if he had learned anything as a result of Natalie's death. "Many things," Rippberger replied. "That Christian Science isn't always effective [and] my understanding of the laws of California aren't what I thought they were." Dunn wanted to know if he and Susan had continued to rely on Christian Science for the health care of their remaining five children. "I've had no call to change my course of action in the past five years," he answered. But then, without prompting, Rippberger told Dunn that shortly after Natalie died one of his other children had shown signs of meningitis. Had the symptoms persisted, he said, he would have called county health officials. "Why would you have called them?" Dunn asked. "I was concerned for my child, for society," he answered.[58]

The jury began its deliberation late on Wednesday, August 2, after emotional closing arguments by Dunn and Mackenroth as well as lengthy instructions from Judge Von der Mehden. On Friday afternoon the jury solemnly filed into the courtroom and delivered a mixed verdict, acquitting Mark and Susan Rippberger of involuntary manslaughter but convicting the couple of felony child endangerment for negligently failing to provide medical treatment for their seriously ill infant daughter. The couple sat nervously staring at the floor while the clerk polled the jury. Not surprisingly, Dunn praised the jury verdict, saying it showed "remarkable intelligence." Mackenroth said the couple would appeal. The *Christian Science Monitor* bemoaned the outcome, claiming it showed how "tenuous" the "American tradition of religious tolerance" had become.[59]

Three months later Judge Von der Mehden announced the terms of the Rippbergers' punishment, imposing a sentence that included five years' probation, five-thousand-dollar fines for each, and three hundred hours of community service. In addition, the Rippbergers were ordered to read the *Family*

Health and Medical Guide, to purchase a thermometer, to attend family health classes, and to report within forty-eight hours any illness of their children lasting more than twenty-four hours. They were required to report any use of a Christian Science practitioner or nurse and to authorize emergency medical treatment for their children at school. Mackenroth immediately gave notice of the Rippbergers' intent to appeal. On January 17, 1990, Judge Von der Mehden upheld the couple's sentence and the conditions of their probation.[60]

The Rippbergers also lost an appeal of their conviction. On the issue of whether the exemption for spiritual healing attached to the state's child neglect statute also shielded Christian Scientists from felony child endangerment and involuntary manslaughter charges, the Court of Appeal bluntly stated, "We cannot accept the proposition that the Legislature intended to carve out an exception that would permit a small segment of our society, with impunity, to endanger the lives of infants who are helpless to act on their own behalf." The issue of whether Christian Science parents are protected from prosecution for child endangerment and involuntary manslaughter under the free exercise clause also has been "decided adversely by our Supreme Court in *Walker.* "Free exercise of religion," the court said further, "is not an absolute right and must be balanced against the rights of others, including one's children. It would be denigrating to the First Amendment if parents could use it as a shield to justify conduct which is life-threatening to an offspring." In brief, the Court of Appeal found that the California Supreme Court ruling in *Walker* eliminated the Rippbergers' basic constitutional and legal defense. The appellate court was bound by that ruling, and it found the high court's "logic of the decision to be irrefutable."[61]

Nearly six years to the day after the fifteen-month-old Seth Glaser died from meningitis while his Christian Science parents prayed, Eliot and Lise Glaser appeared in front of Los Angeles County Superior Court Judge Robert Thomas on charges of child endangerment and involuntary manslaughter. The California Supreme Court's *Walker* decision led the Glasers and Deputy District Attorney Wells to agree to allow Judge Thomas to decide the Glasers' fate based on the transcripts of their preliminary hearing in 1985. The court record included the Glasers' description of the events leading to their son's death as well as the testimony of two doctors who said the infant's life could have been saved if his parents had taken him to a hospital. Judge Thomas ruled there was insufficient evidence to convict the Glasers, noting especially that the infant showed "brief bursts of recovery" during his illness. In making his ruling, he said he had not considered the Glasers' Christian Science beliefs but merely the circumstances surrounding the child's death.[62]

Both sides claimed victory. Wells said, "They won the war, but they lost all the battles along the way." *Walker* ruled that all parents must provide medical care if their child exhibits symptoms that are critical to its health, and a state appeal court concluded there is no religious exemption from child endangerment and involuntary manslaughter charges. When the charges were dismissed Lise Glaser wept. "This is great news," she told the other Christian Scientists attending the trial. "I was praying through the whole thing." Talbot, also present in the Santa Monica courtroom, suggested that the six-year-long court battle was the result of "a basic misunderstanding that conventional medicine is not the only method of care."[63]

The death of four-year-old Shauntay Walker from medically untreated meningitis on March 9, 1984, was the first of the three California cases in which the children's parents were indicted on charges of felony child endangerment and involuntary manslaughter but the last to go to trial. With support from the Christian Science Church, Laurie Walker had waged a five-year legal battle culminating in the U.S. Supreme Court's refusal to review the California Supreme Court's ruling that Walker must stand trial. "We're going to battle," said Walker's attorney Tom Volk as the Sacramento County Superior Court prepared to set a trial date. Volk publicly rehearsed the same arguments the courts had rejected: There is no law requiring parents to provide medical care for a child; the spiritual healing amendment to the child neglect statute precludes criminal prosecution; and, prosecuting Walker would unconstitutionally place her religion on trial. Sacramento District Attorney Steven White didn't bother to rebut Volk's talking points, but said, "The question for the jury to decide is whether—religious convictions aside—a reasonable person would have taken an underweight, unresponsive, ultimately comatose 4-year-old to a doctor during a course of a 17-day illness."[64]

While Walker and the state prepared for trial, the Public Safety Committee of the California Assembly, chaired by John L. Burton, a Democrat from San Francisco, held hearings on a bill drafted by the Christian Science Church and introduced by Assemblyman Nolan Frizzelle, a Republican from Orange County. The bill sought to bolster the law protecting Christian Scientists' spiritual healing practices, exempt practitioners from a duty to report ill children deprived of medical care, and to retroactively dismiss the charges brought against Walker, Glaser, and the Rippbergers. The bill's introduction declared that the legislature had found "certain religious methods of healing [had] a generally accepted record of success." Assemblyman Terry Friedman said he thought that the bill "goes beyond the constitutional free-exercise clause" and that "other questions outweigh religious freedom issues." He questioned why, for example, non–Christian Scientists who decide not to seek medical care are held liable for the death of a child while Christian Scientists are exempt from prosecution. "Why should they be treated differently when the consequence, the result, is the same?" Friedman asked. After much more discussion the Public Safety Committee delayed a vote on the bill.[65]

In June, when the committee again took up the measure, Rita Swan, the president of CHILD, arrived from Sioux City, Iowa, to testify against the bill. Representatives from the California Medical Association, the American Academy of Pediatrics, the California District Attorneys Association, and the California Attorney General's office also spoke against the bill. Al Carnesciali was the primary church spokesperson. After Carnesciali's presentation, Chairman Burton struggled to discover what advantages a Christian Science practitioner brought to a sick child. Burton asked if practitioners learned new prayers during their training. "No. Not new prayers," Carnesciali said, "but how to follow the system of healing that Christian Science teaches." "Which is?" Burton asked. "Is there a different prayer that the practitioner would say than the mother would say?" Carnesciali explained that a practitioner prayed "more actively and more conscientiously." "Than the mother?" Burton asked incredulously.[66]

At this point one of the bill's endorsers, Assemblyman Tom McClintock, a Republican from Orange County, publicly withdrew his support of the proposed bill. "I entered the hearing thinking the issue was religious tolerance," he said. But it was now clear to him that advocates of spiritual healing ignore "a child's right to grow up and to make his or her own decisions." On that note Burton adjourned the hearing, postponing a vote on the bill until January 9, 1990. Christian Scientists lobbied the committee intensely in the interim, but, knowing the bill did not have a majority of backers, the church withdrew the bill hours before the scheduled vote. The move was a rare procedural setback for the church, but, more important, the defeat bolstered the California courts' interpretation of the existing laws.[67]

Six months later more than one hundred Christian Scientists were present in Superior Court Judge Darrel W. Lewis's courtroom in Sacramento to show their support for Laurie Walker, on trial for the death of her child. Volk moved that the charges be dropped because Walker acted reasonably by providing spiritual treatment that legally qualified as remedial care. He filed another motion for dismissal, claiming Walker was the victim of discriminatory prosecution. "Prosecutors throughout this state and nation," said Volk, "have aligned themselves with a private citizen [i.e., Rita Swan] on a personal vendetta against the Christian Science Church." The district attorney, Volk charged, pursued Walker because she followed her religious beliefs, whereas he ignored the deaths of several other children who died under questionable circumstances but whose parents weren't prosecuted. Deputy District Attorney O'Mara acknowledged it was possible some cases fell through the cracks, but there was no evidence of discriminatory conduct on the part of the prosecutors who filed charges against Walker. Judge Lewis denied both defense motions.[68]

Volk used one last legal tactic to avoid a trial and to prepare a record for appeal. Walker waived a jury trial and submitted her case directly to Sacramento Superior Court Judge George Nicholson on the basis of stipulated facts and the preliminary hearing transcript. In this way Walker and the Christian Science Church avoided the spotlight, and Walker preserved her appellate rights. Judge Nicholson found Walker guilty of involuntary manslaughter, placed her on probation, and sentenced her to six hundred hours of community service. The settlement agreed to by O'Mara and Volk also gave some protection to Walker's daughter Tamu. Until December 25, 1994, Tamu's eighteenth birthday, the court required Walker to allow Tamu to decide what form of treatment she preferred for an illness. But if Tamu became dazed, delirious, incoherent, or unconscious in the presence of her mother, Walker must immediately notify the girl's father, with whom Tamu lived, and summon medical aid.[69]

In an interview with the probation department after her sentencing, Walker ignored six years of court rulings to the contrary and insisted the law was not clear, and, therefore, her conduct had not violated the law. She told a newspaper reporter that she was not "criminally negligent or guilty in any way. I relied on God when my daughter was ill," she said, "because I understand and believe that prayer is the most effective healing method available."[70]

According to plan, Walker appealed Judge Nicholson's guilty verdict. In pretrial motions and before the Court of Appeal Walker argued that she was a victim of a national campaign by prosecutors to "go after Christian Scientists." On April 30, 1992, the court upheld Walker's conviction and rejected her complaint that prosecutors and Swan had conspired to convict her and other Christian Scientists. The court found that a newsletter published by the National Center for the Prosecution of Child Abuse reporting on the prosecution of Christian Scientists, among others, and Swan's effort to repeal religious exemption statutes failed to substantiate Walker's claim of victimization.

The court concluded that Walker "fails to show that these facts had any impact on her prosecution."[71]

Five years later Walker's persistence was rewarded. On January 4, 1997, U.S. District Court Judge Lawrence K. Karlton, appointed to the bench by President Carter in 1979, overturned Walker's involuntary manslaughter conviction, ruling that the California law bearing on spiritual healing was so confusing and contradictory at the time of Shauntay's death that Walker's prosecution was a denial of her constitutional right to fair notice. Volk greeted the news by saying, "I'm so pleased. It's been a long time coming." O'Mara too expressed satisfaction with the federal court's decision. The case "has once-and-for-all made it clear what the law is in California," he said, referring to the fact that Judge Karlton's decision applied only to incidents preceding the California Supreme Court's ruling on November 10, 1988.[72]

The California courts found that the religious exemption to child neglect was not a defense against criminal charges of child endangerment or manslaughter. The law unmistakably required parents to provide a child with medical care at that point when a reasonable, prudent person under similar circumstances would act to save a child's life. Members of the Christian Science Church were not shielded from trial and possible punishment for crimes for which nonchurch members would have no protection. The courts furthermore made clear that the First Amendment gave protection to religious expression, but not to all religious conduct. A compelling state interest—for example, the protection of a child's well-being and life—could constitutionally infringe on religious conduct.

3

Ian Lundman

Aᴏᴛᴇʀ ᴛʜɪʀᴛᴇᴇɴ ʏᴇᴀʀs of marriage, Douglass and Kathleen Stuart Lundman divorced in 1984, citing irreconcilable differences about spiritual healing, among other issues. They both had been raised in the Christian Science Church, but during the course of their marriage Doug began to question the validity of spiritual healing and left the church in 1981. The court awarded Kathy custody of the couple's two young children, six-year-old Ian and eight-year-old Whitney, and she agreed to maintain for the benefit of the children medical and dental insurance as provided by her present or future employer. Doug did not ask Kathy for any additional stipulation about medical care.[1]

Less than two years after getting divorced, Kathy, thirty-six years old, married William McKown, a fifty-five-year-old retired former vice president of General Mills who shared her Christian Science faith, including her belief in the efficacy of spiritual healing. Kathy, Ian, and Whitney moved into McKown's home on Lake Sarah in Independence, Minnesota, a small town twenty-three miles west of Minneapolis. Three years later, in the spring of 1989, eleven-year-old Ian died from untreated diabetes, an event setting in motion seven years of criminal proceedings and civil litigation to determine if Kathy and Bill McKown and the Christian Science Church should be held responsible for the boy's death. In the interlude between the end of the criminal proceeding and the beginning of Doug's civil suit against his former wife and the church, the McKowns and Whitney moved to Hawaii, where Bill owned a bed and breakfast inn.[2]

In 1985, the year after his divorce from Kathy, Doug completed a degree in architecture at the University of Minnesota, where he taught for one year before taking a position as an assistant professor in the College of Architecture

at Kansas State University. While living in Manhattan, Kansas, Doug telephoned and visited Ian and Whitney and spoke with Kathy regularly about
how they were doing in school and how their health was. During his visits
with the children, Doug occasionally provided Ian with medical care. Evidence introduced during the civil trial portrayed him as a "very loving father," one who followed Ian's physical and intellectual growth in "great detail."
After Ian's death, Doug moved back to Minneapolis to work, and there he
launched a lengthy, ultimately unsuccessful court battle to gain custody of
Whitney.[3]

About 8 p.m. on May 9, 1989, Kathy, who was listed in the Minneapolis
Yellow Pages as a Christian Science practitioner, called Doug to tell him Ian
was sick, but she did not tell him the boy was seriously ill. Doug offered to
come to Minnesota, but she said that wasn't necessary, and when he asked to
speak with Ian, Kathy said he was sleeping. Seven hours later, about 3 a.m.,
Doug received a call from Kathy telling him that Ian had died. Doug and a
friend left immediately for Minnesota, 560 miles northeast of Manhattan.[4]

Ian died from undiagnosed and untreated ketoacidosis diabetes (DKA). Intermittently ill for several weeks, he ate mints to mask his breath, which had a
fruity aroma (a sign of insulin deficiency), and he lost weight while complaining of fatigue and a stomachache. Beginning on Friday, May 5, Ian's condition grew progressively worse, causing vomiting, dehydration, deep, gasping
breathing, confusion, and excruciating abdominal pain. Kathy hired Mariano
Victor Tosto, a Christian Science practitioner, to give the boy spiritual treatment through prayer. Tosto never visited Ian but prayed at his home for the
boy. Ian could not sleep on the night of May 7 and, feeling frightened, told his
mother he didn't want to be alone. He was unable to keep down any food the
following morning, and Kathy sought additional help. Following church di-
rectives, she called James Van Horn, the Christian Science Church's one-per-
son Minnesota Committee on Publication and public relations. He verified
that she had contacted an approved practitioner, and he notified an official
at the Mother Church in Boston that a child was seriously ill. The downward
spiral of Ian's condition accelerated. He was unable to eat or drink or control
his bladder and became so disoriented he did not recognize his mother.[5]

About 9 p.m. Quinna Lamb, a thirty-seven-year-old, third-generation
Christian Science nurse who had no medical training and had never cared for
a seriously ill child, arrived at the McKowns' home. Lamb found Ian lying in
his own urine, unable to talk or breathe normally. She cleaned the boy up and
changed his bedding. During the next six hours Lamb jotted down notes that

charted Ian's decline and death and her faith that the spiritual healing process undertaken by Tosto from afar would heal Ian. At 11:30 p.m. she noted, "Patient vomiting brownish fluid—called Practitioner—vomiting ceased." At 1 a.m. Lamb wrote, "Patient swallowing—facial spasms—called Practitioner"; five minutes after alerting Tosto, she noted, "Immediate [change]—symptoms gone." But one hour later Lamb wrote, "taking big breaths every other breath, gritting teeth." She called the practitioner again, but this time she noted, "shallow, irregular breathing—eyes fixed." Again she called the practitioner. Neither Lamb nor anyone else with access to Ian on that fateful evening advised taking the boy to the hospital or provided him with medical care. In fact, at trial, evidence showed, as in the cases discussed earlier, that the church trained its nurses to ignore medical symptoms in the belief that naming them would encourage the illness. At 2:36 a.m. on Tuesday, May 9, Lamb wrote, "Patient stopped breathing." Bill called 911 and Van Horn at 3:02 a.m. The police officer that arrived at the McKowns' home described Ian as being "very skinny" and "to tell you the truth [he] didn't even look human." Hennepin County Medical Examiner Garry Peterson ruled the death a homicide on the grounds that Kathy and Bill McKown had failed to seek medical help.[6]

In late September 1989, Robert J. Streitz, the assistant Hennepin County attorney, presented evidence to a grand jury in regard to Ian's death. Medical experts testified about diabetes and its treatment and told jurors that with medical intervention Ian's condition could have been stabilized as late as two hours before he died. Jurors heard testimony as well about Christian Science spiritual healing and the specific methods used in treating the boy. Streitz then defined second-degree manslaughter: "A person who causes the death of another . . . by culpable negligence whereby the person creates an unreasonable risk and consciously takes chances of causing death or great bodily harm to another." A juror asked, "Can you explain child neglect? Is there any sort of statute that would apply?" Streitz answered by reading aloud the state's child neglect statute, including the spiritual treatment and prayer exception: "A parent who willfully deprives a child of necessary food, clothing, shelter [or] healthcare is guilty of neglect. If a parent responsible for the child's care in good faith selects and depends upon spiritual means or prayer for treatment or care of disease or remedial care of the child, this treatment shall constitute 'health care.'" The county attorney asked, "Did that answer your question, ma'am?" The juror responded, "Mm-hmm." After deliberation, on October 10, 1989, the grand jury returned an indictment for second-degree manslaughter against the McKowns and Tosto. The point of the prosecution,

Tom Johnson, the Hennepin County attorney, said, "is to establish that parents have a responsibility regardless of the religious or spiritual beliefs to provide adequate medical care to their child."[7]

The McKowns moved to dismiss the indictments, challenging the state's interpretation of the child neglect statute and its relationship to manslaughter. Judge Eugene Farrell, a "squat and animated" man with a "raffish goatee" and a graduate of the University of Minnesota Law School who had spent a dozen years in private practice before his appointment to the bench, heard the defendants' motion to dismiss on March 26–27, 1990. The McKowns made three arguments: First, the child neglect statute's spiritual treatment provision provided them with an absolute defense against any criminal charge; second, given the broad scope of the spiritual treatment provision it would violate their right to due process for the state to charge them with manslaughter; and, third, there was no probable cause to support the manslaughter indictment.[8]

The record showed that the Christian Science Church had crafted and lobbied hard for the child neglect statute on which the McKowns relied. By conflating the terms *spiritual means* and *health care* the church sought to exempt Christian Science parents from prosecution for child neglect and other criminal charges, regardless of the outcome of spiritual treatment. Peter Thompson, the attorney for Kathy McKown, argued precisely this in a brief supporting dismissal. Kathy acted in accordance with the health care / spiritual means provision, and legislative hearings on the law made it clear there could be no criminal proceedings against parents who followed the law when the "spiritual treatment they have selected and depended upon for their children proves unsuccessful." Prosecuting Kathy McKown "for acting on sincerely held religious beliefs," Thompson concluded, "violates her constitutional rights to freely exercise her religion."[9]

Assistant County Attorney Streitz interpreted the child neglect statute differently. He argued that the phrase "spiritual treatment shall constitute health care" explicitly limited the scope of the prayer exemption to the child neglect statute and therefore did not protect the defendants from a charge of manslaughter. The McKowns, Streitz asserted, had a duty to provide medical treatment in life-threatening situations, to act as a "reasonably prudent man" would.[10]

Judge Farrell swept away the state's argument and granted the McKowns' motion to dismiss their manslaughter indictments. He ruled that the state had failed to show the McKowns acted with gross negligence and recklessness, as required by the second-degree manslaughter statute. In the absence of reasonable evidence to sustain that stipulation, the state's charge that the McKowns consciously created "an unreasonable risk of harm" could not be sustained. Farrell could have stopped there, but he argued further that the child neglect statute and the manslaughter statute had a common purpose and must be read, construed, and applied together. In light of this rule of statutory construction, the religious exemption provision attached to the child neglect statute also protected parents who chose prayer to treat an ill child from a charge of manslaughter. Farrell insisted that the Christian Science Church's "understanding" that they could rely on "spiritual means for health care without the threat of criminal reprisal" meant the state had erroneously informed the grand jury that "the standard of care was that of a 'reasonably prudent man.'" The state's "failure to properly instruct the Grand Jury as to the proper standard of care substantially prejudiced the rights of the defendants." Finally, Farrell found that the McKowns' due process rights had been violated. What he termed the state's inadequate interpretation of the manslaughter statute left the McKowns confused and without fair notice of what behavior constituted criminal conduct. For all these reasons, Farrell dismissed the manslaughter indictments against the McKowns.[11]

Outside the courtroom, the church spokesman Nathan Talbot praised Judge Farrell's decision, saying "it took a certain amount of courage" to dismiss the McKowns' manslaughter indictments. Doug Lundman disagreed, saying to a reporter, "There should be no question that a child's basic right to life and liberty should not be preempted by any adult's personal religious convictions." The county attorney, Johnson, broadly hinted the state would appeal. Two days later prosecutors asked the Minnesota Court of Appeals to reinstate manslaughter charges against the McKowns.[12]

A three-judge panel heard argument on the issue in July 1990. Johnson opened by attacking Judge Farrell's ruling as "clearly erroneous" in that the legislature did not intend the spiritual healing provision in the child neglect statute to apply to the state's manslaughter law. While parents' religious beliefs have absolute protection under the law, their actions do not. By relying only on prayer to cure Ian's illness—by not acting the way a "reasonably prudent man" would and providing medical care—the McKowns negligently caused Ian's death by creating an unreasonable risk. "There is no inherent right to act or not to act to cause the death of a child," Johnson said. The legislature "didn't mean for us to make martyrs of our kids." The appeals court judge Doris Huspeni asked Johnson if his argument didn't place an undue burden on parents to determine when "the line of neglect had been passed." No, Johnson quickly responded, because it is the same decision the law asks a parent to make "between lawful force to discipline a child and force that constitutes child abuse."[13]

Peter Thompson, the lawyer for Kathy McKown, emphasized the part of Judge Farrell's ruling that found the McKowns' right to due process had been violated because they did not have fair notice that the spiritual treatment provision did not protect them from a manslaughter charge. Thompson said the criminal neglect exemption for spiritual healing implied an exemption for overall health care and any serious consequences. "The state would have you believe," he told the court, "that there are exceptions to the exemption, that the law applies only when something can be cured with chicken soup, but not when there is serious illness." Thompson concluded with the puzzling argument that to make the McKowns responsible for analyzing the medical status of their son would be contrary to their experience and to Christian Science practice.[14]

Judge Sandra Gardebring, at forty-three the youngest member of the Court of Appeals, wrote for a unanimous court in October 1990. Without speaking to the First Amendment free exercise and establishment clause issues raised in amicus briefs filed by the Christian Science Church and the Minnesota Civil Liberties Union, the appeals court affirmed the trial court's order to dismiss the manslaughter indictments against the McKowns. Gardebring rejected two of Judge Farrell's conclusions: that the child neglect statute and the second-degree manslaughter statute have a common purpose and must be read together; and that the "spiritual means or prayer" provision attached to the child neglect statute provided an absolute defense to criminal liability. However, she concurred with the trial court's conclusion that the McKowns due process right to fair notice had been violated. Specifically, Gardebring found that the child neglect statute authorized parents to use prayer "without respect to the medical condition of the child" and at the same time the manslaughter statute gave "no notice of when its broad proscription might override the seemingly contradictory permission given by the child neglect statute to treat the child by such spiritual means." For this reason, the court rejected the state's argument that despite the child neglect statute's spiritual means provision a parent could be charged with manslaughter whenever the outcome of prayer treatment led to serious injury or death. Gardebring concluded, "That is unacceptably arbitrary and a violation of due process."[15]

Unwilling to concede defeat, the state announced it would appeal the lower court's decision to uphold dismissal of the manslaughter indictments to the Minnesota Supreme Court. Doug Lundman also looked ahead, joining a small group belonging to CHILD in an effort to persuade the legislature to repeal the provision of the child neglect statute equating health care and spiritual treatment. The chairman of the Senate Judiciary Committee, Sen. Allan Spear, was the chief roadblock to reform. When the Christian Science parents of seven-year-old Amy Hermanson were convicted in a Florida court of third-degree murder in 1989 for withholding medical aid from their daughter (see chapter 1), Spear told his colleagues, "I don't think we want to make a parent who belongs to a religious group and in good faith selects a spiritual means of treatment or care subject to criminal proceedings." The attorney Terry Fleming, representing the Christian Science Church, countered Doug Lundman's emotional testimony about Ian's death. The current law, Fleming told the judiciary committee, represents a "delicate balance" between religious freedom and the welfare of children, and on that congratulatory note Spear tabled Sen. Jane Ranum's repeal bill without a vote.[16]

The House held hearings on a repeal bill similar to Senator Ranum's. In addition to Doug's testimony, Rita Swan shared her personal experience and extensive knowledge about the pitfalls of faith healing, and Joni Clark, a former member of End Time Ministries, a midwestern religious group that discourages medical attention for pregnancy and childbirth as well as disease, talked about the death of her first child as a result of nonmedical treatment. Uncharacteristically, the presentation of the Christian Science official Van Horn got off to a rocky start. He introduced three witnesses whose testimony he intended to bolster the benefits of spiritual healing. A Native American talked about healing ceremonies, but to Van Horn's surprise the shaman concluded his presentation by explaining that his healing rituals and medical care were perfectly compatible. A spokesperson from Minnesota's large Hmong community made the same confession, and a Christian Science mother testified she would welcome repeal because if the exemption no longer prevailed she would not be allowed by law to let her child die. Donna Lundman, Ian's grandmother, a Christian Science practitioner and a witness to her grandson's death spiral, seemed to save the day for Christian Science. She blasted her son's testimony, attributing Doug's grief—the motivation for his effort to bring spiritual healing under the law—to his leaving Christian Science and becoming an atheist. Several senators praised her courage, and the committee tabled the bill.[17]

When political persuasion proved fruitless, the CHILD advocates Maria Castle and Steven Peterson expressed their disappointment and outrage in an op-ed in the *St. Paul Pioneer Press*. Many witnesses, including Christian Scientists, pleaded that the only way to protect children's lives was to repeal the spiritual healing provision. But, as Castle and Peterson pointed out, Chairman Spear never questioned the church's motives behind the request for exemptions: "He never considered how legal validation reinforces a well-meaning family's faith healing delusions and facilitates a child's endangerment. He never sought input from supporters of repeal [or] from victims of the exemptions." Yet, Castle and Peterson concluded, Spear "will feel he has done something wonderful."[18]

While House and Senate legislative committees considered a repeal bill, the Minnesota Supreme Court heard arguments on the state's appeal to reinstate the manslaughter indictments against the McKowns. The court announced its decision in late September 1991. By a vote of four to two the court upheld the two lower court decisions. Justice Esther Tomljanovich, a self-described "lawyer and feminist," wrote for the majority, agreeing with the court of appeals that the McKowns' manslaughter indictments violated their constitutional guarantee of due process of law because they did not receive fair notice that the child neglect statute allowing spiritual healing did not protect them from a charge of manslaughter if prayer failed. The spiritual treatment provision expressly provided the McKowns with "the right to 'depend upon' Christian Science healing methods so long as they did so in good faith. Therefore, the state may not now prosecute them for exercising that right." However, Tomljanovich warned, the court's decision did not mean the state could never prosecute someone whose reliance on spiritual methods leads to the death of a child.[19]

Justice Mary Jeanne Coyne, who as a lawyer had argued more than one hundred cases before the Minnesota Supreme Court prior to her appointment to that court in 1982, dissented. Coyne agreed with the majority that the child neglect and manslaughter statutes were not so closely related as to require that they be interpreted in light of each other, but she also assailed the majority's analysis and its conclusion. Having determined that the two statutes should not be construed together, she wrote, the majority nevertheless held that the McKowns' manslaughter indictments failed to meet constitutional requirements of due process of law because the child neglect statute did not give fair notice that the law's spiritual means or prayer provision did not protect them from a charge of manslaughter. This is nothing more than Judge Farrell's "rejected *in materia* argument garbed in the cloak of due process."[20]

The McKowns' manslaughter defense, Coyne pointed out, relied on that provision within the child neglect statute allowing a parent to use spiritual healing as remedial care, but there is no reason to believe the legislature in-tended that part of the child neglect statute to have any effect on a parent's criminal liability for involuntary manslaughter. The statutory language does not except spiritual treatment from triggering the child neglect statute's pen-alty. Rather, it simply provides that a parent who in "good faith" selects and depends on spiritual means for treatment of his or her child is no more and no less subject to prosecution for gross misdemeanor child neglect than a parent who makes more conventional health care available. Whatever kind of health care is chosen, Coyne continued, a parent who violates the child neglect statute has not acted in good faith but has deviated from the standard of care a reasonable person would provide and, although being aware of the risk created by that deviation, consciously disregarded it. Whatever kind of health care is selected and used, Coyne argued, due process does not require notification that behavior that appears to comply with the requirements of one statute may not meet the requirements of another.[21]

Adhering to a statutory mandate, Coyne maintained, does not limit reli-gious freedom, as the McKowns insist. A parent swayed by religious belief that prayer can heal better than doctors and who fails to call a doctor for an ill child may be acting in a criminally negligent manner. In fact, a grand jury found probable cause to believe the McKowns took an unreasonable risk and consciously disregarded a known risk by ignoring the deadly symptoms leading to Ian's death and returned an indictment for second-degree man-slaughter. Whether there was satisfactory and sufficient evidence to find the McKowns culpably negligent is, Coyne concluded, a "jury question, not a question appropriately decided by this court at the pretrial stage on the basis of a mistaken interpretation of a statute."[22]

Hennepin County Attorney Mike Freeman put a positive spin on the state high court's decision. "Now that the smoke has cleared," he told the *Star Tribune*, "the Legislature needs to ensure in drafting statutes that parents, regardless of their religious persuasion, take all appropriate measures to pro-tect the health of a child. That may require conventional medical treatment in life-threatening situations even if the parents' beliefs are to the contrary." Robert Riach, an attorney for the McKowns, saw the outcome differently. The case reaffirmed, he said, that "Christian Scientists can rely on spiritual treat-ment." The prosecutor Michael Richardson said the court made the "wrong decision," stating that adults have a right to believe what they like, "but . . . cannot sacrifice [their] children for [their] own beliefs."[23]

In May 1991, a month before the state filed its appeal, Doug Lundman filed a civil wrongful death suit seeking monetary damages from his ex-wife, Kathy, her husband, William McKown, the Christian Science Church, Mariano Tosto, Clifton House, a Christian Science nursing facility, and James Van Horn, head of the Minnesota Committee of Publication. The complaint stated that Ian was "in the custody and care" of the McKowns when he began to exhibit signs of illness, weight loss, lethargy, and fruity breath, all symptoms of diabetes. His illness "progressed through stages of vomiting, labored breathing, incoherence, unresponsiveness, excessive urination, inability to swallow, facial spasms, and clenched teeth until he died." Despite these obvious signs of serious illness, the McKowns "failed to provide reasonable necessary medical treatment for the child, and as a result thereof, caused his death." Intentionally or negligently they failed to fulfill a "standard of care which would be exercised by a reasonably prudent person under the same or similar circumstances." Likewise, agents of the Christian Science Church, hired as "counselors and advisors to the McKowns, also assumed the duty of making available reasonable care to the diseased," but they acted negligently in failing to supply or recommend medical care.[24]

Coincidentally, less than two weeks after Lundman filed suit seeking substantial monetary damages, the Christian Science Church launched an ambitious round-the-clock cable television news program despite a balance sheet showing that its newspaper, the *Christian Science Monitor*, was losing eight million dollars each year, and in 1991 its "Total Funds on Hand" were less than half the amount held by the church in 1987. Jack Hoagland, the chairman of Monitor Television, believed the bold move was necessary to carry out the church's mission of delivering objective, thoughtful news to the world. Several media consultants and a number of dissident church members disagreed. Referring to Hoagland and Netty Douglass, the manager of the Christian Science Publishing Society, who were charged with making the church's television news program profitable, one Los Angeles–based media consultant said, "Seldom have two people who knew less about electronic media made more far-reaching decisions about product and finance than these two did." Inside the Mother Church, Stephen Gottschalk, who for more than a decade had served as an advisor to the Committee on Publication, abruptly resigned, angry and alarmed by the amount of money spent in "frantic efforts to update [the church's] image and attract new members" by creating a cable television network.[25]

The Monitor Channel limped through just one year before it collapsed under a heap of debt. Media experts estimated the church lost $500 million, a loss of funds so dire that church officials borrowed $91 million from the employee pension fund, $46.5 million to meet payroll and another $45 million to cover severance pay for 350 workers released from the failed television venture. The transfer of funds was not illegal, but it caused church members and current and former employees to publicly worry about their financial future. Ironically, the church's solution to its financial woes proved more divisive than the fallout from the failed cable news venture and from what church members somewhat dismissively called the "child cases." In the fall of 1991 church officials agreed to publish Christian Scientist Bliss Knapp's once-suppressed book *The Destiny of The Mother Church* by May 1993 in order to receive a bequest from the Knapp estate estimated to be between $75 million and $92 million. According to Knapp's book, Jesus and Mary Baker Eddy were God's two witnesses, "two Great lights [who] appeared on the fourth day of creation," "two great rulers in the heavenly kingdom," he "over the foundations" and "Mrs. Eddy ruler over the gates by which we enter the Holy City." For over forty years the board of directors held Knapp's book to be "incorrect." Gottschalk bluntly labeled the book's argument "nothing short of sacrilegious," and he and a handful of other ranking church officials angrily resigned. Some Christian Science Reading Rooms declared they would not accept copies of Knapp's book, while others accepted it but stated they would not display it. The *Boston Globe* columnist Joan Vennochi called the publication of Knapp's book "in return for a $72 million payoff, a Judas-like betrayal." Despite the controversy the church published the book, rationalizing its deification of Eddy as "broaden[ing] the church's view of Eddy" and saying it was not "an entirely new view." In short, the money made the church financially solvent but ideologically divided. The deal completed, church officials turned their attention, perhaps with a sigh of relief, to a child case, Doug Lundman's suit against the church.[26]

The McKowns, the church, and the church's agents made the same arguments in a motion to dismiss Lundman's civil suit that they had successfully made in the criminal case, namely, that they were protected by the statute permitting prayer as an alternative to medical care and that being forced to obtain medical care for Ian would have violated their right to free exercise of religion. Judge Sean J. Rice, appointed to the Fourth District Court in 1987, just six years after his admission to the bar, denied the motion to dismiss, ruling that a duty exists for parents to protect children against unreasonable risk of harm and that the suit focused on the defendants' actions or inactions rather than on their beliefs. By adducing clear and convincing evidence Lundman subsequently won the court's approval to add punitive damages to his lawsuit against the church and its agents.[27]

Lundman's wrongful death lawsuit began Monday on July 19, 1993, in Minneapolis. His attorney, James H. Kaster, a trial lawyer with a specialty in employment litigation, told the *Minneapolis Star Tribune* that Lundman's was the first civil case in the country to go to trial that involved a death in which a Christian Scientist used prayer rather than medicine as a healing method. "This is a case of the death of an eleven-year-old boy who died for the religious beliefs of others. He had no choice," Kaster told the jury in his opening statement. The defendants were negligent because they did not provide medical care for the boy. Rather, as Ian's condition became progressively worse, his mother made several telephone calls in search of additional spiritual healing help, including one to Mariano Tosto, a practitioner hired to pray for Ian, another to Van Horn, titular head of the church in Minnesota, who gave nonmedical advice, and a third to a Clifton House administrator who sent Quinna Lamb, a caregiver without medical training. No one recommended medical care, and no one questioned Kathy Lundman's complete reliance on spiritual healing.[28]

The next day the trial lawyer Terrence J. Fleming of Minneapolis, a graduate of Harvard Law School in 1981 who was representing Kathy McKown, told the jury she drew on her knowledge of, and experience with, spiritual healing. When Ian's condition worsened and became critical, she "could do only what her religious faith told her to do." It would have been "unthinkable" for Kathy to begin experimenting with medical care, Fleming argued, because she had no experience with it. Kathy acted as she did, the lawyer concluded, "because she loved her son." The defense attorneys for the other appellants also emphasized their clients' deeply held religious belief in the efficacy of spiritual healing. Wendy J. Wildung, Van Horn's attorney, made the most surprising argument. She shifted blame away from the church executive to Doug Lundman by insisting there was no merit in the claim that Van Horn should have urged McKown to seek medical care for Ian when Doug, who was aware of his son's illness, didn't call a doctor.[29]

"I was Ian's father," Lundman told the six-woman jury at the end of the second week of the trial. "I should have found a way to learn the circumstances. I should have prevented [Ian's death.]" Speaking quietly and carefully, he reconstructed the telephone conversations he had with his former wife and with his mother, a Christian Science practitioner, in the hours before Ian's death. Both women had said Ian was sick, but they assured Doug the boy's illness wasn't serious. Doug's mother did add that the boy seemed frightened. Doug offered to drive to Minneapolis from Kansas State University, where he was working, but Kathy said there was no reason to do that. Yet at 3 a.m. she called to tell Doug that Ian had died. When he arrived in Minnesota, Doug told the jury, he met with a funeral director to plan Ian's memorial service and cremation. He first asked to see his son's body. When the funeral director objected, Lundman said he told the director he would call the police if necessary. The director relented, and Doug spent an hour with Ian's body. In response to Kaster's question about how he felt four years later, Doug replied that since his son's death he had suffered from clinical depression.[30]

Holding a Bible and speaking with calm conviction, Kathy McKown testified at length about her personal knowledge of the protection Christian Scientists enjoyed under Minnesota law and about her deep, unshakable faith in spiritual healing. As examples of illnesses that prayer had cured she mentioned Ian's impetigo (a common skin infection) and warts. When Kathy recounted the days leading up to Ian's death she began to cry as she described trying to feed him liquefied gelatin on the last day of his life. Until that moment, she said, she had not considered his life to be in danger. She responded to what she now perceived as a crisis by calling Van Horn and Clifton House, and arranged to hire the caregiver Lamb. Under cross-examination Kaster asked Kathy why she had not asked Ian if he preferred spiritual treatment. She replied that she didn't feel her son, being only eleven years old, could make such a decision. Kathy added that the day before Ian died she asked him, "Are you part of the team?" a question perhaps meant to elicit his agreement with Christian Science practices. "I am," he said.[31]

In closing, Fleming echoed his opening remarks, asserting that Kathy did what was natural considering her lifelong experience as a Christian Scientist who used prayer for healing. "To abandon that when things were getting worse and try something new wouldn't make sense," he told the jury at the end of the five-week trial. Kaster challenged the defense's contention that Kathy's decision to stick with prayer was natural and understandable. If it were you, he asked the six women jurors, wouldn't you do anything to save your child's life? Kaster branded Ian's death a team effort. According to its policy, the church plays a major role when a child is seriously ill: Van Horn advised Kathy and her husband, recommended a practitioner, and suggested they call a Christian Science nurse. It's the jury's decision as to how to calculate the money damages, Kaster said, but without doubt Lundman should be compensated for the loss of his only son.[32]

After seven hours of deliberation a jury found the defendants' negligence was deliberate, demonstrated a serious disregard for the rights of others, and was a "direct cause of the death of Ian Lundman." The jury returned a $5.2 million verdict in compensatory damages against the McKowns, the Christian Science Church and its agents, and for Doug Lundman's loss of the companionship of his son. Ian's sister Whitney, who was seventeen years old, was to share in the damage award. In addition, the jury determined the degree of liability attributable to each of the defendants. It found Kathy and William McKown responsible for roughly a third of the damage award and the church and its agents liable for the remainder. All were held jointly liable for damages, so that if one could not pay, the award could be assessed against the other defendants. After discussion with the attorneys, Judge Rice told the jurors they could be asked to determine if punitive damages should be assessed against the seven defendants.[33]

In fact, within days Rice ordered the jury to consider punitive damages against the First Church of Christ Scientist, Boston. Each side presented brief arguments by financial experts. A Minneapolis certified public accountant called by Lundman said the church had a net worth of $136.9 million. Donald Bowersock, a former executive at the management consulting firm Arthur D. Little and at the time the church's managing treasurer, said that when funds earmarked for specific purposes were excluded, the church had a deficit of $83 million in unrestricted funds. Numbers aside, Kaster told the jurors that if they wanted to change church policy on spiritual healing when children are involved, "it's by punitive damages against the church." Warren Christopher contended that Lundman had not shown that the defendants deliberately acted negligently. There was no intent on the part of anyone connected to the church to harm Ian Lundman. The jury disagreed, finding that the church had acted with deliberate disregard for Ian Lundman's rights and safety, and awarded $9 million in punitive damages.[34]

Now free to speak, the jurors wanted it understood that their verdict was not about religion. "This wasn't a case about religion, it was about health care, the protection of children and the rights of children," said Kerry Deason, a warehouse worker. The most difficult part of the jury's task, she said, was deciding an appropriate amount to compensate the child's father. "People may think we're criticizing religion," the jury forewoman, Judy Hanks, said, but "it was more about providing health care." Another juror, Angela Brandon, thought the church was "more concerned with their public image than with the child's welfare."[35]

Opinion outside the courtroom varied widely. Swan cautiously applauded the jury's verdict, while an attorney and spokesperson for the church and Stephen L. Carter, a professor at Yale University and the author of the best-seller *The Culture of Disbelief: How American Law and Politics Trivialize Religious Devotion,* found fault with the case's legal outcome. Swan had flown from Sioux City, Iowa, to Minneapolis to listen to final arguments and await the jury's verdict. She told the *St. Paul Pioneer Press* that Doug Lundman's lawsuit and the $14-million-plus damage award represented a "partial victory" and said she hoped "it will persuade the church it simply must tell people to take sick kids to a doctor at the same point any other reasonable person would." Christopher thought the "key issue was the [McKowns'] subjective belief, not the objective results. They believed that spiritual treatment would work and that Ian would be cured through prayer." Writing in the *Christian Science Monitor,* Carter saw the court's Lundman decision and the U.S. Supreme Court's subsequent choice not to review the case as a major blow to freedom of religion and to a parent's right "to rely on their religious faith" to help them make the best possible choice for their child. A "family's religious freedom," Carter concluded, "should not be limited by what other families would do."[36]

Medical ethics experts were divided about the outcome of the case. Michael Paulson, a law professor at the University of Minnesota and an expert on church–state issues, said the jury sent a "troubling message about religious freedom." Its verdict is an example of "courts trying to punish a church for what it believes and teaches to its members," said Paulson. The physician Ronald Cranford, a nationally recognized expert on medical ethics, disagreed: "To let someone die from a treatable problem is wrong," he said. "I hope the verdict sends a clear message to that effect." After all, Cranford added, "religious freedom has its limits."[37]

Ian's death and the trials that followed plunged Doug Lundman into an emotional cauldron. A thoughtful, gentle, introspective man, he became deeply depressed, feeling guilty for not having intervened quickly enough to save Ian's life. He also had felt anger seize control of his body when he learned that prayer had been the only treatment used to save his son. In the months after that moment he had come to terms with his anger, seeing his rage as absurd. But joy has not been a part of his life since Ian's death, he said during a post-trial telephone interview from his home in Cambridge, Massachusetts: "Children have no one looking out for them but their parents. If I'd been there, he would be here now. I have to live with that."[38]

He nevertheless described himself as a religious man, but he no longer believed in absolutes. Rather, Lundman said, "religion is like good poetry. It is filled with ambiguity." Without mentioning his former wife or the practitioner who prayed by Ian's side while he slipped into a diabetic coma and died, he characterized Christian Scientists as sincere but added quickly, "Their sincerity is insidious." He now saw the events surrounding his son's death as a "true tragedy." Ian was the hero whose fatal flaw was the trust he placed in adults: "His trust was a virtue and it destroyed him."[39]

Four years after his son's death and a few days after a Minnesota jury awarded Lundman $5.2 million in compensatory damages and $9 million in punitive damages to be paid by the Christian Science Church, Lundman acknowledged he had reached the end of the "legal road." The size of the jury award meant little to him. "I don't get Ian back and nothing can change that," he said. "But maybe because of this case some other child may not have to have the experience Ian had. Maybe."[40]

In October 1993 Kathy McKown filed a motion asking the court to reduce the amount of compensatory damages for which she was found liable. She held that the verdict was out of line with other child wrongful death awards and that Lundman's decision to live in Kansas after he and Kathy divorced showed he did not have a close relationship with Ian. Judge Rice rejected the latter argument, but he ruled that $1.5 million was "the highest compensatory damage award a reasonable jury could have given under the facts of this case." The Christian Science Church argued that the $9 million in punitive damages assessed against it should be overturned because it violated public policy and the freedom of religion guaranteed by the U.S. and Minnesota constitutions. But Rice ruled that the award promoted public policy by discouraging the church from "allowing another child to die when the child could have been saved by using reasonable methods of health care." The church announced its intention to appeal the District Court's ruling to the Minnesota Court of Appeals.[41]

Judge Jack Davies, who simultaneously served in the Minnesota Senate and taught at William Mitchell Law School for a quarter century before being appointed to the appeals court in 1990, spoke for the court. His balanced, reasonable, creative analysis set aside the punitive damages that the Hennepin County jury had ordered the church to pay in connection with Ian's death, but he held that Christian Science parents must seek conventional medical care when a child is seriously ill. Davies's ruling also clarified who had a legal duty to Ian to provide care.[42]

Davies gave three reasons punitive damages against the Christian Science Church could not be imposed. First, he found no evidence the church directly interfered and weak evidence that it played a part through its agents, the caregivers. Second, amicus briefs submitted by a group of eleven religious organizations made a compelling argument for finding unconstitutional the imposition of punitive damages meant to force the church to change its teaching. However, Davies added, "we do not grant churches and religious bodies a categorical exemption from liability for punitive damages." His third reason for not allowing punitive damages was that he thought there was no "clear and convincing evidence" the church showed a "deliberate disregard" for the rights and safety of others. The church's only contact with Ian came when Van Horn told church officials in Boston that a Christian Science parent treated her seriously ill child using spiritual healing. "Knowledge by itself," Davies ruled, "is insufficient to support an award of punitive damages."[43]

Davies turned next to the other appellants: the McKowns, Tosto, and Lamb. They asserted that religious freedoms guaranteed by the Minnesota and U.S. constitutions precluded an award of compensatory damages because permitting the case to go forward put the Christian Science religion on trial, and allowing a jury to assess the reasonableness of the four appellants' conduct amounted to a constitutionally impermissible evaluation of their genuine religious beliefs. Davies rejected that argument. Citing familiar U.S. Supreme Court decisions—*Cantwell v. Connecticut* (1940), *Prince v. Massachusetts* (1944), and *Reynolds v. U.S.* (1879)—Davies ruled that the four Christian Scientists were "free to believe what they will—and to teach and preach what they believe. But, when beliefs lead to conduct, the conduct may be subject to regulation." The constitutional test for interpreting the free exercise of religion clause is called a balancing test, the judge said, because it balances state against religious interests. Specifically, the balancing test weighed the state's compelling interest in protecting the welfare of children against the McKowns' claim that the free exercise clause protected their religious conduct. Using that test, spiritual healing could constitutionally be regulated by statute.[44]

Although the child neglect statute in Minnesota allows for some accommodation to the Christian Science religion, Davies argued, the statute cannot be read as authorizing reliance on prayer as the sole treatment for seriously ill children under all circumstances. The statute simply indicates the legislature's willingness to tolerate spiritual healing—"up to a point." But the court rejects the argument that the legislature "has sanctioned prayer alone to treat a child battling a life-threatening disease." Davies also rejected two "less-restrictive" alternatives suggested by Christian Scientists: a reporting requirement and reliance on criminal liability. For several reasons, he deemed, neither a reporting requirement nor criminal liability is likely to work effectively.[45]

The McKowns argued in addition that the judgment for compensatory damages should be dismissed because the criminal court had ruled that their constitutional right to due process had been violated for failure to satisfy the fair notice requirement. But Davies countered that this is a "civil action based on common law negligence." And the rules of common law are always adapting to new conditions, interests, and usages "as the progress of society may require." For this reason, he said, the due process requirement of fair notice has not been violated.[46]

Finally, Davies asked, who had a duty to provide Ian with care and what was the standard of care? Minnesota law determined there was a duty when a "special relationship" existed between the parties. A special relationship existed when one person has custody of another who is "vulnerable and dependent" on someone who holds "considerable power over the dependent's welfare." Kathy McKown, a custodial parent, acknowledged she owed a duty to protect her son from harm. The other appellants argued, however, that they did not have a duty of care and that the trial court erred in finding they each had a special relationship with Ian.[47]

Bill McKown argued that he did not have a legal duty to Ian because he was a stepparent and because Kathy was solely responsible for making decisions about Ian's health care. The record, Davies noted, provided ample evidence contradicting McKown. During Ian's final days McKown was fully aware of the seriousness of his condition and frequently acted as a caregiver. He carried Ian from his bed to the table so that the boy could be offered food and drink, and he made several telephone calls on Ian's behalf. Finally, although McKown did not remain awake throughout the night when Ian died, he testified that he spent "most of that night "in the doorway [to Ian's room] making sure I could be summoned for help, if necessary." These facts, Davies concluded, supported a conclusion that McKown knew of Ian's helplessness and had accepted a responsibility to protect him. A special relationship existed between the two, and he cannot "hide behind the natural parent." The law required McKown "to step forward to rescue Ian."[48]

Lamb, the nurse, and Tosto, the practitioner, also claimed they did not have a duty of care. Judge Davies strongly disagreed, saying Lamb had a brief but "special relationship," including custody and control of Ian, a helpless, gravely ill boy she had accepted responsibility to care for and to protect by furnishing her professional services for cash wages. When she arrived at the McKowns' home she found Ian "lying in his own urine, unable to walk, talk, or breathe normally." She cleaned him, changed the bedding, and read hymns and prayers to the boy. That was all she was hired to do, she maintained. To recommend medical care, she argued, would have been antithetical to Christian Science nursing. But Davies pointed out an official church publication, *Legal Rights and Obligations of Christian Scientists in Minnesota,* that warns parents that their right to use spiritual healing "in lieu of medical treatment will continue to be respected by public officials so long as [the officials] are assured that *effective* care is being given our children." That warning, Davies argued, "logically extends beyond parents." Lamb had a professional duty to provide Ian with lifesaving care. She was therefore unable to hide behind pure Christian Science doctrine or Kathy's authority and control. Protecting a child's life "transcends any interest a parent may have in exercising a religious belief."[49]

Judge Davies found that Tosto also had a special relationship with Ian and a duty of care. He accepted a responsibility to serve Ian, and through frequent conversations with the boy's mother and nurse he held considerable power over Ian's well-being. Tosto argued he was subject to Kathy's control and was engaged by her only to provide Christian Science care. As in the case of Lamb, Davies flatly rejected those arguments. Tosto, he said, cannot "hide behind mother." As a professional caregiver he had a responsibility to acknowledge that spiritual healing was not succeeding and "to persuade mother to call providers of conventional medicine, or persuasion failing, to override her and personally call for either a doctor or the authorities."[50]

Finally, Davies focused on the standard of care to be used in determining if Bill McKown, Lamb, and Tosto had breached their respective duties of care. They argued that Minnesota's child neglect statute authorized spiritual treatment "in all circumstances." But if the statutory standard did not apply, the proper standard was a "reasonable Christian Science professional," not the "reasonable person" standard used by the trial court. Davies rejected both arguments, writing, "We will not embrace a negligence standard that would ignore the rights of Ian Lundman." Rather, Davies created a "reasonable person—who is a good-faith Christian Scientist" standard of care. Under this standard a parent may exercise genuinely held religious beliefs, but when he or she is "put to a choice between fidelity to religious belief or serious injury and potential death to the child—judged by the law's general acceptance of conventional medicine—the child's right to life prevails."[51]

In the common law tradition, Davies noted that his ruling served as a notice to "all professional Christian Science caregivers that they cannot successfully disavow their professional duty to a child by deferring to a parent as the ultimate decision-making authority." At the same time, Judge Davies concluded, Lamb and Tosto were not "agents of the church" whose acts were "authorized by the church." There was no evidence the church had a right to control Lamb's and Tosto's performance in caring for Ian. That means the trial jury could not lawfully find the church was a principal in an agency relationship relating to the boy's care. Therefore, the Christian Science Church did not owe a duty to Ian. For this reason, Davies set aside the $9 million in punitive damages the trial court had ordered the church to pay.[52]

Swan praised Judge Davies's decision as "an important development historically," one marking the first time a court had mandated that Christian Science parents, practitioners, and nurses must seek conventional medical care rather than relying solely on prayer when a child is seriously ill. Deborah Georgatos, a church lobbyist, told an audience at a child abuse conference that the court's decision would not change church practices: "It does not change our statutory protection because it was based on common law negligence." Carter weighed in on the controversy. In an essay published in the *Christian Science Monitor,* he celebrated the use of prayer to heal and the right of parents to make what he euphemistically termed "religious decisions for children," for seriously ill children. He trivialized the Minnesota court's decision that parents and caregivers owe a common law duty to protect a minor child from serious harm or death by comparing it to a hypothetical mother in Seattle who sent her four-year-old son off to Nepal believing he was a lama. When he reached adulthood could the unhappy boy sue his mother for exercising her faith?, Carter asked. "The answer," Carter jocularly wrote, "at least in Minnesota, is evidently yes."[53]

Given the public and legal controversy in the case and the church's desire to challenge the award, both Kaster and Christian Science officials indicated they would appeal Davies's decision to the Minnesota Supreme Court and, if necessary, to the U.S. Supreme Court. Two months after the appeals court filed its decision the state high court declined without comment to review the case against the Christian Science Church. Although presented as an urgent issue of religious freedom, with an importance to Christian Scientists that "can scarcely be overstated," Kathy and Bill McKown, Lamb, and Tosto failed to persuade the Supreme Court to hear an appeal of the $1.5-million damage judgment the jury had awarded Douglass and Whitney Lundman. Victor Westburg, an official at the church's headquarters in Boston, responded defiantly: "We'll continue to practice our religion as we have for over 100 years."[54]

4

Ashley King

JOHN AND CATHERINE KING'S neighbors in the affluent neighborhood of Paradise Valley, Arizona, described the King's daughter, eleven-
year-old Ashley, as a friendly, bright girl who talked confidently with adults
and loved to help her mother care for a stable of quarter horses the family
owned. During the academic year 1986–87 Ashley did well in math, language
arts, and reading at Cherokee Elementary School. The summer before she
started attending middle school she won a State Certificate of Achievement
for reading twenty-five books. But Ashley earned average grades in social
studies and science and health. Her parents, members of the Christian Science Church, did not want her to participate in health education.[1]

John King grew up in California in a middle-class home where Christian
Science played a prominent but sometimes divisive role. John's parents, Eb-
enezer and Helen, divorced in 1942 when he was seven years old, and his
mother and grandmother moved the family from Michigan to southern California. Five years later Helen married Thomas King, whom John and his older brother, William, considered their father. The boys attended Palos Verdes
High School, where John excelled as an athlete and won election as student
body president. He graduated from the University of Southern California in
1957 and served two years as a lieutenant in the U.S. Navy. After being hon-
orably discharged he pursued a career in real estate, which in 1973 took him
to Menlo Park, California, where he became vice president of L. B. Nelson
Corporation, a property management firm. There, John met the twenty-four-
year-old Beverly Jean Guth in a Christian Science reading room in the Bay
Area where she worked. The couple married six months later, in April 1975.
Beverly, who changed her name in 1980 to Catherine Justine, had grown up
in Belmont, California, the younger of two girls. There was a religious divide

within the household: the girls' mother was a Christian Scientist, but their father was strongly opposed to the church. Partly as a result of the division, Catherine had a turbulent relationship with her father. At the age of seventeen she left home to attend San Jose State College and graduated from there in 1972 with a degree in home economics. At the same time, she embraced Christian Science, convinced it "answered all her questions and provided a way of life for her." She and John lived in Mill Valley, an upscale community four miles north of San Francisco, before moving to Paradise Valley in 1983.[2]

Early in November 1987, about three months shy of her twelfth birthday, Ashley developed a limp, thought to be a recurrence of a problem that earlier in the school year had caused her to give up dance instruction and to remain on the sidelines during physical exercise class. Catherine, an attractive thirty-seven-year-old woman with blue eyes and brown hair cut in a bob, prayed for her daughter and employed Dorothy Douglas, a Christian Science practitioner with thirty years' experience, to initiate spiritual treatment for Ashley. Douglas spoke with Ashley by telephone every day and claimed she visited Ashley once or twice a week. Catherine allowed Ashley to stay home from school "when she wanted to." For a short time she collected Ashley's school assignments so she could keep up with her classmates but found that too burdensome, and Ashley did not return to school after mid-November. Although Christian Science treatment had been under way for two months, by the end of December Ashley had difficulty breathing when she hobbled from her bedroom to the family room to watch television. In retrospect, Catherine ambiguously concluded that Ashley's "condition was probably terminal by medical standards by December." But because the Kings had experienced "numerous beautiful healings in the past through prayer" they held to the belief that Ashley would be healed.[3]

Catherine's faith helped her put a positive spin on the decline of her daughter's health, transforming her worldly relationship with Ashley to something ethereal and elevating her seriously ill child to near-mythical status. She wrote later, "Our love for each other was as pure as can be gained on earth. She was my best friend. She would never hesitate to give me advice or words of wisdom. I always valued the thoughts she would share with me. Nobody can really understand unless they have experienced a relationship that is somewhere between here and heaven. It so transcended just the parent/child roles. In fact, Ashley was so incredibly beyond her years I often had to remind myself who was the mother and who was the child."[4]

Shortly after Christmas vacation Ashley's sixth-grade teacher, Tammy

Vandenberg, arranged to visit Ashley. Catherine King brought the teacher into the living room, where Ashley lay motionless in a sleeping bag on the couch. Vandenberg thought she seemed very withdrawn and in pain. The teacher tried to talk with Ashley, but it was fruitless, she later recalled, because King repeatedly interrupted, speaking for Ashley. Vandenberg and two friends returned on February 12, but King turned them away, saying, "Oh, she's doing fine." During another failed attempt to see Ashley six weeks later, King caused Vandenberg to shudder when she said, "We finally have come to the point where you place God before your own life."[5]

In January 1988 a social worker in the Scottsdale School District contacted the Kings and recommended they officially withdraw Ashley from school and petition the state to permit her to be homeschooled. Overwhelmed with caring for Ashley—making meals, grooming her, keeping her clean, and praying for her—Catherine said she preferred that a teacher come to their home. However, when she learned that the program required a physician's approval, she opted for homeschooling. She later stated she officially withdrew Ashley from school on January 25, but as late as May the school authorities at Cocopah Middle School were not aware that homeschool papers had been filed for Ashley. Rather, it appears Catherine had initiated her own curriculum. She made Christian Science the center of Ashley's education. *Science and Health* became an English text, the *Church Manual* served as a government lesson, and mother and daughter learned about music from the Christian Science hymnal. "I just incorporated everything we did into a learning experience," King wrote.[6]

Catherine's memory was that Ashley did not become bedridden until April. At least from that time forward she lay in a big feather bed, diapered and unable to move. A large tumor covered her right thigh. On May 2, prompted by the school district's social worker, Doris Wilson, the school nurse at Cocopah asked the Paradise Valley Police Department to check on Ashley's welfare. Detective Edwin A. Boehm, who had served fourteen years with the Haworth, New Jersey, police department before moving to Arizona in 1984, contacted Charlene Craig, a caseworker for the state's Child Protective Services (CPS) and interviewed Wilson and the school principal. Boehm went to the Kings' home, where he knocked at the front door and "heard a female voice, but no one answered." He also interviewed a neighbor, who said she hadn't seen Ashley for months. Craig followed up Boehm's visit by calling King and explaining her role with CPS and the statutory power she possessed to investigate Ashley's welfare. She made an appointment to visit Ashley at

3 p.m. the next day. When Boehm and Craig arrived at the King home they were met by John and Catherine King, Dave Barton, a spokesperson and lobbyist for the Christian Science Church in Arizona, and Madeline Anderson, a practitioner who was filling in for Douglas. Barton, a tall man with glasses and a receding hairline, lectured Boehm and Craig about the value of spiritual treatment and the church's statutory exemption from prosecution for child abuse. Catherine refused to allow the two investigators to see Ashley until Craig said she could obtain a court order.[7]

Catherine told Boehm and Craig not to sit on or bump Ashley's bed and instructed the two investigators not to look at Ashley's leg because that would interfere with the spiritual healing process. She said she had put a pillow on Ashley's leg to make her more comfortable. Boehm and Craig introduced themselves to Ashley and explained they were concerned about her. She said she was fine and not in pain. Boehm later told a grand jury that Ashley was covered by a sheet and therefore nothing below her neck could be seen. She didn't move at all during their conversation except to speak, which she did in short, breathless sentences. Asked to describe the girl's appearance, Boehm said, "She was extremely white, ashen colored—to be specific, death color." Craig asked Ashley where her leg was swollen. Around the knee, the girl said. At the moment the caseworker asked Ashley to be more specific, Craig realized Catherine King was outside the door listening. She rushed into the room and said to Ashley, "It's OK to say where," but before Ashley could speak, King said, "The swelling was the knee and just above."[8]

After speaking with Ashley for a few more minutes, the investigators asked to talk with Anderson alone. She told Boehm and Craig she would not volunteer information, but she would answer their specific questions truthfully. When asked to describe the condition of Ashley's leg, she told them "there was a swelling on Ashley's leg the size of a watermelon." Boehm now realized that King had misled him when she said she had placed a pillow on top of Ashley's leg. This information led Craig to inform the Kings of CPS's policy and procedures. She told them their religious beliefs would be respected, but "CPS needed to determine if Ashley was at medical risk." King insisted that Christian Science spiritual treatment alone would heal Ashley, and later the same day, Douglas, Ashley's full-time practitioner, contacted Craig and explained Christian Science treatment. In emphasizing the efficacy of spiritual treatment she made two remarkable statements: Ashley "had been walking on her leg until just recently," and she did not consider Ashley's condition life-threatening because "God is life."[9]

When she arrived at her office the day after visiting the Kings, Craig called Dr. Mary Rhimza, described Ashley's condition, and asked what those symptoms might indicate. Rhimza suggested several possible diagnoses but concluded she "could think of no benign condition which could fit the description." Craig recognized the need for swift action, but at every step Catherine King created obstacles that slowed the process of getting Ashley to hospital. Craig called the Kings' home and told John he should contact a practicing physician who could see Ashley. He did not object, saying he would ask Barton for a recommendation. When, by early afternoon, she hadn't received the promised response, Craig called the King home again and spoke with Catherine. Although she gave no details, Catherine said they had not been able to find a doctor. She proposed transporting Ashley to a nearby emergency clinic if female physicians and ambulance attendants could be found to do the job. Craig said she would try to comply with those requests and, while waiting for confirmation that a team of women physicians was available, Craig spoke again with Catherine. The caseworker informed her "it was imperative" that Ashley be examined within the next twenty-four hours. Catherine raised another issue: the family did not have medical coverage. Craig had anticipated that problem and told King that CPS would pick up the bill for the ambulance and the attending physicians. That information led King to abandon the idea of the emergency clinic in favor of having a doctor come to her home. Craig reminded King that an exam would include X-rays and blood work, which could not be carried out in her home. Nevertheless, King ended the conversation by giving vague assurances that she would continue to "work on getting a doctor," someone who wouldn't traumatize Ashley. The latter comment troubled Craig. She told King that the "attitude she displayed to Ashley was very important" and that she feared her "apprehensive feelings were being transmitted to Ashley." While the child "allegedly was committed to Christian Science practice," Craig added, she believed Ashley "was very dependent upon her mother's approval and 'coaching.'"[10]

About 9:30 a.m. the next day Craig told Catherine King that CPS had arranged for a doctor to come to their home. During the phone conversation King enthusiastically told Craig she had discovered a lesion near the bottom of Ashley's leg that was draining, which King believed indicated that, together with Ashley's feeling of "forgiveness," a healing was in progress. Craig, Boehm, and Dr. Fred Dickie, an intern at Scottsdale Memorial Hospital, went to the Kings' home and were allowed to see Ashley. Dickie's examination revealed a massive growth on the child's leg, a rapid heartbeat, and serious difficulty breathing, which led him to determine she needed to be examined more fully at a hospital. Craig explained to the Kings that, if necessary, she could get a temporary custody order allowing CPS to obtain medical attention for Ashley. The Kings agreed to cooperate, and paramedics transported Ashley to Scottsdale Memorial Hospital.[11]

At the hospital, physicians determined that Ashley had a malignant tumor on her leg measuring forty-one inches in diameter and extending from just above her knee to the groin area. X-rays revealed that the bone in her right leg was fractured in two places, eaten away by the cancerous growth, and that the cancer had spread to her lungs. Craig noted that the medical staff was "visibly outraged" by Ashley's condition, aghast at the size of the tumor, and disgusted that she had arrived at the hospital on a "thoroughly soiled sheet." When the examining physician informed the Kings of his diagnosis, they denied the seriousness of Ashley's medical condition. In fact, Catherine contended that a number of similar cases had been healed through Christian Science treatment, and she asked if Ashley could be taken to Upward View, a Christian Science nursing facility. The examining physician refused and told the Kings he wanted Ashley to be transferred to Phoenix Children's Hospital. When the Kings balked, Craig again reminded them she would, if necessary, obtain a temporary custody order.[12]

At Phoenix Children's Hospital, Dr. Paul Baranco, a pediatric oncologist, confirmed the diagnosis of osteogenic sarcoma, "an extremely painful cancerous tumor of the bone" that usually develops during a period of rapid growth in adolescence. He also found that Ashley's heart had become enlarged as a result of having to work so hard to pump blood that was collecting in her thigh. In fact, Baranco believed that at the moment Ashley was more at risk of congestive heart failure than of succumbing to the cancerous tumor. Because of her enlarged heart, he noted, Ashley's lungs could not be seen well enough in the X-rays to determine the extent of the cancer there.[13]

Late Friday afternoon on May 6, Baranco recommended that Ashley be admitted to the hospital, but Catherine King refused to allow her to be admitted. Without hesitation Craig initiated the process allowing CPS to assume temporary forty-eight-hour custody of Ashley. Craig noted that both parents were "very sincere" in their belief that spiritual treatment would heal Ashley, but she characterized Catherine's reliance on faith as more "dominating." By contrast, she and others portrayed the fifty-four-year-old, gray-haired John King as "less religiously principled." He stated, for example, that he was not opposed to medicine or doctors, but he wanted to support Ashley's decision to rely on Christian Science. Catherine also seemed to defer to Ashley, but some hospital observers noted that she exerted enormous influence over her daughter's decisions. Several hospital nurses, for example, claimed that when her mother was present Ashley denied feeling any pain but when alone with a nurse she confided, "I'm in so much pain." Unlike her husband's seeming openness to medical treatment, Catherine expressed no tolerance for it. Rather, she blamed the medical care Ashley received at hospital for the child's increasingly serious condition. "Because of [Ashley's] intense resistance to the medical [treatment]," King wrote to a friend, "her condition became such that after 6 nights in the hospital she could not be returned home for care but had to be brought to Upward View." Faced with temporarily losing custody of their daughter, the Kings contacted Barton, intending to fight for their beliefs.[14]

Baranco made it clear he would not permit Ashley to be released because of the seriousness of her situation. Her hemoglobin count was 2.4 grams per deciliter, a level "almost incompatible with life," as a healthy girl her age would have a count of 12 to 15. Ashley's pulse rate was 140 beats per minute, about twice the normal rate. The size of the cancerous tumor on her leg and the accompanying pain made it nearly impossible for her to move, causing extensive bedsores. The fact that she had been using diapers and changing herself—an extraordinarily difficult and painful maneuver—meant she often lay in her own excrement, which had caused serious skin deterioration on her buttocks and in the vaginal area. An abnormal accumulation of fluid also affected her right labia. For all these reasons, Baranco recommended amputating Ashley's leg. He explained that the amputation would not save Ashley's life since the disease had progressed too far, but it would relieve the pain and aid in her hygiene.[15]

Catherine King manifested no understanding of, or curiosity about, Baranco's analysis. She blamed the hospital, asserting that Ashley's cancerous leg had become larger at the hospital and that "any feces or urine" found on her bedsheets "was the result of her being terrorized" by the prospect of hospital care. Baranco conceded that some bleeding could have taken place en route to the hospital, but he emphatically held that Ashley's tumor hadn't occurred overnight and that the problem of hygiene "has been ongoing." A few moments later, while complaining to Craig about Baranco, King offered a scientifically unfounded explanation for the growth of Ashley's tumor. The tumor grew larger, she said, when two or three weeks ago she bathed Ashley with hot water.[16]

When Barton arrived at the hospital he and Baranco had a heated discussion about what treatment was best for Ashley. Barton insisted Ashley was not in pain and claimed that Christian Science treatment had been effective in curing bone cancer and other serious diseases. Baranco dismissed both claims as unfounded. The two men also argued about whether the state could order the Kings to provide medical care for their daughter. Barton cited a state law that allowed Christian Science parents to rely on spiritual treatment for their child and Baranco responded sharply that that right was not absolute. Eventually an agreement was reached by which Ashley would remain at Phoenix Children's Hospital and receive pain medication through the weekend. If cardiac arrest occurred, one attempt would be made to revive her. A meeting of all interested parties was scheduled for Monday.[17]

On May 9, in the boardroom at the hospital, Baranco outlined Ashley's condition to the Kings, Craig, Paul Matte, an assistant attorney general, Dave Barton and his wife, Laura, the administrator of Upward View, and attorneys for the Kings and Ashley. Baranco explained that had the child received medical treatment earlier there would have been a 50 to 60 percent chance that the cancer would not have spread. Currently, Ashley's condition was inoperable, and she had less than a 3 percent chance of survival. Baranco continued to recommend amputation of her leg in order to aid in the child's hygiene and relieve her pain.[18]

Over the next three days, two intertwined questions dominated discussion among the hospital professionals: was Ashley in pain and, if not, could she implicitly give consent to withhold medical care? Following Baranco's presentation, Matte asked if Ashley's threshold for pain could be determined or if the human body had a natural ability to produce a painkiller. No one around the conference table had a definitive answer to those questions. But on the basis of his brief interview of Ashley, Dr. Richard Spiegel, a fellow in child psychiatry at Phoenix Children's Hospital, questioned the validity of Ashley's denial of pain and her alleged high threshold for pain. Barton, however, talked about the efficacy of Christian Science treatment. As the meeting ended, a consensus emerged that additional evaluations of Ashley's pain level were needed together with insight into whether she was personally responsible for her decision to forgo medical care or under the strong influence of her mother. Dr. James Joy, a pediatric psychiatrist at Phoenix Children's Hospital, and Dr. Brian Yee, a private psychiatrist employed by the Kings, took on the task of finding answers to those key questions.[19]

At this point Baranco stepped out of the fray, discouraged and angry. He later told an investigator:

This had to be the most disturbing, depressing case I have ever seen in my 25 years as a physician. I think that sums it up. I have seen a lot of nasty things. I've seen child abuse cases. I've seen patients dying of malignancies because of complications, because of therapy or disease. I have never seen a patient presented with this kind of a situation. Could have been totally avoided. Just [as] disturbing in my mind, the courts would not support something to be done with the child. Not that we could have cured her. Just given her a chance to live a somewhat longer life—quality of life, while she did have some time.[20]

On May 11 Matte convened a follow-up meeting to discuss the new information gathered about Ashley's health. Joy reported he was struck by the "intensity with which [the Kings] professed their beliefs" and, manifesting little awareness of Christian Science, expressed surprise that a cosmopolitan, college-educated couple would deny the obvious seriousness of their child's illness. He said Ashley was uncooperative, denied being in pain, and said she had been "harshly treated" and "didn't want the surgery." Then she refused to answer any more questions. From these two very brief interviews Joy drew four far-reaching conclusions: Ashley was not in pain; he found no evidence of parental coercion in Ashley's decision about medical care or her Christian Science beliefs; Ashley's "deep-rooted belief" legitimized her denial of medical care and her commitment to Christian Science treatment; and, given her commitment to spiritual healing, it would be "devastating" to amputate her leg.[21]

Craig voiced an abundance of contrary information supplied to her by nurses. An admitting nurse, Sue Jacoby, reported that when she asked Ashley how she was sleeping, the child replied, "I haven't slept in so long." When asked why, Ashley said, "I'm in so much pain." Ashley's primary care nurse, Kellie Kluever, said that when King was in the room Ashley denied being in pain, but when Kluever and the child were alone, Ashley admitted she was indeed in pain. On one occasion when King returned to the room unexpectedly and found Ashley crying, she told her, "You're not in pain, you're afraid." Jeannie Blose, the eighth-floor nursing coordinator, told Craig she had overheard King tell Ashley she "was going to have to learn to deal with pain." Perhaps aware of the nurses' views, King approached Craig and said, "Please talk to Ashley, she'll tell you she's not in pain."[22]

Yee, Barton, and Catherine King also contributed arguments for Matte's consideration. On the question of whether to amputate Ashley's leg, Yee argued that if it were done she would need the support of her family to recover and "it was doubtful she would get this support." Although healing is a distinctive aspect of Christian Science, Barton said, it is also "a way of life," a religious discipline that is meant to shape every aspect of life. If, for whatever reason, that goal isn't successfully realized Christian Scientists don't "give up to try something else." As she had from the outset, King played a major role in the decision-making process. At home and in the hospital she seemed omnipresent, and her message never wavered: Ashley was a "consecrated Christian Scientist," wise beyond her years, free from pain despite the presence of an advanced cancerous tumor, traumatized by doctors and nurses, and convinced she would die if operated on or forced to remain in the hospital. All the decisions rejecting medical care King attributed to Ashley.[23]

At the conclusion of the meeting, Matte decided not to file for a petition of custody. On May 12, seven days after Craig and Boehm had made contact with Ashley, the child was transferred to Upward View. Catherine King refused to sign any papers. The two parties agreed that a new caseworker from CPS would monitor Ashley's care at the Christian Science facility.[24]

At approximately 7 p.m. on Sunday, June 5, 1988, Ashley died at Upward View. She lived for 12 years and 129 days before succumbing to bone cancer that had metastasized to her lungs. Her parents were at her bedside. Dave Barton prayed with the child, and Laura Barton, formerly a medical nurse, said, astonishingly, that Ashley "had been making progress" and "her passing was a surprise to us all." She described the child's death as "very quiet and peaceful," adding she was not in pain. Since leaving the hospital Ashley had not received pain medication.[25]

More than a year after Ashley's death, Catherine King concluded with "absolute certainty that the right treatment had been given all along." According to her, she did not influence the decision of the twelve-year-old Ashley to reject medical care in favor of Christian Science treatment. She claimed Ashley was intelligent and mature enough to be personally responsible to choose a treatment for her illness and that she consistently chose spiritual treatment. As Kent Greenfield, a professor of law at Boston College, points out, however, "Sometimes people are actually *not* responsible for their own decisions when they are under the powerful psychological influence of authority figures." A grown person and certainly a child can be manipulated by an authority figure to their detriment because the psychological power of authority is immense. There is an abundance of compelling evidence testifying to the powerful influence King exerted over her daughter, although she and her legal team masked that influence by creating the myth that Ashley alone was responsible for making treatment decisions. King insisted that the doctors and nurses at the hospital traumatized Ashley and that she adamantly refused medical treatment. Perpetuating to the fullest extent the myth about Ashley's autonomy and her reputed deep Christian Science faith and its efficacy, King stated that her daughter suffered no pain, an argument that deflected responsibility from King to Ashley and at the same time gave her credit for tutoring and raising a perfect Christian Science child.[26]

Esther Muñoz, a six-year veteran at Phoenix Children's Hospital assigned to care for Ashley, established a caring relationship with the child that quietly and briefly challenged King's psychological dominance over her. Shortly after Ashley's arrival at Phoenix Children's Hospital, a physician ordered her to undergo a computerized tomography scan, but King refused to agree to the procedure. "The longer we waited to do it," Muñoz explained, "the more Ashley would worry about it." Muñoz and Ashley talked about the procedure, and Ashley agreed "to go ahead and get it over with." But remembering how painful the move from her home to the hospital had been, she asked Muñoz for pain medication. King didn't want her to have medication, as to have agreed to the provision of medicine would have violated her Christian Science beliefs and been an admission that pain existed. But she relented, saying Ashley "was old enough to make a decision on her own." With that, Muñoz arranged for a morphine drip, and the move from one hospital floor to another went smoothly. When Ashley returned to her room, Muñoz confronted the problem of Ashley's hygiene. King insisted Ashley was solely responsible for changing her own diaper, an enormously difficult task given the fact that any movement caused Ashley to suffer excruciating pain. For that reason Ashley often spent an entire day with a soaking wet diaper and a wet bed that caused discomfort, odor, and the deterioration of the skin underneath her cancerous leg, buttocks, and groin. Still, King did not help Ashley, and she forbade Muñoz to do so, despite the nurse's expressed willingness to assist. Muñoz solved the problem by making use of a specially designed bed used for burn patients. Called a clinitron bed, it uses resin beads through which air is blown, and pulling drainage down into the beads, at the same time reducing pressure on the patient's body. The bed made Ashley much more comfortable, but it did not eliminate her pain. King's faith-based approach was to deny the existence of pain and therefore to insist that Ashley did not need and should not ask for medication or help to relieve pain and the discomfort that accompanied it. Muñoz's commitment "to take care of Ashley and meet [her] needs" and her medical training gave her a different perspective and created a different result. She knew "bone pain is one of the most severe types of pain," and she knew Ashley was suffering without medication. She "was very irritable," and "didn't want to talk to anybody," but when she was given morphine that dulled the pain "she would talk, could carry on a coherent conversation and was a very pleasant, cheerful child."[27]

By providing Ashley greater comfort, relief from pain, and affection, Muñoz unknowingly shook Ashley's Christian Science faith and challenged King's dominant influence. On Ashley's last day at the hospital, at a time when her mother and her religious, legal, and psychiatric advisors had convinced state authorities to allow Ashley to be moved from the hospital to Upward View, Ashley asked Muñoz if "we could take off all her IVs and do what they [mom and dad] want us to do, could she please stay here, as she likes her nurses and doesn't need to be moved." But neither Ashley nor Muñoz had control at this point. According to King, during the final month of her daughter's life she and Ashley gloried in their commitment to Christian Science. "I'm so grateful that God brought me here," Ashley allegedly said to her mother, "because had I stayed in the hospital and had the operation I would be dead now."[28]

On August 3, 1988, a grand jury in Maricopa County returned a "True Bill," charging John and Catherine King with negligent homicide and felony child abuse for failure to obtain medical care for their daughter Ashley. At their arraignment thirteen days later the Kings entered pleas of not guilty to all charges and were released on their own recognizance. When asked for comment, Catherine King's attorney, Robert J. Hooker, a defense lawyer and former judge from Tucson, responded testily to published remarks made by Maricopa County Attorney Tom Collins, a former marine, who was quoted as saying, "Any person who calls himself a Christian wouldn't let a dog die like this." "Let me tell you what I think about Mr. Collins' comments," Hooker told reporters. "They are either motivated by one of three things, or a combination of all of them: Ignorance, politics, or religious bigotry." Hooker later added, "Any indictment that is a result of any one of those things is inappropriate and improper. I suspect," he continued, that Collins "is attempting as best he can to prejudice this community not only against [the Kings], but Christian Scientists." Collins fired back by saying religion has nothing to do with the case, which in reality "deals with man-made laws that impose a duty on people to care for children who cannot care for themselves." He didn't stop there: "The law doesn't allow a child to die because people are trusting in God to prevent it. Just as it doesn't allow somebody to park a baby carriage on a railroad track and trust that God will prevent a train from going by." Deputy Maricopa County Attorney K. C. Scull, who was assigned to try the case, attempted to quiet the rhetorical storm stirred up by his boss. "Religion is not going to be the argument in this case," he said.[29]

Scull was whistling in the dark. The issues of religion and child abuse burst onto the scene before the Kings' case was even properly under way. In April 1988 an eighteen-year-old woman named Debra Ann Forster had pleaded guilty to two counts of attempted felony child abuse stemming from an incident in May 1987 in which she left her two children, ages eighteen months and six months, alone in a sweltering apartment in Mesa, Arizona, for two days. Both infants were dehydrated and near death when discovered by Forster's ex-husband. Maricopa County Superior Court Judge Lindsey Ellis Budzyn sentenced Forster to use birth control for the rest of her childbearing years. Along with liberals, religious fundamentalists, and feminists, the American Civil Liberties Union protested the order, arguing that it violated her reproductive freedom, and the Roman Catholic Church objected that the sentence violated her religious beliefs (Forster was Catholic). Forster's public defender appealed the sentence.[30]

Before the outcry surrounding Judge Budzyn's sentence in the Forster case had abated, she was by chance assigned to the King case. Criminal procedure rules in Arizona allowed a defendant to request that the court change a judge assigned to a criminal case. First Catherine and then John King filed a motion for a change of judge. Budzyn was an obvious target for Hooker, but his second use of the rule was an early hint that he intended to pursue an aggressive style aimed at putting the state on the defensive. Hooker, whose criminal law practice had earned him a reputation as a "champion of the underdog" passionately committed "to fighting against government abuses of civil and personal rights," charged that Judge Budzyn was "biased and prejudiced against [the Kings] by reason of her deep-seated opinions about the underlying allegations of child abuse and child neglect." Prosecutor Scull responded by arguing weakly that Hooker had not established Budzyn's bias and prejudice toward the defendants. Aware that the issues raised by the Kings at trial would be controversial enough even without regard to Budzyn's record, Judge Thomas W. O'Toole granted Catherine King's peremptory right to remove Judge Budzyn and a short time later also granted John King's motion to remove Budzyn's replacement, Judge Barry G. Silverman. On September 28, O'Toole transferred the King case to Judge Ron Reinstein, a former deputy county attorney (1974–85) whom the *Phoenix New Times* labeled "compassionate, thoughtful and even-handed."[31]

A week before Judge Reinstein assumed control of the case, the Kings filed a motion with the trial court to dismiss the charges against them or, alternatively, to send the case back to the grand jury. The Kings held that they had been denied a "substantial procedural right," or due process, during the grand jury proceedings. They pointed to a ruling by the U.S. Supreme Court holding that due process required an unbiased grand jury and a fair, impartial presentation of the evidence. These are vague phrases perhaps, but the Kings maintained that Scull had violated these fundamental safeguards. Among other alleged procedural violations, the Kings asserted that Scull inadequately questioned the grand jurors about their exposure to media coverage, failed to advise the jurors of an Arizona statute exempting Christian Science parents who treated their child with spiritual healing from a charge of child abuse, and used hearsay medical evidence that violated patient–doctor privilege. These errors of omission and commission had the effect of misleading the grand jury, undermining its impartiality, and therefore denying the Kings a substantive procedural right.[32]

In clear, sharp prose Scull refuted each of the Kings' points. The defendants' charge that some grand jurors might have been unqualified because of exposure to media coverage of the case is "mere conjecture" and ignores the procedural rule governing prejudice. The rule applies only to prospective jurors who may be prejudiced "by knowing a defendant or the attorneys involved, or by having formed an opinion about the case prior to" the start of legal proceedings. A county attorney read that rule to the jurors and asked if it applied. No one disqualified himself or herself. He did not refer to the Christian Science exemption during the grand jury proceedings, Scull declared, because that provision is found in the Children's Code and is not applicable to the criminal charges of negligent homicide and felony child abuse. "If the legislature had intended the so-called exemption to apply to the child abuse defined in the Criminal Code," he wrote, "they would have specifically said so and they most clearly did not." Finally, Scull insisted, the doctors and nurses at Children's Hospital did not breach physician–patient privilege because in fact the law specifically requires doctors and nurses to report suspected cases of child abuse: "There is no privilege for the defendants to hide behind."[33]

In its reply to the state's arguments, the defense elaborated on its two most compelling points. First, the Kings insisted the exemption statute was relevant to their defense. While the extent of the accommodation was an issue to be resolved at trial, the prosecutor should have made the grand jurors aware of the statute. By failing to inform the grand jurors that Christian Scientists in Arizona may be exempt from a charge of child abuse, the Kings

argued, Scull had "impermissibly manipulated the grand jury by withholding important factual information." Second, allowing Robert Eckhoff, a state
investigator, to present hearsay testimony about Ashley's physical condition
and to imply the Kings unilaterally removed their daughter from the hospital
constituted "prosecutorial overreach" and deprived the Kings of their "substantial procedural right to a fair and impartial presentation of evidence."
Therefore, the court should grant the defense motion to dismiss or return the
case to the grand jury.[34]

On October 24, 1988, following oral argument, Judge Reinstein denied the
Kings' motion to dismiss, but he granted their motion to remand the case
to the grand jury. The court's order supported two of the state's key arguments: the grand jury need not be informed of the statute possibly exempting
Christian Scientists from a charge of child abuse; and testimony from doctors
and nurses about Ashley's condition and treatment did not breach the physician–patient privilege. However, Reinstein found Eckhoff's testimony to be
"incomplete and therefore misleading, such that it denied the defendants a
substantial procedural right to a fair and impartial presentation before the
grand jury." The grand jury also should have been told the Kings did not
unilaterally "spirit the child away from the hospital" to Upward View, but
instead that a number of people interested in Ashley's welfare participated in
that decision.[35]

On October 31, three days before the 102nd Maricopa County Grand Jury
convened, Hooker had two letters "hand delivered" to Scull outlining how the
grand jury should proceed in order to reach a decision free of prosecutorial
and media influence. Hooker's letters and argument characteristically manifested what his friend and fellow attorney Nat Schaye called "Bob's dogged
determination on behalf of his client" and his firm belief that the criminal
justice system "must change." The specific changes in the ways the grand jury
operated were borrowed by Hooker from Sigmund G. Popko, a clinical law
professor at Sandra Day O'Connor College of Law, and, like Hooker, a longtime member of Arizona Attorneys for Criminal Justice. About a year before
Hooker sent his letters to Scull, Popko gave a seminar in Tucson on advanced
trial skills, later published as "Arizona's County Grand Jury: The Empty
Promise of Independence." Hooker's letters to Scull adopted Popko's grand
jury reforms. "It is not my intent," he wrote, "to tell you or the grand jury how
to conduct its investigation." Despite this disclaimer, there followed a list of
specific requests: the state should not set forth the charges which it thinks
should be brought, but should provide the jurors copies of "all applicable

statutes," including "all statutes which sanction Christian Science treatment";
the state should not paraphrase or recite what a witness said but call every
witness personally; the state should not influence the grand jury but allow it
to "deliberate and determine on its own whether the Kings should be indicted and on which charge;" finally, Hooker demanded that every grand juror
be carefully and fully questioned "to ensure they have not been influenced in
any way by the publicity that has gone on in this case." He concluded with a
warning: "I assure you that when reviewing the grand jury transcripts, this
area will be given very close scrutiny."[36]

On November 22, 1988, the grand jury declined to indict the Kings on a
charge of negligent homicide. The couple was indicted for felony child abuse,
a lesser charge to which they entered pleas of not guilty at their arraignment
on December 6. From this point forward Hooker seemed less concerned
with preparing for a trial than with building an exhaustive record to support
a successful appeal. Over the next six weeks Hooker filed nine motions with
the court, including a forty-six-page motion asking Judge Reinstein to dismiss the case or to return it, yet again, to a grand jury. The defense charged
the prosecution with "knowingly misstating the facts," failing to pursue possible juror bias stemming from the "extensive media coverage," improperly
inquiring into the defendants' religious beliefs, introducing evidence about
Ashley's pain after May 6, when the state had assumed temporary custody
of the child, and questioning Ashley's competence "to make a decision regarding religious freedom and suggesting any preference she expressed was
merely the result of coercion by her parents." At the conclusion of this litany
of alleged violations of due process, the Kings weakly urged the court "to
consider the cumulative effect of all the irregularities upon the entire grand
jury proceeding."[37]

Scull's response labeled the Kings' motion nothing but "a rehash" of their
earlier argument absent any evidence that "the defendant was denied a substantial procedural right." He refuted each point, beginning with the defense
accusation that he deliberately misstated testimony in order to manipulate
the grand jury's outcome. Such a personal attack, he wrote, was "baseless,"
nothing more than a "form of character assassination which the defendants
seem to persist in making their motions." The defense also fails to prove their
vague charge of juror bias stemming from publicity about the case or to link
it to the deprivation of a substantial procedural right allegedly denied to the
defendants. In regard to the defendants' religious beliefs and practices, the
"defense attorneys want to have their cake and eat it too." Along with Talbot,

the Kings were permitted to talk for hours to the grand jury about their religious beliefs and practices. To argue that the state cannot ask any questions about their beliefs and practices "is ludicrous in the extreme." In fact, Scull continued, the state has consistently stated that the Kings "cannot martyr their child to their religious beliefs." Finally, Scull wrote, whether a twelve-year-old child is competent to make life and death decisions "is a matter that will be brought out at trial." For the reason stated, the defendants had clearly not been denied a substantial procedural right, and therefore their motion to dismiss or remand should be denied by the court.[38]

In reply, the Kings elaborated on their original arguments to dismiss, but they also raised other legal and constitutional issues. The couple argued that their "religious freedom defense" was unique to Arizona and therefore all three major cases cited to the grand jury by the prosecution were without value. According to the defense, neither *Matter of Appeal in Cochise County, Arizona* (1982) nor *Commonwealth of Pennsylvania v. Barnhart* (1985) gave the jurors proper legal guidance, and the reach of *Prince v. Massachusetts* (1944) was greatly exaggerated.[39]

In the Arizona case, a mother took her six-year-old son Therial to the emergency room, where he was pronounced dead on arrival. Because of the circumstances of the child's death, a physician contacted the Arizona Department of Economic Security, and two caseworkers subsequently interviewed the mother. In response to questioning, the mother explained she "believed in miracles and that God's will should be done," and accordingly, she continued, if any of her other seven children became ill she would not take them to a doctor. The Department of Economic Security then filed a petition requesting that the family's living children be declared dependent, subject to state control. On appeal, the Arizona Supreme Court ruled as follows: "There was not sufficient evidence to warrant State interference with the fundamental right of the parent to custody and control of his or her child, particularly to 'monitor' the health of the child when there is no known medical danger and when providing medical care is contrary to the parent's religious beliefs." Whereas Scull had used the court's decision to bolster his argument that he had provided the grand jury with good, current legal advice to help it understand the issues in the King case, the defense insisted that *Cochise County* was not on point because King was not a "state intervention case." That is, the *Cochise County* court sought to balance the parents' right to religious freedom with the state's right to intervene in order to protect the life and health of living children. The defense argued that because Ashley already was dead, the Kings' case presented different legal issues. The state's intervention was not intended to balance the well-being of the child and religious freedom. Rather, the state sought to punish the Kings and "chill and modify the religious beliefs and practices" of all Christian Scientists, an act which, according to the defense, violated the First Amendment.[40]

The prosecution and the defense also disagreed sharply over the interpretation and applicability of *Barnhart*. In the state's view there were "many striking similarities" between *Barnhart* and the King case. Justin Barnhart was a minor child of parents who were lifelong members of the Faith Tabernacle Church, a religious group that eschewed medical care in favor of God's power to heal. After a five-month struggle, Justin succumbed to cancer. The boy's death sparked a state inquiry that eventually led a jury to convict the parents of involuntary manslaughter and endangering the welfare of a child. In upholding the conviction, the Pennsylvania Superior Court noted that the parents had an absolute right "to raise their child according to their beliefs but when the child's life is endangered the parent's religious beliefs must give way to the state's compelling interest to protect a minor child's life and welfare." The King defense attacked *Barnhart* as "nothing more" than a "poorly reasoned" "lower appellate court opinion" that failed to make the distinction "between intervention cases and the state interest in a criminal prosecution." In short, the prosecution's use of *Barnhart* seriously misled the grand jury.[41]

Finally, Scull and the Kings advocated diverse interpretations of *Prince v. Massachusetts*, the case most often cited in disputes involving religion-based medical neglect. As we have seen, the case turned on the right of Sarah Prince and her nine-year-old niece to sell Jehovah's Witnesses pamphlets on the street in the city of Brockton, a practice that violated a Massachusetts child labor law. Prince challenged the enforcement of the law, claiming it infringed on her religious liberty. The U.S. Supreme Court's opinion held that the First Amendment's protection of religious freedom did not give parents absolute authority over their child. The state had a role as guardian of juveniles. "Neither rights of religion nor rights of parenthood are beyond limitation," Justice Wiley Rutledge wrote. "Parents may be free to become martyrs themselves. But it does not follow they are free, in identical circumstances, to make martyrs of their children before they have reached the age of full and legal discretion when they can make that choice for themselves." Using these powerful admonitions, the Maricopa County attorney argued that *Prince* "stands squarely for the proposition that rights of religion can be limited and controlled by the State when in the practice of that religion a child's health or well-being may be threatened." In its reply, the defense insisted that *Prince* "was limited to its facts" and therefore stood for the "very narrow proposition" that the state had a right to infringe on the First Amendment only when it conflicted with child labor laws.[42]

On March 1, 1989, Judge Reinstein announced his ruling on the defense motion to dismiss or remand the 102nd Maricopa County Grand Jury's indictment of John and Catherine King for felony child abuse. He acknowledged how contentious the process had been. "After sifting through the charges, countercharges, and polemics on both sides of this issue," Reinstein wrote exasperatedly, "it is clear that this was *not* a perfect grand jury presentation. In fact, it was far from it." But, he wrote, the law doesn't require a perfect hearing, only one in which the defendants were not denied a substantial procedural right. The state made many mistakes: it should have done more to discover potential bias and prejudice toward Christian Scientists among grand jurors; it should have more tightly controlled the angry testimony of Dr. Paul Baranco; and it should not have cited *Cochise County* and *Barnhart* as "authority for an 'instruction' in a criminal case." Although these mistakes should not have occurred, the Kings had an opportunity to "neutralize" the prosecutor's alleged "inflammatory and irrelevant" remarks about Christian Science during their lengthy, uninterrupted testimony to the grand jury, and the prosecutor's legal instruction was "harmless" because "there is no recognized religious belief exemption to a criminal case prosecution." In fact, Arizona law recognizes a compelling state interest that outweighs "the parents' right to practice their religion, at least where a child's medical condition is grave or seriously impaired." Considering all these reasons, Judge Reinstein denied the defendants' motion to dismiss or remand.[43]

If the court or the prosecution thought they were finished with Hooker's pretrial motions, they were mistaken. Twenty-seven days after the court's ruling, the defense team filed a fifty-six-page motion for reconsideration, asking Judge Reinstein to change his mind. Much of what the attorney Glenda Edmonds, a forty-five-year-old former social worker just beginning the practice of law, wrote was old news, but she made three new arguments. First, she attacked the court for failing to utilize its alleged broad "supervisory powers" to wrest control over a deeply flawed grand jury process from the county attorney's office. The court mistakenly believed dismissal or remand could be ordered only if the defendant had been denied a substantial procedural right. To the contrary, the court can—must—use its "inherent supervisory powers" to avoid becoming a "partner in prosecutorial misconduct." Second,

Edmonds argued, the defendants had a right to an evidentiary hearing, and the court was wrong to deny it. The court's error prevented the defense from demonstrating that during the grand jury process the state's witnesses gave "inaccurate and misleading testimony" and the prosecutor deliberately "misled" the jurors. Third, the prosecutor's purposefully inaccurate "legal instruction" to the grand jury forced the defense to distinguish the cases he cited. In it's ruling, however, the court did not have to decide if Arizona's "recognized religious belief exemption" extended to felony child abuse. As a result, the defendants are now "burdened with an unfavorable 'law of case' that deprives them of a substantial defense." To remedy this untenable situation the Kings asked the court to delete that sentence from its order or to dismiss the case.[44]

Scull responded promptly, briefly, and confidently with a motion asking the court to deny reconsideration. Arizona Rules of Criminal Procedure stipulate that a court shall not reconsider an issue previously decided "except for good cause." Generally, a successful reconsideration is based on some "new factor" or raises an issue the court had not previously considered. The Kings' motion raised no new issues, Scull wrote, tongue-in-cheek, except for their suggestion that the court "boldly proclaim a general and unlimited 'supervisory power' to remand to the grand jury whenever the Court should deem it appropriate, where no Arizona court has found such a power before." Scull lightheartedly dismissed as well the so-called new factors advanced by the Kings: their *Walker* discussion failed to establish the California case as an authoritative interpretation of Arizona statutes; and they failed as well to explain how and why Arizona's Christian Science exemption could be "forcibly 'read into' the criminal code when the legislature didn't write it there." Viewed in this light, the motion raises "the tiniest suspicion that this paper blizzard is intended as much to delay and exasperate the weary traveler as it is to provide this court with new vistas." In sum, he concluded, the motion adds nothing new, fails to show good cause, and should be summarily denied.[45]

On the same day the state filed its motion to deny reconsideration, it took a second bite of the apple by submitting a response to the defendants' motion for reconsideration. Scull's argument in the two motions was similar but more fully and seriously stated in the second piece. He began with the usual bromide: The freedom to believe in any religion is an absolute right protected by the U.S. and Arizona constitutions, but the right to religious conduct is not absolute. A religious practice may be infringed on, for example, by the state's compelling interest to protect the life and well-being of a child. As a result, Arizona has enacted laws establishing "objective responsibilities"—

food, housing, and medical care for a seriously ill child—to which all parents must comply. The state may not grant a religious exemption to a statute spelling out an objective parental responsibility. Therefore, no religious defense exists either in Arizona law or in the constitutional protection afforded the free exercise of religion. Although the Kings' religious beliefs may shed light on their "state of mind" during the commission or omission of the criminal behavior with which they are charged, that element cannot constitute a separate defense.[46]

The Kings asserted that the Christian Science exemption written into the state's child dependency statute permitting a court or CPS caseworker to temporarily remove a child from parental custody when evidence shows a parent has failed to provide reasonable care and treatment to the endangerment of a child's health and well-being also applied to a criminal charge of child abuse. The argument linking the two statutes, Scull insisted, rests on the thin reed that the "similarity of purpose" between the two statutes "creates an inference that the legislature intended for an exemption in one to apply to the other." In fact, the opposite inference applies—namely, that the legislature knew what it was doing when it used a different definition of abuse and omitted mention of an exemption in the criminal child abuse subsection. More to the point, even if the Christian Science exemption could somehow be applied to a criminal charge, "it would not provide the Kings with a defense in this case" because the statute simply states that a child receiving Christian Science treatment shall not be considered an abused child "for that reason alone." If, however, the court found a child's life endangered despite spiritual treatment state intervention and a criminal charge would be justified.[47]

In this case, Scull argued, the Kings did more than pursue a course of spiritual treatment. As early as November 1988 they realized that Ashley's condition was serious enough to take her out of school and that the swelling in her leg indicated a serious illness. Still, they watched her condition steadily deteriorate despite Christian Science treatment. "Whatever protection the Arizona legislature intended to provide for faith healing," Scull wrote, "it surely never intended to allow a child to die who might have lived had her parents sought medical attention."[48]

The state must have the ability to impose a criminal penalty in response to a parent's failure to seek medical treatment for a seriously ill child for religious reasons. The defendants' argument that the state's interest ceased to exist when Ashley died "is myopic in the extreme." Obviously, the state can do nothing more for Ashley, but the Kings' criminal behavior must be punished if for no other reason than that prosecutions such as this represent the state's best hope of deterring similar behavior and saving other children from suffering under like circumstances. The logical outcome of the Kings' argument would prohibit the state from prosecuting for murder a believer in a religion that practiced human sacrifice "because the victim is already dead." The state has a compelling interest in doing everything constitutionally possible to protect the lives of children. Whether the Kings' acts and omissions constituted a violation of the felony criminal child abuse statute is a question for a jury to decide. But no separate religious exemption exists.[49]

In his conclusion Scull pounded home his key arguments. The Kings received a fair grand jury hearing. They were not denied a substantial procedural right, and therefore they are not entitled to a new grand jury. Sensing this outcome, the Kings had tried to convince the court that minor procedural errors should cause the court to evoke its heretofore unused supervisory power to order a new grand jury. In fact, the Kings mistakenly believed the law on child abuse did not apply to Christian Scientists. The law is clear, Scull concluded: their "leap of faith" is legally permissible, but the "sacred duty to protect a child's life by every means possible falls both on parents and the state." Religious belief is no excuse for child abuse and no defense to prosecution.[50]

Following this major face-off between the Kings and the state, a new flurry of motions, including a boilerplate motion waiving the Kings' right to a speedy trial and a motion to compel discovery of "all historical information that could mitigate or negate defendants' guilt," slowed the pace toward trial. However, Judge Reinstein's ruling on May 5 marked a turning point in the case. He denied the Kings' motion for reconsideration as well as their request that the court strike his statement establishing as case law that the Kings' religious beliefs was not a defense in a criminal case. "For the most part," Reinstein wrote, "the defendants motion is a 56-page rehash of the original motion." The judge also wistfully ordered that all future motions and responses be limited to fifteen pages and replies to ten pages.[51]

One month later the state filed a motion asking the court to prohibit the defendants from offering what it termed highly prejudicial evidence, namely, a catalogue of photos of Ashley and several lists of books she read. The ploy was intended to show she was raised in a loving household and that she was sufficiently mature to make her own decisions about which form of treatment to choose. Scull argued that the Kings' strategy appeared to be designed "to evoke sympathy from the jury" and to support an argument that the alleged "'maturity' of an 11 or 12 year-old" relieved the parents of their legal duty to properly to care for the child. The first will inflame the jury, and the second is without legal basis. The court should thereby preclude the Kings from submitting the photos or the book lists as evidence. The Kings responded that the book lists indicated Ashley's "mental and intellectual maturity" and that she was "capable not only of understanding the tenets of the Christian Science religion and adopting those tenets as her own religious belief system, but also of meaningfully insisting upon her right to exercise her religious conscience and her right to privacy." This argument was said to be relevant to the question of the Kings' decision to support their daughter's assertion of her religious rights. The photos, Edmonds asserted, "serve to controvert any suggestion of sinister religious fanaticism."[52]

Scull seems to have gauged these arguments as being weak or meant to lay a basis for an appeal. He responded immediately, blasting the defense's assertion that Ashley's alleged maturity gave her legal and constitutional protection to practice her religion, to reject medical care in favor of spiritual healing. There is no authority in Arizona law to support the proposition that a "mature child" could constitute a defense of the criminal offense of which the parents have been indicted. Until Ashley reached the age of eighteen years, Scull detailed, the Kings were responsible for her care "regardless of how mature she may have been." Similarly, the fact that the Kings took photographs of their daughter had nothing to do with whether they negligently failed to perceive that without medical care Ashley's illness was likely to lead to her death. Further, the state did not believe that photos show Ashley's "religious understanding and commitment, the extent of her intellectual maturity, or the reasonableness of Defendants' failure to provide medical care when she became seriously ill."[53]

While Judge Reinstein prepared his decision, the Kings sought unsuccessfully to petition the Arizona Supreme Court to obtain review of the Court of Appeal's decision to decline jurisdiction over the Maricopa County court's refusal to exercise its supervisory power over the Kings' grand jury and to waive once again their right to a speedy trial. These legal decisions pushed their trial date to the front burner and created an incentive to reach a plea bargain. The two sides negotiated for nearly a month before agreeing to a deal. At 4:45 p.m. on September 1, 1989, just fifteen minutes before the deadline set by County Attorney Scull, Catherine and John King arrived at Judge Reinstein's courtroom and entered no contest pleas to reckless endangerment charges. (While no contest is technically not an admission of guilt, the court treats it the same as a guilty plea.) The parties agreed that the crime did not involve moral turpitude and that its factual basis was contained in the evidence presented to the grand jury. In addition, upon successful completion of probation, the undesignated endangerment charge would be designated a misdemeanor.[54]

Although the very favorable plea agreement negotiated by the Kings allowed the couple to evade their legal responsibility for Ashley's death, it did not shake their belief that they were being persecuted by the state for their commitment to Christian Science. This feeling stemmed largely from their unwillingness to understand the law's distinction between belief and practice. John's statement that, had he been told his "religious beliefs were wrong, he would have either chosen not to have children or have moved to another state" because he did not wish to violate the law revealed his flawed understanding. In fact, the law respects and protects from majority attack all religious views, but actions that threaten the rights of others—in this case the well-being of a child—may be reasonably regulated. Lacking an understanding of this basic constitutional principle, the Kings grudgingly consented to abide by the law but publicly and privately scorned it. John once said to a reporter, "That anybody would accuse me of child abuse makes me want to throw up." Catherine even claimed that she had suffered "far beyond cruel and unusual punishment standards" because she had been "lambasted in the headlines day after day" for her daughter's death and because she "had been deprived of having more children because I cannot raise them according to my highest sense of right."[55]

In addition to seeing herself as a victim, Catherine King distorted the truth to support the "Cause." "We realize that because this is a 'child case' which has gained public attention," she wrote, "it is an important one for our beloved Cause." For this reason she repeatedly denied that Ashley suffered any pain and claimed just two weeks before her death that she was making progress toward restoring her health. Both for the record and in private letters attached to the case file Catherine made statements that contradicted known facts. She told a friend that "vicious attacks had been made on her in the Grand Jury proceedings." She also incorrectly told another Christian Scientist that because of Ashley's "intense resistance" to hospital care she could not go home "but had to be brought to Upward View at the state's orders."[56]

Catherine King, weeping and leaning against her attorney, seemed to be emotionally drained during the brief court proceeding at which she and John pleaded no contest to a child endangerment charge. The couple tried to avoid the press when leaving the courthouse by ducking into a stairwell. The Kings made no comment after their court appearance, but they later stated they accepted the plea because they believed they "could not convince a jury to suspend their bias towards religious healing." Scull refused to discuss why the deal was offered, but, he noted, he never intended to put the Kings behind bars. The plea agreement put other practitioners of spiritual healing on notice that they could face criminal charges if they failed to provide medical care for seriously ill children. Attorney Hooker said the deal was better than he expected. "I don't think there's a case in this courthouse that the defense wouldn't jump at a chance to take a misdemeanor regardless of what the facts are," Hooker said. "The state got what they wanted out of this, which was some kind of message." Privately, he later added a tougher assessment. It's a serious question, Hooker wrote to Judge Reinstein, "whether it is the function of the criminal justice system to send messages or to alter behavior of religious groups. The Kings were made pawns in a struggle between the State and the Church over the practice of religious beliefs."[57]

In addition to opposing counsel trading barbs on the courthouse steps, Judge Reinstein received a handful of opinionated letters, and a few people shared their personal views about the case in the press. A woman who identified herself as a Catholic wrote to Reinstein expressing her worry that "if Freedom of Religion wins in this case, then people are really going to take it to the limit such as Satanic Cults." At the same time, a person named Donna believed that "children cannot be dying because of their parents' beliefs." An anonymous letter writer challenged the judge's remark, reported in the press, that the state had a compelling interest in providing medical care to seriously ill children. "When I see the state give live birth to children," she wrote, "I'll agree with your views. That day will never come though, and the God who gives life does not want the state usurping parents' rights and I feel on judgment day you will have to answer to our Creator for enforcing your anti-Christian views on Christians." The *Arizona Republic*'s balanced coverage of Christian Science included an article about Dave Barton and his family and one about Paul Michener, a fifty-one-year-old farmer who lived in Ohio and who, as a nine-year-old, had his leg "ravaged in a horrible gasoline fire." For two years he lay on a couch in agony waiting for the open wounds on his leg to heal in response to the prayers of his mother, a Christian Scientist. "If she had used some common sense along with the spiritual sense," Michener said, "my leg probably would be fine today."[58]

Max Bessler, the supervisor of the Adult Probation Department, received letters about the Kings from Christian Scientists eager to appear respectable, intelligent, and successful. George Gregg began a letter testifying to John King's good character by noting that Christian Science had been "lambasted and so unjustly and ignorantly portrayed in the media and by the prosecutors in this and other cases" that he thought it might be useful to educate Bessler. A short lesson about Mary Baker Eddy's teachings led Gregg to conclude that King "deserved credit, rather than condemnation, for his efforts to turn mankind away from its worship of materiality that is proving so ruinous today." Repeating charges first made by Catherine King, Jan Forrister told Judge Reinstein that King endured "vicious attacks made on her by the Grand Jury" and that she "has been persecuted and tormented by the public and the media—all for adhering to her religious beliefs, a constitutionally guaranteed right."[59]

On September 26 Judge Reinstein sentenced John and Catherine King to three years' unsupervised probation. He also ordered John to complete 100 hours of community service and Catherine 150 hours. Finally, Reinstein stipulated that upon successful completion of their three years' probation, the endangerment charge to which the couple had pleaded no contest would be designated a misdemeanor, allowing the Kings to avoid the negative impact of a felony conviction. Catherine plunged into her community service one week after sentencing. On Tuesday morning, October 3, at 7:30 a.m. she began work at the Cherokee School library, where Ashley had browsed for books two years earlier. After five days at the school library, she and her husband sought to fulfill their obligation at a Christian Science Reading Room in Scottsdale, a choice Reinstein promptly overruled. Catherine then worked a dozen nine-hour days at the Phoenix Zoo, a thirteen-hour day at Missing Mutts, and then completed her requisite number of community service hours on December 2, 1989, by working sixteen hours at the Arizona Transit Association's Roadeo. John fulfilled his community service on February 23, 1989.[60]

One week after John completed his community service, Catherine wrote to Judge Reinstein asking that the couple's offense be designated a misdemeanor and that their probation be ended. Catherine contended that her study aimed at securing a degree in paralegal studies and her intention to apply for admission to law school, as well as her husband's listing in the *Arizona Real Estate Bulletin* as a person convicted of a felony, jeopardized her future and her husband's career. She added, argumentatively but not entirely correctly, "It cannot be said by anyone what the outcome would have been at our trial. Since the time we entered our plea agreement, the subsequent two Christian Science cases to be decided in California and Minnesota have both been dismissed by judges." Reinstein forwarded the Kings' letter to Scull, who took the position that the couple should serve their full sentence, noting that Catherine King had not set forth any "undue or unforeseen hardships" and that he failed to see the relevance of the cases she cited. Without referring to Scull's comments, Reinstein rejected the Kings' request on the grounds that it was not customary to terminate probation before at least half of the original term imposed had transpired. Twelve months later, on April 24, 1991, Reinstein granted the Kings' motion for termination of their probation and designated the endangerment offense a misdemeanor.[61]

No one who watched Ashley die or followed the Kings' legal struggle doubted that Catherine and John loved their daughter. That was the single point of agreement. There was considerably less certainty about the efficacy of spiritual healing and about the degree of protection Arizona law and the U.S. Constitution provided the Kings' religious behavior and, conversely, for the need of state intervention to protect the well-being and lives of children. The defense attorney Robert Hooker used all of his considerable legal skills to defend the Kings' right to practice their religion. At the same time, the state prosecutor K. C. Scull committed the state's resources to prosecuting the Kings for their failure to provide medical care for Ashley. He and the court had no doubt that the law prohibiting child abuse had to be enforced. In the end, the two men agreed to a plea bargain.

That small step did not resolve the larger problem created by the tangled web of faith and reason spun by the Christian Science Church, but it did suggest compromise was possible. Arizona law, after all, did not forbid spiritual healing, but it did mandate that parents of a "seriously ill" child must seek medical care. The law and religious parents could quibble about the point at which an illness could be classified as serious, but the fact is, the law invited common sense and compromise. Because the King case did not go to trial, the Arizona Supreme Court was not asked to review Judge Reinstein's case law ruling that the state's Christian Science accommodation did not protect religious parents from a criminal charge of homicide or felony child abuse. All that can be said is that Scull and Reinstein did not think so. At the same time, both men accepted a plea bargain that reduced the charge against the Kings to a misdemeanor, manifesting the law's flexibility—or perhaps its weakness.

Neither John nor Catherine King allowed common sense or flexibility to creep into their faith. Despite the fatal outcome, the Kings remained firm believers in what Catherine termed the Cause. Both parents insisted that a twelve-year-old child, whom neither the law nor the Christian Science Church considered an adult, had determined their choice to reject medical care. They shifted their parental responsibility to Ashley, maintaining that the child had freely chosen spiritual healing. But some nurses at Phoenix Children's Hospital overheard Catherine bullying Ashley and therefore were not surprised the child mimicked her parents, denying her pain and demanding that the medical staff surrender control to her, just as her parents did. Esther Muñoz ignored Ashley's blinkered belief and treated the child kindly, dulled her pain with medication, and stroked her forehead. For a moment Ashley was free to be a kid whose care was in the hands of a kind, knowledgeable adult. However, like the good child she was, she wanted most of all to please her parents and to embrace their belief that spiritual healing would prove pain and death an illusion. To impose on a twelve-year-old girl stricken with cancer the burden that she was responsible for whether she lived or died is unconscionable.

5

Robyn Twitchell

THE MANSLAUGHTER TRIAL of the Christian Scientists David and Ginger Twitchell for the death of their two-and-a-half-year-old son Robyn took place in 1990 in the shadow of the Christian Science Mother Church in Boston. It capped a decade in which the tragic deaths of Christian Scientists' children and shocking abuse of children roiled the nation, especially Massachusetts. The Twitchells' trial was thus fought at a fever pitch and gave rise to a popular struggle over the meaning of the state's religious exemption provision, the degree of constitutional protection granted a religious practice, and the right of families to be left alone. Three years after a jury found the Twitchells guilty of involuntary manslaughter, a reform coalition convinced the Massachusetts legislature to repeal the state's religious exemption statute.

Children's advocates in Massachusetts eventually succeeded, despite the wealth and power of the Christian Science Church. In addition to the full panoply of legal and political arguments, children's advocates emphasized a simple core idea that resonated with legislators and the public: the death of a child by religious exemption was intolerable. Those who championed greater protection of children embraced the democratic process, whereas many people, in the face of a public relations campaign portraying Christian Scientists as "your neighbors" and loving parents, perceived the church as hierarchical, secretive, coldly ideological, and more concerned with defending itself than with saving a child's life.

Massachusetts was one of eleven states that attached a religious exemption to its child abuse statute prior to the passage in 1974 of the federal Child Abuse Prevention and Treatment Act (CAPTA). The exemption followed the involuntary manslaughter trial of thirty-one-year-old Dorothy Sheridan, a single mother and a Christian Scientist charged with failure to provide medical care for her five-year-old daughter Lisa. For three weeks as the child struggled to survive, Sheridan and two Christian Science women certified by the church as qualified to heal prayed for Lisa's good health. Their efforts failed, and Lisa died of pneumonia in her home on Cape Cod about 1:30 a.m. on March 19, 1967.

In his instructions to the jury at the close of Sheridan's three-day trial, Judge Eugene Hudson referred to a section of the state's child neglect law that called for criminal misdemeanor penalties for any parent of a minor child who "willfully neglects or refuses to provide . . . proper physical care." Judge Hudson ruled that "proper physical care" included "medical attention." A jury deliberated just forty-five minutes before finding Sheridan guilty, and the court sentenced her to five years' probation.[1]

In December 1968, after the Sheridan trial, David Sleeper, a senior church official, lectured at the First Church of Christ, Scientist, in Hyannis, Massachusetts. He elevated God's law above the legal system that convicted Sheridan. "Human law," he stated, has "nothing stronger to support it than human belief. God's law *rebukes* claims of another law. There is *no* law that subverts God's law. Divinity will prove its evidence. Divine authority supports our rights. It is not for the courts or the legislature to provide us our freedom." Sleeper urged parents not to succumb to the "enchantments of medicine and its claims of power" and not to be afraid to rely on "Christian Science practice for yourself and your children."[2]

In the fall of 1971 the Christian Science Church quietly lobbied the Massachusetts legislature to add a religious exemption provision to the child support statute used to convict Sheridan. The amended law stipulated that a child would not be considered neglected or lacking proper physical care "for the sole reason that he is being provided remedial treatment by spiritual means alone in accordance with the tenets and practice of a recognized church or religious denomination by a duly accredited practitioner." Christian Science was not publicly mentioned during the deliberations over the amendment or during the legislative debates, but the language left no doubt the church had crafted the law to protect its adherents from prosecution.[3]

The exemption statute of 1971, along with excerpts from other Massachusetts laws affecting Christian Scientists' religious practices, were compiled by the Mother Church's Committee on Publication in a frequently updated booklet, *Legal Rights and Obligations of Christian Scientists in Massachusetts.*

The booklet, which was distributed to church members as a guide to action, emphasized religious accommodations in the state's laws and tutored church members in ways to avoid alarming school officials when a child was absent owing to illness and how to obtain assistance from the church when requesting that a child be exempted from school physical exams and from health science classes. Beginning in 1975 the booklet included, without attribution and without quotation marks, an excerpt from Massachusetts Attorney General Francis Bellotti's opinion about the 1971 amendment to the child support law requiring a parent to provide "proper physical care." The law, Bellotti wrote, referring specifically to the amendment, "is a criminal statute and it expressly precludes imposition of criminal liability as a negligent parent for failure to provide medical care because of religious beliefs." However, in his official opinion, not reprinted in *Legal Rights,* Bellotti added that the clear intent of the state's child abuse and neglect reporting statute "is to require that children of such parents be provided services whenever the need arises." As printed, the single sentence seemed to give unequivocal support to the church's argument that no criminal charges could be brought against a Christian Science parent who withheld medical care from a child. David and Ginger Twitchell claimed that the statement as it appeared in *Legal Rights* guided their decision to rely exclusively on prayer treatment for their son.[4]

There is no official prohibition in Christian Science doctrine about receiving medical care, but resorting to such care contradicts the church's fundamental belief, namely, that medical science treats the material body whereas to Christian Scientists the only true reality is spiritual, "God, the Divine Mind." Christian Science healing practices easily lead to the conclusion that medical and spiritual treatment cannot be reconciled. The Twitchells were firm adherents of radial reliance, which, as we have seen, demands complete disavowal of medical care as a means of dealing with sickness. In a television interview after the death of his son, David Twitchell made this difference clear. "If we were closer to God," he said, "we could have stopped it from happening in that way. I blame myself."[5]

David Twitchell was born in 1955 to parents who were Christian Scientists, and his maternal grandmother was a certified practitioner devoted full-time to healing through prayer and spiritual treatment. He joined the Mother Church in Boston at the age of twelve, signing an application affirming that he would "follow in the Christ Jesus' footsteps who healed those around him of sin, sickness, and raised them from the dead." After graduating from high school, according to a later story in the *Boston Globe,* David was offered a scholarship at a state university, but he turned it down in favor of attending Principia College in Elsah, Illinois, a small liberal arts college linked to the Christian Science Church. He met his future wife, Ginger, at the college. Financial problems forced the young couple to leave Principia after two years, and David completed a degree in political science at the State University of New York at Stony Brook. After graduating he worked briefly in the secular business world before beginning a career as a manager of Christian Science nursing homes. In 1986 David managed the Chestnut Hill Benevolent Association, and the couple and their two children, Jeremy, five, and Robyn, two and a half, lived in nearby Hyde Park, Massachusetts.[6]

Robyn's fatal five-day-long illness began on the evening of April 3, 1986. After the family had eaten a light supper Ginger heard the boy crying. David took the boy to the bathroom, where he screamed in pain and vomited repeatedly. Robyn's condition lasted throughout the night. The next morning Ginger called Nancy Calkins, a fifty-one-year-old Christian Science practitioner with twelve years of experience. In accord with printed advice from the Mother Church, Calkins spoke with Nathan Talbot, the sole spokesperson for the Committee on Publication for Massachusetts of the First Church of Christ, Scientist and the manager of Committees on Publication around the world. Robyn continued to vomit and to sleep intermittently throughout the day, growing pale and weak. The infant's condition had not improved by Saturday, April 5, and Ginger again called Calkins, who came to the Twitchells' home to pray for and with the child. Ginger called Calkins on Sunday morning to report that Robyn still could not hold food down. Because healing had not occurred, Calkins called Talbot and recommended to Ginger that she arrange for a Christian Science nurse to visit Robyn. Calkins made another visit to the Twitchells' home on Sunday evening to pray for Robyn. A nurse, Linda Blaisdell, arrived on Monday morning. Blaisdell had no medical training, her only goal being to make patients comfortable. She helped bathe Robyn and showed Ginger how to put small bits of food into his mouth. Robyn vomited repeatedly.[7]

On Tuesday, April 8, David stayed home from work to help Ginger care for Robyn, and the child appeared to be improving. But at 8 p.m., after a bath, Robyn vomited feces. Alarmed, Ginger called Calkins, who again came to the Twitchells' home and prayed and sang. Robyn appeared to be very weak. The parents and Calkins briefly considered contacting a physician, but they decided against it. Less than an hour later, Robyn began to have spasms, his eyes rolled up, and he lost consciousness. Calkins called Talbot and told him she thought the "baby had passed." He advised calling an undertaker to remove Robyn's body. At 10:10 p.m. David called Waterman's Funeral Home and was told the funeral home would not take Robyn's body until the police or the medical examiner had released it. David was advised to call 911. Approximately thirty-five minutes later Waterman's alerted the medical examiner's office, which immediately dispatched an ambulance to the Twitchells' home that arrived just before 11 p.m.[8]

David met the paramedics at the curb and led them into the house, where they found Robyn lying alone on a rug in the upstairs hallway. His body was cold and stiff, and he had no vital signs. A paramedic carried the child downstairs to the ambulance and began resuscitation efforts and other emergency medical procedures. The ambulance arrived at Carney Hospital at 11:16 p.m., and Robyn was pronounced dead at 11:27 p.m. An autopsy performed the next day concluded that the cause of death was a bowel obstruction attributable to Meckel's diverticulum, a congenital anatomical abnormality. Dr. Aubrey Katz, a pediatrician at Children's Hospital, later testified that the condition is diagnosable and treatable, and the prognosis is excellent.[9]

In the weeks after Robyn's death the Twitchells moved first to North Attleboro, Massachusetts, and then to Brentwood, New York, where David took a position as manager of Open Gate, a Christian Science retirement home. In the meantime, the Boston Police Department, the Department of Social Services, and the Suffolk County district attorney's office began an investigation into Robyn's death. On the basis of that preliminary investigation, Suffolk County District Attorney Newman A. Flanagan, who had recently completed a term on the U.S. Attorney General's Task Force on Family Violence, appointed John A. Kiernan as special assistant district attorney for the case and ordered an inquest. West Roxbury District Court Judge Lawrence D. Shubow conducted the investigatory proceeding into Robyn Twitchell's death. The parties filed memoranda of law, and Judge Shubow heard testimony from witnesses under oath in December 1986. His report, delivered to the district attorney on December 18, 1987, provided evidence that a crime had been committed.[10]

Judge Shubow concluded the "affirmative acts and failures to act of David R. Twitchell, Ginger Twitchell, Nancy Calkins, Linda Blaisdell, and Nathan Talbot, individually and collectively, contributed to the death of Robyn Twitchell." Calkins "aided and reinforced the parents in exclusive reliance on spiritual healing," and she "collaborated in withholding from Robyn the opportunity and right to receive other modalities of treatment." Shubow labeled

Blaisdell's advice "about what and how to feed [Robyn] reckless behavior . . . done in ignorance of what was making Robyn sick and added to his burdens." In addition to encouraging everyone concerned to rely exclusively on spiritual healing, when told of Robyn's death Talbot "advocated a course of action contrary to the law and thus prevented earlier attempts to resuscitate Robyn Twitchell than occurred." Finally, Shubow noted, Blaisdell, Calkins, and Talbot interfered with the "natural parental instinct to seek other help from any available source." In focusing "only on the presumed benefits of their sense of religious healing they unlawfully ignored the best interests of the child."[11]

Because an inquest is an investigatory proceeding, Judge Shubow acknowledged his report to be "merely commentary utterly devoid of the force of judgment." He did offer "one judge's view" of the applicable law. He found "compelling" reasons for and against prosecution of David and Ginger Twitchell for involuntary manslaughter. He warned that no matter how carefully a prosecution is crafted and no matter how precisely it is rooted in specific conduct outside the realm of prayer, "it will inevitably be portrayed and generally be perceived as an attack on the Christian Science religion." But the validity of the church's belief in spiritual healing is not the issue. The practice "would not even have been considered had [it] not been presented as the explanation and justification for conduct that otherwise would be beyond any conceivable defense at all." Although Judge Shubow's report reviewed both the spiritual and medical treatment of Robyn Twitchell's controversial death, he concluded that "he died unnecessarily."[12]

On the basis of Judge Shubow's report and other evidence developed by prosecutors, District Attorney Flanagan presented the case to a Suffolk County grand jury, which indicted David and Ginger Twitchell for manslaughter on April 22, 1988. The three church officials rebuked in Shubow's report were not indicted. The district attorney's office speculated that the grand jury might have concluded the parents had primary responsibility to properly care for their children. David and Ginger Twitchell were arraigned in Suffolk Superior Court on May 2, 1988.[13]

Rikki Klieman, the Twitchells' flamboyant, highly regarded lawyer, responded angrily to the indictment, telling the *Boston Globe*, "I don't think this is a crime, period." Talbot also found fault with the law, which he expressed in terms well rehearsed in earlier cases. Robyn's parents "acted in accord with the law as they understood it," the spokesperson for the Mother Church said in a statement meant as the opening shot in a public relations campaign. "No one would think of prosecuting grief-stricken parents in the hundreds of sad instances where children have died under conventional medicine. It is obvious that what is being put on trial here is not the action of individual parents, but a public policy, a healing practice, and a way of life for many families." An editorial in the *Boston Herald* defended the First Amendment's protection of all religious beliefs but rejected the Twitchells' argument that the free exercise clause "fully shields their refusal to provide medical care to their child." David and Ginger loved Robyn, but as "firm adherents of 'radical reliance' [they] condemned their little boy to die." Apparently, the *Herald* concluded, "preserving their church's doctrines was more important than preserving their son's life. However broad our tolerance of diverse religions, it cannot be made to stretch that far."[14]

While the legal battle in Boston and in courtrooms across the country focused on whether a state's religious exemption law permitted or prohibited a parent's use of spiritual healing for a seriously ill child, the Twitchells' indictment also spurred a national debate on rights. Speaking for a variety of religious groups, constitutional scholars argued that the First Amendment's free exercise clause protected both beliefs and actions. "I think freedom of religion doesn't mean anything unless it goes beyond belief to action," stated the attorney William Ball, a leader of the Christian Legal Society, who convinced the U.S. Supreme Court that the Amish should be exempt from compulsory state education laws. Other lawyers disagreed, among them Wendy Mariner, a professor of health law at Boston University who repeated the Supreme Court's traditional position: "You can believe anything you want, but there are limits to the conduct" the Constitution protects. Advocates and observers on both sides of the Twitchell case realized that a legal victory for the Christian Science Church would strengthen the argument for constitutional protection of all religious conduct.[15]

Six weeks after the indictments were handed up, Klieman and Stephen Lyons, a lawyer from Boston with extensive medical malpractice experience, filed a motion in Superior Court to dismiss the indictments for manslaughter against the Twitchells. The defense argued that the Commonwealth of Massachusetts failed to adequately demonstrate the crime of manslaughter and that neither the common law nor Massachusetts statutory law required parents to provide conventional medical care rather than "other recognized types of remedial health care, such as Christian Science healing." The Commonwealth countered that the nineteenth-century common law cases cited by the defense were no longer good law because "contemporary community standards of culpability on this issue have changed." Similarly, the state insisted the 1971 law allowing an exemption for spiritual treatment did not apply "when other factors exist, such as significant trauma or serious illness." Even if the statutory religious exemption does provide a defense to neglect, Assistant District Attorney Marcy Cass stated, "there is no reason to believe that the exemption precludes imposition of liability under the manslaughter statute." Finally, the defendants argued that criminal prosecution for not seeking medical care for their child contravened their religious beliefs as protected by the First Amendment's free exercise clause. The Commonwealth, on the other hand, contended that while the First Amendment's protection of religious belief was absolute, its protection of religious conduct was not. Specifically, Cass held, the state has a compelling interest to protect children, and therefore the prosecution of the Twitchells did not violate their First Amendment rights.[16]

A year after the Twitchells' indictment Superior Court Judge Sandra Hamlin denied a defense motion to dismiss manslaughter charges against the couple. Among other cases, Judge Hamlin cited *Commonwealth v. Gallison* (1981), in which the Supreme Judicial Court (SJC) of Massachusetts affirmed a mother's manslaughter conviction for failing to realize that her child's vomiting, high fever, and breathing difficulty constituted a substantial risk of death and that her failure to act was "wanton and reckless conduct." Similarly, the Twitchells' failure to seek medical care despite Robyn's deteriorating health created "a substantial and unjustifiable risk of harm." Judge Hamlin's thirty-two-page decision also rejected the Twitchells' constitutional arguments. Attorney Klieman immediately announced she would appeal the decision to a single justice of the SJC to decide whether to refer the case to the full bench or send it back to the Superior Court for trial. Justice Herbert P. Wilkins heard the appeal and, without commenting on its merits, rejected the defense motion, noting the issue "can be dealt with adequately on the appellate level only after a trial."[17]

While the Twitchell case moved slowly through the judicial system, children's advocacy groups and legislators mobilized to repeal the state's religious exemption statute. The campaign began when Kenneth Casanova, a graduate of Hamilton College in Clinton, New York, who was living and working part-time in Boston, read about Robyn's death. Like many people who followed the story, he was saddened by the child's death and shocked to learn that a prosecution was questionable because of the Massachusetts law shielding Christian Scientists. Casanova made some phone calls. He talked directly to Talbot, who followed up their conversation with a short letter, a handful of articles about spiritual healing, and an invitation to a Wednesday evening meeting at which Christian Scientists gave testimonials about personal healing experiences. During that same initial burst of energy Casanova telephoned the Suffolk County district attorney's office and his Massachusetts state representative, John E. McDonough. Casanova also contacted Rita Swan of CHILD, Jetta Bernier, a longtime professional advocate of legislative programs to prevent child abuse and, since 1984, the executive director of Massachusetts Citizens for Children, headquartered in Boston. With the later addition of Kiernan these men and women formed the nucleus of the coalition to repeal the state religious exemption statute.[18]

By chance, McDonough, a graduate of Boston College who successfully plunged into politics in 1985 when he won a seat in the Massachusetts House representing the Boston neighborhood of Jamaica Plain, was cochair of the Joint Committee on Health Care when Casanova contacted him about Robyn's death. McDonough agreed to look into the issue and urged Casanova in the meantime to build support for an anticipated bill aimed at repealing the religious exemption law. Late in the 1988 legislative session, McDonough filed a bill, H.B. 4728, amending the 1971 law (chap. 273, sec. 1) exempting spiritual treatment from penalty for neglect or lack of proper physical care by adding the clause, "unless medical care is necessary to protect the child from suffering serious physical harm or illness."[19]

Casanova contacted other Massachusetts children's groups, among them the Massachusetts Society for Prevention of Cruelty to Children (MSPCC), the Massachusetts Department of Public Health, the Commonwealth's Office for Children, the Massachusetts Council of Churches, and the Massachusetts Catholic Conference. On advice of counsel, the MSPCC's board decided not to support McDonough's bill. The secretary of human services and the director of the Office for Children refused to support H.B. 4728 because each agency allegedly feared their other legislative priorities could be jeopardized by an effort to amend the state's religious exemption law. The Council of Churches also opposed the proposed bill, citing a grab bag of reasons, including "delicate problems of relations with the Christian Science Church," the small number of children who suffer from spiritual treatment, the shortcomings of "high technology medicine," and, curiously, "undermining the principle of separation of Church and State."[20]

By the spring of 1989, however, when McDonough's bill was before the Joint Judiciary Committee, Casanova had brought into the coalition a number of committed and energetic organizations and individuals. Swan, a ten-year veteran of legislative campaigns and a savvy lobbyist for children's rights, asked CHILD contributors in Massachusetts to call and write every member of the Judiciary Committee urging support for H.B. 4728. Likewise, Bernier rallied supporters of Mass Kids and personally wrote to the Judiciary Committee chair, Rep. Salvatore DiMasi. "We contend," Bernier wrote, "that treating children for medical conditions through spiritual healing, even if under the auspices of an established church, places vulnerable children in serious jeopardy." The American Academy of Pediatrics jumped on board, and its lobbyist in Boston, Edward J. Brennan Jr., immediately sent each member of the Judiciary Committee a report of the academy's bioethics committee that placed responsibility for the unnecessary death of children on states' religious exemptions laws. Speaking for the Massachusetts Medical Society, Dr. Joseph J. O'Connor urged Chairman DiMasi to act to "ensure that innocent children do not suffer irreparable harm or even death needlessly."[21]

The American Jewish Congress was the only religious group to engage the issue. After discussions with several groups, including the Christian Science Church, the congress's executive director, Sheila Decter, proposed an alternative to the McDonough bill. She sought support from Rep. Byron Rushing, an African American and an advocate of unfettered religious liberty. "Since we have a certain amount of expertise and interest both in the issue of religious liberty and the welfare of children," Decter's letter to Rushing began, "we have been following the [Twitchell] case closely." She proposed a compromise: recognizing the right of "*adult* believers in spiritual healing to choose such treatment for themselves at *any* time and authorize it for their children in the ordinary course of minor childhood illnesses" but permitting the state to intervene if the child's life or long-term health is threatened. Neither Rushing nor the coalition backing the McDonough bill embraced Decter's alternative proposal, and eventually she pledged the prestige and resources of the American Jewish Congress to back the coalition's amendment requiring parents to provide medical care to protect children from serious illness and physical harm. "How any religious group can believe that God has provided" physicians and medicines, Rabbi Simeon J. Maslin wrote in the *Jewish Exponent,* "and yet forbid their use is quite simply beyond my understanding."[22]

A number of individuals prominent in the Boston medical community also joined the coalition's effort to amend the state's religious exemption statute. Dr. Eli H. Newberger, the director of the Children's Hospital's Family Development Study and a member of the state's Child Abuse Prevention Board, told the Judiciary Committee that he believed the McDonough bill would "get the word out that children need to be protected not only from parental abuse and neglect, but from the treatments in the guise of religious faith which can cause them damage because of medical neglect." In a letter to the Judiciary Committee, Leonard H. Glantz, a professor of health law and the associate director of the Boston University School of Public Health, argued that "the obligation of the state to prevent parents from inflicting damage or death on a child does not vary depending on the religious beliefs of the parent." Alan Dershowitz, a law professor at Harvard University, used much more colorful language to make the same point: "Letting a child with a treatable illness die in the name of Christian Science," he said, "is not very different from the Ayatollah Khomeini giving 12-year-old kids tokens to heaven to put their bodies on the line in the name of Allah."[23]

Casanova's unpaid lobbying work followed a pattern. He worked to bring additional individuals and new groups into the coalition to amend the religious exemption law to require parents utilizing spiritual healing to obtain medical care when a child is in danger of serious physical harm or illness. He telephoned legislators to ask their position on the McDonough bill and followed up with a letter and an informational packet. Casanova then made personal visits to the legislators he had called, bringing additional information, including a brief analysis of significant court decisions and newspaper columns and articles favorable to the coalition's position. He also created and circulated widely a six-page fact sheet listing eighteen reasons H.B. 4728 should be supported. Finally, Casanova repeatedly lobbied members of the Judiciary Committee. He kept a scorecard, a running tally of the representatives' position and the reasons they held the view they did.[24]

The Christian Science Church fiercely opposed the coalition's effort to amend the exemption law. The church's power lay in its influence and organization, not in its numbers. Chosen by the church's board of directors, a self-perpetuating body, Nathan Talbot was solely responsible for monitoring and correcting any perceived unjust criticism made of the church by the press or general public. His public comments often were tart and blunt. Of McDonough's rewording of the state's child abuse law, Talbot sarcastically said the amendment would mean, "You can pray as long as it doesn't count." Trained as a lawyer but not licensed to practice in Massachusetts, Talbot articulated the principles of the church for outsiders and produced the *Legal Rights* booklet. To implement his broad authority he had access to enormous financial resources, a full-time professional staff, open access to the *Christian Science Monitor,* a full-time paid lobbyist, several lawyers on retainer, and dozens of assistants whose job it was to serve as a link between the Committee on Publication and local churches. (Every state and about 120 countries have Committees on Publication.) Tall, gray-haired, patient, and persistent, the lobbyist Warren Silvernail repeated Talbot's message every day at the Massachusetts State House: H.B. 4728 jeopardized the religious freedom won by our forefathers; H.B. 4728 would substitute state intervention for loving parents' judgment about what's best for their child; H.B. 4728 would substitute mistake-prone medical care for the proven successes of spiritual healing.[25]

In the run-up to the Judiciary Committee hearing for H.B. 4728 every Massachusetts legislator received a packet of materials from the Committee on Publication. Some of the literature set a moderate tone, stressing Christian Scientists' reasonableness, social responsibility, and respect for the law. Under the heading "Some Thoughts About the Accommodation of Religious Practices," the committee wrote the following: "Generally lawmakers have recognized that in the absence of an emergency medical situation no one should be forced to participate in any activity which would compromise his strongly held religious beliefs. Thus laws mandating certain activities or duties for all usually take into consideration the religious sensitivities of those for whom strict compliance would mean submitting to practices or procedures contrary to their beliefs."[26]

Another piece was headlined "From Your Christian Science Neighbors," and began,

> Many of you have read about us. On the whole, you've seen us through the eyes of others. In fairness, you may want to hear some of the story that has not been told. We share with you a profound love of children. They are our hope and joy. No parent who loves his child would sacrifice that child to religious beliefs.
>
> Some have argued that the issue is a child's right to life versus religious freedom. Not so. When a responsible method of spiritual treatment is employed, the issue is one of intelligent choice of the method most likely to make the child well.[27]

A question-and-answer fact sheet distributed to legislators by Silvernail took a militant stance. Question 1 asked, will H.B. 4728 "take away freedom of religion?" The answer: "Yes, of course." Questions 2 and 3 asked if the proposed change in the law would result in "excessive state intervention into family privacy." In fact, the answer went, "excessive state intervention into the privacy of families is already causing serious concern, even among those not particularly sympathetic to spiritual healing." Amending the existing law, according to the fact sheet, would "compel medical attention whenever a child gets a nosebleed." A follow-up question and answer acknowledged that the state had a duty "to mandate that parents provide children with adequate health care" but insisted that conventional medical treatment should not be the only reasonable method of care permitted. A concluding argument asked why loving, grief-stricken parents who acted out of sincere religious beliefs should be prosecuted. "It seems unreasonable," the church declared, "to compound the tragedy of a child's death by punishing such parents when no form of treatment—whether medical or spiritual—has a perfect record."[28]

Two articles linking religious freedom and the alleged shortcomings of modern medicine were included in the pamphlet. Arthur Dyck, the Mary B. Saltonstall Professor of Population Ethics at the Harvard Divinity School, contended in an interview that appeared in the *Middlesex News* that prosecuting the Twitchells for the death of their child "is a dangerous violation of the couple's constitutional right to freedom of religion." There is no law requiring parents to be medical experts, Dyck argued, and "while a doctor might be ruled negligent because he failed to diagnose an ultimately fatal condition, parents cannot be held to the same standard."[29]

Item number 9 in Silvernail's packet was a reprint of a column from March 1988 by Dr. Robert Mendelsohn, the author of a nationally syndicated column titled "The People's Doctor" that regularly criticized the medical profession. Mendelsohn accused the American Academy of Pediatrics of engaging in "religious warfare" because it recommended eliminating religious exemption laws. "By attacking religious exemptions from medical care," the People's Doctor wrote, "the Religion of Modern Medicine is attempting to establish hegemony over other religions. So you and your church leaders should be concerned about this drive for power."[30]

The hearing on H.B. 4728 held by the Judiciary Committee on March 15, 1989, drew a large crowd. Casanova and Silvernail had rallied their troops. The process appeared chaotic. The committee had scheduled a single hearing session on a number of bills, and advocates were called randomly, not according to their interest in a particular bill. Of about a dozen people who spoke, some were for and some against amending the existing exemption law. Several people on both sides prepared testimony but, growing tired of waiting, left without speaking.[31]

When his turn came, Casanova spoke about his reaction to Robyn Twitchell's death. "The boy did not have to die," he said quietly. "He had his whole life ahead of him. He died because his parents, as Christian Scientists, chose to rely exclusively on spiritual healing—prayer—and would not seek medical attention for their son, even when his condition became life threatening." Casanova went on to say that the proposed bill would not eliminate the ambiguity a religious parent with a sick child might confront, but, he concluded, quoting the California Supreme Court, "The law is full of instances when a man's fate depends on his estimating rightly. The matter of degree that persons relying on prayer treatment must estimate rightly is the point at which their course of conduct becomes criminally negligent."[32]

Talbot spoke for the church, beginning by praising the Massachusetts legislature. "Ever since the discovery of Christian Science by Mary Baker Eddy in 1866," Talbot said, "efforts have been made to eliminate healing through spiritual means alone. Throughout the years Massachusetts legislators have been steadfast in their protection of religious and personal rights." He asked the Judiciary Committee to add to its bill the following compromise language: "A child shall not be deemed to be neglected or lack proper physical or health care if his parent provides the child with treatment in accordance with the tenets and practices of a recognized religious method of healing with a reasonable record of success in lieu of medical care."[33]

Seven months later, by a vote of 9–5, the Joint Judiciary Committee reported out H.B. 4728 favorably. But the bill reached the House floor too late to be acted on in the 1989 legislative session. Casanova and the coalition took heart from their small victory and prepared for the next year by discussing legislation not merely to amend but to repeal outright the state's religious exemption statute. For the 1990 spring legislative session, however, the coalition decided to submit a bill in the same language as its earlier proposal. The Christian Science Church shifted its strategy. Its bill retained a religious exemption but disingenuously added a provision that allowed a court to order medical care for a sick or injured child. On April 12 child advocates and Christian Scientists crowded the State House basement hearing room to debate the merits of the proposed bills. "We're not talking about a tummy ache," said Dr. Lawrence Wolff, chief of pediatric hematology at New England Medical Center. "We're talking about appendicitis, which [left] untreated can kill a child." William Beard, an attorney and a Christian Scientist, expressed an opposite point of view: "This bill takes the choice away from the parent and has a chilling effect on the practice of Christian Science." Two weeks later the Joint Committee on Health Care decided not to act on either bill during the current legislative session because the Twitchell trial had begun.[34]

Almost exactly four years after Robyn Twitchell's death, Judge Hamlin denied a defense motion and set a date for jury selection. The defense attorneys
sought to suppress statements the Twitchells made to a doctor, social workers, police, and prosecutors in the days and weeks after Robyn's death. Their
grounds for making this request were that the couple had not been warned
their statements could be used against them in a criminal trial. Judge Hamlin
ruled the couple had made the statements voluntarily and knowingly: "In
each and every one of the statements made by the Twitchells, I find that as
both responsible, law-abiding citizens and Christian Scientists, they were
anxious to explain the circumstances surrounding Robyn's death and their
religious beliefs."[35]

Meanwhile the Christian Science Church had launched a media campaign
created by a political consulting firm in New York and an advertising com-
pany in Boston. Full-page ads appeared in major Boston-area newspapers
during the week before the scheduled beginning of the trial. In the center
of the two-page spread was a photograph showing several young African
American boys playing in the fountain that dominates the Christian Science
complex in Boston and, in the background, the dome of the Mother Church.
The banner headline asked, "Why Is Prayer Being Prosecuted In Boston?"
In text that appeared beneath the headline, readers were told the Twitchells'
prosecution was selective and contrary both to the law and to religious freedom: "Today, it is the prayers of Christian Scientists. Tomorrow, it may be the
prayers of those in other established religions. Perhaps your religion." On the
facing page was a section titled "Some Questions and Answers About Christian Science," including the crucial question about whether a member may
seek medical care. The answer referred to "free moral agents" but mentioned
neither children nor the argument in *Science and Health* against using both
medicine and spiritual healing.[36]

Dershowitz responded with an op-ed piece in the *Boston Herald*. The
Christian Science Church, he wrote, "denies that if parents were permitted to
choose prayer instead of medicine, 'children would be sacrificed to religion.'
But whatever the benevolent intentions of the parents, the malevolent result
is precisely that an otherwise curable child is allowed to die because, in the
words of the church, 'medicine and spiritual means are incompatible.' That
is sacrificing children to religion." Christian Science parents argue that their
method has a good record of success in curing illness, Dershowitz continued.
They may be right in circumstances "where the empirical evidence is questionable or close. But where the issue is beyond real scientific dispute, the

state must have the power to compel parents to treat their children medically until they become adults." The right to prefer prayer to medicine must not be extended to children too young to understand the consequences of the decision made by their parents, Dershowitz concluded, because it "may deny them the right to life itself."[37]

On the eve of the Twitchells' trial, the forty-two-year-old special assistant district attorney John A. Kiernan, who before entering private practice in 1988 had served for eight years as chief of homicide in the Suffolk County district attorney's office, and Rikki Klieman, the attorney for the Twitchells, aggressively outlined their case to the public. "The question is clearly and purely one of what is appropriate parental conduct," Kiernan said. "The predominate right is the right of a child to life. It's not really a conflict, but a balancing act between constitutional rights and appropriate parental conduct, between the freedom to believe and the freedom to practice," Kiernan continued. "We are saying that the right to practice is limited when the child is facing serious harm or death." The church's media blitz rankled Kiernan: "To suggest we are prosecuting prayer is ludicrous. We applaud the use of spiritual healing." But, he added, "when a parent is confronted with a situation where a child is seriously ill, they cannot exclude medicine." By relying exclusively on Christian Science healing, the Twitchells acted with reckless disregard for the health of their son: "Religious practice is subject to regulation by the state. Belief is not. There's a whale of a difference, particularly when dealing with a baby."[38]

Klieman, an undergraduate theater major at Northwestern University who held a law degree from Boston University and in 1983 was named by *Time* magazine as one of the five best female trial lawyers in the United States, countered Kiernan's remarks by charging that prejudice against the Christian Science Church lay at the heart of the case. "This district attorney wants to put the Christian Scientists out of business," she exclaimed. My clients, Klieman argued, "chose a system of health care which they believed was excellent." After four days during which Robyn's illness ebbed and flowed, he appeared to get better, and a day before he died he went outside to play. She argued further that the 1971 religious exemption amendment to the state's child neglect law recognized spiritual healing as an alternative to medical treatment. For that reason alone the Twitchells should not be prosecuted.[39]

Jury selection began on Tuesday, April 18, 1990, following an order issued by SJC Judge Neil L. Lynch that questioning of prospective jurors must take place in an open courtroom. Potential jurors were asked thirty questions, including whether their religious affiliations or opinions about medical care would affect their impartiality and if they knew any Christian Scientists or had read anything about spiritual healing. Of the nearly 650 people interviewed, the great majority of those excused were found to have formed an opinion against the Twitchells. The defense seemed to prefer childless career women whereas the state was eager to select parents. A jury of eight women and four men, including a secretary, a waitress, a graphic artist, and a former Roman Catholic priest, was empaneled on May 1.[40]

The trial began in Courtroom 808, Suffolk County Superior Court, on Friday morning, May 4, four years and twenty-six days after Robyn's death. Opening arguments were given in the afternoon. District Attorney Kiernan spoke for an hour, describing the pain caused by Robyn's bowel obstruction as it expanded and sometimes contracted, eventually cutting off the blood supply and causing the bowel to die. Robyn screamed and vomited. The Christian Science practitioner Nancy Calkins prayed, but Robyn knew no relief, Kiernan told the jury. After a sleepless, anxious night Ginger Twitchell called Talbot and asked about *her* legal rights. The next day she asked Calkins to pray for Robyn at their home, an unusual request, as practitioners routinely prayed for an ill person at a distance. On Sunday the Twitchells and Calkins called Talbot a second time, again expressing concern about their rights. By Monday, April 7, Robyn's pain had increased, causing him to double over and clutch his gut. "These aren't symptoms of a cold or the flu," Kiernan told the jury. "These are signs and symptoms of a dying baby." The next day Robyn vomited feces, and by Tuesday evening he had the dry heaves followed by seizures and then lay still. The Twitchells and Calkins followed Talbot's instructions. David Twitchell called a funeral home and was told to call 911, but he waited thirty-nine minutes before doing so. By the time the paramedics arrived Robyn's body was cold and stiff. David and Ginger Twitchell were "indifferent" to the "natural consequences of their child being desperately ill." Tears streamed down Ginger's face as Kiernan spoke.[41]

Klieman also made an emotional opening statement. She began by reading Matthew 10:26, "'There is nothing concealed that will not be disclosed, or hidden that will not be known.' . . . Oh, if the truth were only so simple and straightforward." Robyn died "cradled in his father's arms," she said. A rare genetic birth defect that could not easily be detected or remedied by medical intervention had caused the boy's death. "The Commonwealth can't show you," Klieman told the jury as she paced back and forth, that "medical care would have saved this child." The Twitchells were law-abiding parents devoted to their children and did everything humanly possible in using a proven method of healing they believed in and had seen work for three generations in their families. No parent could have known the seriousness of the child's illness, said Klieman. Naturally, they were worried and wanted to do the right thing. Talbot said they were fully protected and cited *Legal Rights and Obligations of Christian Scientists.* Klieman told the jury, "I will be back and speak to you again, and I trust you will enter a just verdict of not guilty."[42]

The state began its case on May 7 as Kiernan called twenty witnesses, including the paramedics, three surgeons, police officers, a worker from the Department of Social Services, some of the Twitchells' neighbors, the medical examiner, and Calkins. To establish that the Twitchells acted in a criminally reckless manner by not seeking medical help, Kiernan called Charles McNamara, an emergency medical technician. McNamara estimated that the boy had been dead between forty-five minutes and two hours by the time he and his partner arrived at the Twitchells' home. "I touched him. I could tell right away. Cold is cold," he told Kiernan. On cross-examination, Klieman won agreement from McNamara that the boy's smaller body could cause postmortem rigidity to set in quickly.[43]

Dr. Margaret Greenwald, a medical examiner, was one of the physicians whom Kiernan called. Greenwald told the court the bowel obstruction that killed Robyn could have been diagnosed and medically corrected. According to her, tissue in a foot-long section of the infant's bowel twisted and caused the obstruction triggering his death over a two- to three-day period. Under cross-examination Greenwald admitted she knew of cases in which people with bowel obstructions died while under medical care. Dr. William Hendren, the chief of surgery at Children's Hospital in Boston, told the jury that Robyn's death from a bowel obstruction—his small intestine became twisted underneath a remnant of the umbilical cord that failed to disappear after birth and a fibrous band from a previous infection—was a catastrophe that could have been prevented by medical diagnosis and surgery up until the time the boy died. Asked by Kiernan whether Robyn would have been able to chase the family cat shortly before his death, as a Christian Science practitioner had testified, Hendren said, "In my experience, that would be totally impossible. I think that is pure fantasy." In the final stages of life, another physician testified, Robyn would have suffered severe dehydration, sunken eyes and cheeks, and an inability to urinate. On Robyn's last day of life his obstructed bowel would have been intensely painful, and the infant would have been "limp, unable to support his own weight, and unable to roll over." He probably was delirious and slipping in and out of consciousness.[44]

At the beginning of the third week of the trial the prosecution called Michael Dery, an employee of the Department of Social Services, and William Powers, an investigator for the Suffolk County district attorney's office. After Robyn's death, Dery had interviewed the Twitchells in their Hyde Park home after receiving a report that the couple had not sought medical care for their son. The Twitchells told Dery they had considered seeking such care but decided to rely solely on prayer. Among other revelations, Ginger told Powers that Robyn gave her a "pleading look" on the evening he died. Under cross-examination by Klieman, Dery acknowledged he had told the Twitchells any information they provided would remain confidential, and Powers admitted he had not taken notes during his conversation with Ginger and David. On redirect, however, Kiernan rehabilitated both witnesses. Dery stated that when the couple admitted they had not sought medical care for their son the law required him to send his report to the district attorney's office. Powers added that his testimony about the Twitchells' interview came from notes he made the following day.[45]

Calkins, who had treated Robyn during the last five days of his life, broke a four-year silence about the case when she waived her Fifth Amendment right and testified as a hostile witness for the prosecution with the aim of countering what she perceived to be Kiernan's portrayal of the Twitchells as uncaring parents. Calkins told the court she believed physical pain and illness were illusions caused by "errors of the mind," "such as fear, hatred, envy and dishonesty." The main test of a practitioner, she said, is, "Can you heal?" Applicants for practitioner must submit three healings to the Mother Church for approval. In answer to Kiernan's question, Calkins admitted there is no medical verification of the healings. "The truth heals anything," Calkins said, "a stubbed toe or a severed arm."[46]

Calkins's second day of testimony afforded more evidence about spiritual healing and Robyn's deteriorating condition. In order "to focus the jury's attention on what is reasonable parental conduct," Kiernan grilled Calkins about the specifics of spiritual healing. The defense counsel objected after nearly every question. The exchange with Calkins went as follows:

Kiernan: Is it true that matter does not regulate a child's bowels or
   temperature?
Calkins: Yes.
Kiernan: Do you believe bacteria causes infection?
Calkins: No.
Kiernan: What causes infection?
Calkins: Fear.

Kiernan: How do you get rid of a baby's fear?
Calkins: The parent and the baby must be treated together.

Kiernan next asked Calkins about Robyn's last day of life. Calkins said Robyn had "ups and downs" during his five-day illness, but on Tuesday "he had a super good day." "Mrs. Calkins," Kiernan said, "he died Tuesday." "I know he did" she said, "but he had a super good day."[47]

Calkins said that when she prayed for Robyn he smiled and hugged his teddy bear. But a few moments later the infant shivered, rested his head against his father's chest, and died. Kiernan asked Calkins how she knew Robyn had died. "I just got a funny feeling in my stomach," the practitioner replied.

Kiernan: Did you check to see if he was breathing?
Calkins: No.
Kiernan: Did you check his pulse?
Calkins: No.
Kiernan: Did you press on his chest?
Calkins: No.
Kiernan: Did you breathe into his mouth?
Calkins: No. I didn't do anything humanly to the child.

Calkins said she prayed briefly for Robyn's resurrection and then called Talbot.[48]

Klieman and co-counsel Lyons exploded. They asked Judge Hamlin to throw out the defendants' indictments or declare a mistrial based on the "prejudicial impact" of Kiernan's "attempt to turn the trial into a litigation of religious beliefs." Hamlin denied the defense motion. During her third day on the witness stand, under cross-examination by Klieman, Calkins insisted that the Twitchells thought Robyn had a case of the flu and that his death was sudden and without warning.[49]

The defense opened its case nearly two weeks after Kiernan's examination of Calkins brought headlines. Klieman put two Christian Science friends of the Twitchells, Barry and Susan Wills, on the stand. The Willses had taken care of Robyn for about two hours on April 5 while David and Ginger celebrated their wedding anniversary. They said Robyn was playful and didn't cry or appear to be in any pain. The boy did "spit up," Barry Wills said," but otherwise appeared to be normal. The Willses buttressed the argument that Robyn did not show any symptoms of a life-threatening illness. Under Kiernan's cross-examination, Barry admitted he had not seen Robyn for the next three days, when, according to medical experts, the boy's illness would have caused vomiting and severe pain.[50]

David Twitchell's testimony was meant to be the centerpiece of the defense. A gangly man, David was wearing a gray suit and a muted tie, sported a chevron mustache, and wore his long, dark, straight hair parted on the left side so that it created a long bang ending just above his right eyebrow. David leaned forward in the witness box, looking up at his questioner. Several times he broke down in tears while describing his son's death but regained his composure enough to say firmly that Robyn appeared to get better on the day he died. "He was alert, he was more active, and when supper was ready," David recounted, his voice trembling, "he came traipsing in behind us, climbed up on his chair and wanted to eat." But after he fed Robyn a few spoonfuls of baby food, the child vomited. "I had never seen him vomiting that suddenly or that strongly before," David said. "I picked him up and carried him to his room." Several hours later Robyn died.[51]

On his second day of testimony, David told jurors he had tried Christian Science prayer to heal a severely decayed tooth but went to a dentist when the pain became constant and affected his attitude toward his family and work. He received Novocain during the subsequent root canal procedure. Klieman wanted to use the episode to show that medical use did not conflict with Christian Science treatment, but the tactic may have backfired because David's admission about visiting a dentist and taking a painkiller contrasted starkly with his decision to withhold medical care from his son.[52]

The next day Klieman asked Twitchell if he was familiar with the church-published handbook *Legal Rights and Obligations of Christian Scientists*. Twitchell said a phone conversation he had with Talbot a few days before Robyn's death guided him to a passage in the handbook. The passage, Twitchell said, allowed a Christian Science parent to "treat their child through prayer, rather than to turn to a medical doctor." Klieman asked David to point out key passages in the booklet. David thumbed through it but could not find the key passage, the religious exemption provision amended to chapter 273, section 1, of Massachusetts General Laws. Klieman suggested David be allowed to mark the passages at his leisure while at home, but Kiernan insisted that he point out the passages there and then. Flustered, Klieman opened the booklet to the correct pages. Twitchell still could not find the exemption provision, a tacit admission that perhaps the law did not guide his actions. At the conclusion of this clumsy exchange, Klieman offered to place the *Legal Rights* pamphlet in evidence. Judge Hamlin excused the jury and held a voir dire on the question of whether that portion of the publication containing the attorney general's statement should be admitted. The judge excluded the evidence. The next day David testified that he had relied on the exemption during Robyn's illness. When asked what had refreshed his memory, he said an audience member had reminded him of it, whereupon Judge Hamlin warned the audience, which included many Christian Scientists, against coaching the witnesses.[53]

On the first day under Kiernan's relentless cross-examination, Twitchell grudgingly admitted that if he were again faced with the same circumstances that killed his son, he "would give medical science a chance." But he added later that he did not think it was a mistake to rely solely on prayer because he "still didn't think it's for sure they [doctors] could have saved him." His next answer brushed away any ambivalence. "Pain," he explained, "has no right to exist because God did not authorize it." "As a father, shouldn't you have tried everything to help your little boy?" Kiernan asked at the close of Twitchell's fourth day on the stand. Despite some ambivalent moments, Twitchell's answer reflected the depth of his belief in spiritual healing. He had been taught, he answered, that spiritual healing and medical science "would tend to cancel each other out, and [an illness] could become worse."[54]

The final witness for the defense, the pathologist Edward Sussman, countered the prosecution's claims that Robyn would have lived had his parents taken him to a hospital for treatment of a bowel obstruction. In Sussman's view, two congenital defects in the boy's bowel that were difficult to detect caused his death. To dramatize his diagnosis Sussman stood in front of the jury box and used his necktie to show jurors how Robyn had died from a twisted bowel. Under cross-examination, however, Kiernan elicited from Sussman an acknowledgment that, granting the accuracy of his hypothesis, Robyn would have showed signs of severe pain two to three days before he died.[55]

Near the conclusion of the trial Kiernan learned that the Christian Science nurse Linda Blaisdell had kept a record of Robyn's illness. On June 19 Blaisdell's notes were brought into court. They badly undermined the defense's case. Under "nature of difficulty" Blaisdell had written, "Child listless at time, rejecting all food, moaning in pain, vomiting." When recalled to the stand she admitted lying about the whereabouts of her notes during her previous testimony. Still, she was not repentant. When Kiernan confronted her with the notes, Blaisdell attempted to drain them of their commonsense meaning, resolutely stating, for example, that her notes describing Robyn as "moaning in pain" and "vomiting" referred to discrete episodes and were not meant to suggest a serious illness.[56]

Klieman and Kiernan made their closing arguments on July 2. The fifty-four-day trial pitted spiritual healing and constitutionally protected religious freedom against a parent's duty to a child as defined by the state and the limitations of the state's religious exemption statute. The two attorneys framed their arguments within these large themes while reiterating the facts of Robyn's illness as each wanted the jury to interpret them. The prosecutor's witnesses testified as to how obvious and painful Robyn's illness must have been during the last days of his life and what reasonable parents would have done. The defense chipped away at the prosecution's case by getting doctors to admit that children sometimes die even while in a doctor's care and rejected the state's claim of parental neglect by pointing out that the Twitchells followed Christian Science spiritual healing, sought the help of a practitioner, a nurse, and a senior church official.

Outside the court, Bostonians gave voice to sharply divergent opinions about the importance of the Twitchell case. A clergyman from the area gave a dire slippery slope warning after offering a boilerplate expression of sympathy. "No one wants a child to suffer unnecessarily," he said from the pulpit, "but we also must remember that no one should have his/her religious faith left unprotected by the law." A columnist for the *Boston Globe,* Bella English, flipped the minister's priorities: "While lawyers, politicians and ministers jabber about religious rights, Robyn Twitchell is dead. He will never get a chance to exercise his religious rights."[57]

Wearing a red, white, and blue dress on the eve of the July 4 holiday, Klieman described the prosecution's case as being replete with "speculation, exaggeration, and distortion." During a seventy-five-minute argument Klieman's voice became increasingly more indignant, emphatic, and emotional. To demonstrate the flaws in the state's case, she made three major arguments. First, none of the eyewitnesses, including David Twitchell, testified they believed Robyn was seriously ill. In fact, some of the witnesses believed the boy's health was improving. The prosecution's expert medical witnesses testified about the symptoms accompanying a typical bowel obstruction, but none of the physicians had seen Robyn before his death, and all of them ignored evidence that Robyn suffered from a rare congenital disease that struck suddenly and was difficult to diagnose. This means, Klieman argued, that the Twitchells stand accused of a crime they could not foresee.

Second, Klieman shifted blame for Robyn's death from the Twitchells to the Christian Science Church. A church official counseled the use of spiritual healing, and state law protected parents who relied on prayer. David and Ginger followed that advice. The Twitchells "are the last people who should be on trial," she said. "Maybe they made a mistake, but you can't convict them for that."

Third, Klieman told the jury that David and Ginger loved their child. "Could you find that beyond reasonable doubt, the Twitchells were so uncaring, so unfeeling, they just let their child die? They did not choose or think or decide about martyring their child," Klieman said. Here she held up a photo taken on April 5, 1986, showing David and Ginger and Robyn smiling. This photo, she said, coming full circle in her closing, does not "exaggerate, speculate or lie."[58]

In his closing remarks Kiernan began by focusing on Robyn and on the part his parents and religious exemption laws played in his death. Little boys are normally a whirlwind of activity, but during his last five days of life Robyn was still and quiet and in pain. He was a very sick little boy, and his parents knew that, as the Twitchells' actions during their son's illness show. Kiernan read the state religious exemption statute, which he characterized as the result of "massive church lobbying." It misled parents as to their duty. Robyn's death was not an isolated incident, the prosecutor stated, listing 8 recent deaths and mentioning 150 known deaths of children whose parents relied solely on prayer since the 1970s.

"Everybody's talking about Mr. and Mrs. Twitchell's rights. What about Robyn Twitchell?" asked Kiernan. "They can deprive themselves of medical care, but they can't deny it for a baby." The U.S. Supreme Court had ruled on this issue. He read from *Reynolds v. United States* (1879), focusing on the court's distinction between religious belief and conduct and pointing out that the state constitutionally could punish criminal activity regardless of religious beliefs. From *Prince v. Massachusetts* (1944) Kiernan read that the right to practice religion freely does not include liberty to expose a child to ill health or death. "Parents may be free to become martyrs themselves," he quoted *Prince*. "But it does not follow they are free, under identical circumstances, to make martyrs of their children before they have reached the age of full legal discretion when they can make that choice for themselves."[59]

Kiernan accused the Twitchells of using a double standard when it came to medical care. David Twitchell testified he underwent a root canal procedure in which he was injected with Novocain after prayer had failed to heal his decayed tooth. Ginger Twitchell received sutures and an anesthetic after the birth of Robyn. But they denied lifesaving medical care to their son.

"What allows them to use a doctor for themselves and not for their boy?" Kiernan asked. "What is it? Where do they justify that? . . . The course of conduct they chose for their son falls outside that which is rational, reasonable, and acceptable. Arrogance is perhaps not a word that easily fits David and Ginger Twitchell. But it is unabashed, unbridled arrogance, painful pride, that puts your own intellectual belief over the life of a child."

Finally, Kiernan reminded the jurors, "the law that parents must do everything in their power to protect their children is older than written law. It was the law when we were living in caves. This law is so fundamental that it is part of the very social contract."[60]

After a lunch break Judge Hamlin instructed the jury as to the law. The jury must decide the seriousness of Robyn's illness and whether the parents displayed "wanton and reckless" conduct by not getting him medical help. In order to find the Twitchells guilty of involuntary manslaughter, Hamlin told the jury, they must find that the state proved four elements beyond a reasonable doubt. First, that the Twitchells had a duty as parents to provide medical care for their seriously ill child. Second, that the couple failed to carry out that duty. Third, that the parents' failure to provide medical care amounted to wanton and reckless behavior, defined as conduct a reasonable person would have known would result in harm to the child. Finally, that the parents' failure to provide medical care caused Robyn's death.

Judge Hamlin also told jurors that religion was not a defense to the crime of manslaughter. The state's child abuse exemption law, which recognizes faith healing as a valid treatment for children, Hamlin said, does not absolve parents of their duty to "provide medical care" to a seriously ill child. For the jury to find the Twitchells guilty of manslaughter the prosecution must prove that they breached their legal duty to provide medical care for their child because that failure constituted wanton and reckless behavior. Hamlin instructed the jury that it was up to them to determine whether Robyn was at risk of death and whether the Twitchells recognized this risk.[61]

The case was given to the jury at 4:30 p.m. on July 3. After fourteen hours of deliberation and four requests for Hamlin's advice, the jury returned a guilty verdict shortly after 5 p.m. on July 4. David and Ginger Twitchell stood holding hands and looking directly at the jury. The couple showed no emotion when the jury forewoman, Jolyne D'Ambrosio, read out the guilty verdict. Several jurors wept as they filed out of the courtroom. Judge Hamlin denied a defense motion to poll the jurors individually to determine if they all agreed with the conviction.[62]

Outside the courtroom David Twitchell thanked the jurors, saying they had no choice but to find him and his wife guilty, given Judge Hamlin's instructions. "This has been a prosecution against our faith," he said. Standing beside her client, the defense attorney Klieman was visibly upset and harshly critical of Judge Hamlin. The judge instructed the jury that "the law requires medical care. The law does not say that," she snapped. Klieman said the verdict would be appealed, and she was "100 percent confident of winning." Talbot agreed that the verdict would be overturned. "We are in midstream," he said. "I don't think the church is in trouble." Whistling in the dark, he added, "Spiritual healing is progressing."[63]

Kiernan praised the verdict: "It will certainly send out a message that when a child is in need of medical care, in addition to spiritual care, then the obligation of the parent is to provide medical care." He added that the prosecution was not an analysis of Christian Science but "an assertion of the rights of children." District Attorney Flanagan echoed Kiernan. "These jurors stood tall," he said. He promised to prosecute any other parents whose child died under circumstances similar to those of Robyn Twitchell's death.[64]

Acting swiftly to calm jurors' fears that the Twitchells' involuntary manslaughter conviction could carry a penalty of up to twenty years in prison, Judge Hamlin indicated at a sentencing hearing that she intended to impose probation rather than incarceration on the Christian Science couple. She admonished the defense lawyers for their public critical statements. "Justice must be tempered with mercy," Kiernan told the judge. Therefore, the Commonwealth believed the primary purpose of the Twitchells' sentence should be to "deter future conduct that would endanger children." Following the hearing, Lyons was visibly angered: "I've learned in this courtroom the First Amendment goes only one way." While the defense was reprimanded, Lyons charged, the hearing had become a "press conference" for the court and the district attorney.[65]

Just two days after the Twitchells were found guilty of involuntary manslaughter, Judge Hamlin sentenced the couple to ten years' probation with the condition they obtain regular medical checkups during that time for their three surviving children and with the proviso that if a child became seriously ill the parents would seek medical help immediately. Talbot criticized the court's sentence. "It's the state's effort to re-educate Christian Scientists into its own view of what health care should be regardless of how effective Christian Science healing is," he said. Kiernan, who had returned to private law practice at the conclusion of the trial, vehemently disagreed. "This is not a contest between medicine and religion," he said. "It's a marriage of the two."[66]

The nationally syndicated columnist Ellen Goodman joined the fray. "It may be that we are more willing these days to acknowledge the power of the mind over matter," she wrote, "and it also may be that we are less confident about the efficacy of professional medical care. But "rejecting the germ theory doesn't make it less a fact." People sympathize with the Twitchells, Goodman wrote, "but to side with them in the 'treatment' of their son is to abandon both Robyn and reason."[67]

The legal community divided over Judge Hamlin's jury instructions. Some lawyers questioned by the *Boston Globe* called Hamlin's instructions erroneous and predicted the verdict would be overturned on appeal. Hamlin, legal critics said, should have informed the jurors about the 1971 amendment, which Christian Scientists argue exempts them from criminal prosecution when they rely on spiritual healing. Other lawyers praised Hamlin's rulings. One judge, who spoke anonymously, contended that the 1971 law was vague, not included in the state's homicide statutes, and therefore could not be used as a defense in a criminal trial.[68]

While legal experts disagreed about Judge Hamlin's instructions, there was widespread agreement among child rights advocates that the state's religious exemption statute should be repealed. The Twitchells' conviction, the *Boston Herald* editorialized, was not about "freedom of religion, but about who ultimately has the final say when the life of a child is at stake." The "state's interest in protecting the life of a minor child supersedes the right of parents to raise their child as they see fit." But the Massachusetts law exempting spiritual healers from the child abuse law may have led the Twitchells to think they also were exempt from a charge of manslaughter. "This pernicious and dangerous exemption should never have been enacted: the Legislature must repeal it," concluded the *Herald*. Although he thought the SJC would, and should, reverse the Twitchells' conviction, Laurence Tribe, a law professor at Harvard, argued as well that the exemption should be repealed.[69]

Talbot and other religious leaders pledged to fight any attempt to repeal the state's religious exemption law, holding that doing so would undermine religious freedom. Talbot announced a campaign to win added protection for spiritual healing. "Other churches will come to the help of the Christian Science Church," predicted Martin E. Marty, a professor at the University of Chicago, "because while they may not like what the Twitchells practiced, they think a principle is at stake." He added, "Religions should define religions, not governments."[70]

Robyn Twitchell's tragic death engendered a broad discussion about the

First Amendment. More than an abstract clash between church and state, the boy's death pulled into the discussion ordinary men and women across the Commonwealth who thought deeply and carefully about religious freedom and its limitations. How was a parent's constitutionally protected right to practice her or his religious faith to be weighed against the unnecessary death of a child? The Christian Science Church claimed the First Amendment protected a parent's right to rely on spiritual healing. The state argued it had a responsibility to protect the life and well-being of all children and to enact laws to achieve that end. To resolve the dilemma posed by these conflicting perspectives, a broad spectrum of people seemed instinctively to embrace a formula articulated by the U.S. Supreme Court more than four decades before Robyn's death. A parent's freedom to believe and practice his or her faith is protected by the First Amendment's free exercise clause, but a parent is not free to impose her or his religious practice on a minor child. No Massachusetts court expressly articulated that rule during the long struggle to achieve justice for Robyn Twitchell, but a broad swath of people embraced that argument. In this way the people defined the First Amendment's meaning to include common sense and compassion. That is Robyn's legacy.

6

Repeal of Religious Exemptions

Except in Massachusetts, the public debate that followed the unnecessary deaths of children whose Christian Science parents had denied them medical care did not lead to repeal of the confusing religious accommodation statutes on which prosecutors and defendants alike had depended. In the wake of lengthy, contentious legal proceedings in Arizona, Florida, Minnesota, and California, there were calls for repeal of exemption laws, but despite encouragement from some state courts, powerful editorials, efforts by CHILD and the American Academy of Pediatrics, legislators could not be moved to repeal the law or extend greater protection to children. However, South Dakota, Hawaii, and Maryland, states not directly affected by the "child cases" that roiled the nation in the 1990s, joined Massachusetts in successfully repealing statutes exempting from prosecution parents who treated a seriously ill child by spiritual means alone.[1]

Legislators contacted by the *Phoenix Gazette* while Ashley King lay dying saw no reason to repeal the state's provision exempting Christian Scientists from child abuse or neglect charges. In their opinion the religious exemption statute "hadn't been abused." Several Florida legislators who had voted for a religious exemption publicly stated after Amy Hermanson's death that they had no idea the exemption would endanger children. As late as 1998, six years after the Florida Supreme Court overturned the Hermansons' conviction on the grounds that the state's religious proviso "created a trap that the legislature should address," not a single legislator had stepped up to sponsor a repeal bill. "You would think when the Supreme Court says your work product is defective," said Karen Gievers, a lawyer and children's advocate in Florida, "you would go back and fix it, but most of our legislators feel like they have better things to do than protect children." In fact, according to Stephanie

Olin, the staff director for the House committee on family law and children, the Florida Supreme Court's ruling confused legislators. The criminal portion of the child abuse statutes, Olin claimed, made no provision for religious exemption. Such an exemption is found only in civil statutes. "Someone found guilty of something like third-degree murder shouldn't have access to the religious exemption defense," she said angrily.[2]

Children's rights advocates, including Rita Swan, the president of CHILD, and members of that organization, testified before legislative committees in nearly a dozen states. In California and Minnesota, opponents of religious exemption laws highlighted the deaths of Shauntay Walker and Ian Lundman, but no exemption repeal bill came to a floor vote. "What's significant now about the Walker case," the *Sacramento Bee* wrote in 1992, "is that the ambiguity that misled Laurie Walker, and that may have led to her child's death, remains on the books, a tribute to legislative venality and cowardice. The state Supreme Court has settled the ambiguity, though perhaps not with the clearest logic. But it would be far better if the Legislature had the courage to get rid of the Christian Science exemption altogether."[3]

Against a somewhat different backdrop, South Dakota became the first state to repeal the religious exemption attached to a parent's statutory duty to provide a minor child with food, clothing, shelter, medical attendance, and other remedial care. The new statute also included "religious healing practitioner[s]" among persons mandated to report child abuse or the death of a child resulting from abuse and authorized a court to order medical treatment for a child "under treatment solely by spiritual means." The bill's passage on February 28, 1990, came about primarily through the work of Swan, Joni Clark, the Reverend Geri Smith, a pastor from Sioux Falls, and the South Dakota legislators John Timmer, Jean Beddow, and Dr. Richard Belatti. More than a dozen church organizations as well as the South Dakota Chapter of the American Academy of Pediatrics and the South Dakota Department of Social Services joined the effort.[4]

Clark had just graduated from high school when she married Gary Cooke, a onetime student at Northwestern University who followed Charles Meade, a self-proclaimed religious prophet, to Sioux Falls, South Dakota, in 1973. Meade founded End Time Ministries, preaching an apocalyptic gospel centered on positive confession theology, or Word-Faith. He stressed the inherent power of word and thoughts, allowing all persons to control their own future by what they said and by how well they used spiritual laws. At the same time, Meade rigorously controlled every aspect of life within the church, prohibiting his followers from reading books and newspapers and from listening to the radio and watching television. He condemned the medical profession, preaching that sickness was a result of sin and nonbelief that only prayer could heal. In Sioux Falls this belief led to the death of at least five newborn babies during home deliveries that were not attended by licensed health care providers.[5]

Joni Cooke's first pregnancy at the age of twenty-three was extraordinarily difficult. She experienced blinding migraine headaches, exhaustion, swollen joints, and labored breathing. Unable to stand, she lay in bed one afternoon as her husband yelled at her to get up. Lying down was admitting defeat, he told her. Being tired is a sin because God's people are empowered with supernatural stamina. Joni delivered the baby at home alone a month before her due date: the baby, Libby, weighed less than four pounds and struggled to breathe. Meade told Joni only prayer would help. Four days after being born, Libby stopped breathing, vomited blood, and died. A doctor later told Joni that Libby would have had a 99 percent chance of survival if she had been born in a hospital.[6]

Over the next several years Cooke gave birth to four healthy girls, but along the way she became convinced that the women and children of End Time were paying too steep a price for their membership in the church. "I saw children suffering," she later recalled, "at the same time, adults, particularly men, would sneak off to doctors." In 1984 Meade and his followers, approximately 125 families in Sioux Falls, including Joni and Gary Cooke and their children, moved to Lake City, Florida, to establish God's perfect community on earth. In the fall of 1986 Joni rebelled and left End Time Ministries, divorced her husband, and returned to Sioux Falls with her four daughters to begin a new life under her maiden name, Clark. She enrolled in Sioux Falls College en route to acquiring a law degree and began telling her story to community groups. In the summer of 1989 she spoke to a service club in Sioux Falls that included state representative Timmer, who was shocked by what he heard. "We have laws that protect animals better than we do humans," he said. Timmer and Clark later joined Swan and Reverend Smith, who had counseled many former members of End Time Ministries, at a conference held by parents whose children had joined the move to Meade's earthly utopia in Florida. With help from the parents' support group and a cluster of churches and children's advocacy groups, the four led a campaign to repeal South Dakota's religious shield laws.[7]

By January 1990, when the South Dakota legislature convened, thirty-two of the seventy representatives and fourteen of the thirty-five senators had signed on to the repeal bill as co-sponsors. Clark, Smith, and Swan arrived in the state capital, Pierre, on January 30 to "work the floor" and found a Christian Science lobbyist also at work. More disconcerting, they discovered that some of the co-sponsors were not fully committed. "We're not out to lift anyone's religious freedoms," Representative Beddow told doubters. "We just want to prevent the suffering and death of children." After a volatile hearing that left the House committee divided, the committee chairman, Jerry Lammers, floated a compromise. He proposed adding to existing law a clause allowing court-ordered medical treatment of children. The Christian Scientists accepted, but Swan's group declined, Swan arguing that the exemption had to be repealed to make it clear that parents had a duty to care for their children. The committee voted 7–5 against repeal.[8]

When Clark, Smith, and Swan returned to Sioux Falls, they immediately set to work to change the status quo. Smith called her former parishioners and asked them to call legislators. The parents' support group rallied their members on weekends. Swan faxed to the governor's office copies of all the exemption laws in other states. Representative Timmer told his colleagues, "Prayer does have power and God can heal, but you also have to make use of the things that God has provided." This last-ditch effort led Lammers to draft a bill removing nearly all religious exemptions from South Dakota laws.[9]

The attorney Jim Olson, a Christian Scientist who had testified earlier against repeal, now said the church could "live with" the bill. It sailed through the House 65–0, although a few days later the Christian Science lobbyists were urging senators to vote against the bill. When the senators discovered that these same lobbyists had agreed to the bill in the House, the Senate passed the bill unanimously. When Gov. George Mickelson signed the bill into law he singled out Clark's work for praise. "I hope you realize," he wrote, "you are the primary reason why House Bill 1314 is becoming law. Your willingness to endure the pain of telling your story in the public hearings of the legislature will be rewarded with saved lives in the future. Because you put yourself through the ordeal of publicly explaining your story, many additional children will be spared unnecessary pain and injury. I want you to know how much I admire your courage."[10]

In the summer of 1991 Hawaii took steps to repeal its religious exemption provisions in response to notification from the U.S. Department of Health and Human Services that the state was not in compliance with federal regulations. Hawaii law exempted parents of children treated by spiritual means

from being considered medically needy under child abuse or neglect reporting requirements, making the state ineligible for federal child abuse prevention funds. Debbie Lee, the assistant program administrator for Child Protective Services, located within the state's Department of Human Services,
was alarmed. Belying the myth that Hawaii is a paradise in every respect, the
state had a very high rate of child abuse. From 1989 to 1991 Hawaii had one
of the country's highest death rates for abused children under the age of one
year and was among ten states with the most infant deaths per one hundred
thousand births. Lee and Lori Nishimura, of the Honolulu Department of
Prosecuting Attorney, contacted Swan for information about what reporting
statutes other states had enacted and about court rulings on religiously based
neglect. Swan responded with a wealth of information and exhorted Lee and
Nishimura to work to repeal Hawaii's religious exemption rather than merely
amend the reporting requirement.[11]

Winona E. Rubin, the director of human services in Hawaii, wrote to the
Senate Committee on Judiciary on February 14, 1992, to argue for repealing the religious exemptions for child abuse and neglect. Her contention
rested on three points: first, because the state was not in compliance with
CAPTA reporting provisions, Hawaii would be denied more than two hundred thousand dollars in federal grants from the National Center on Child
Abuse and Neglect; second, a long list of child advocacy agencies supported
repeal, including the American Academy of Pediatrics, the American Medical Association, the National Committee for Prevention of Child Abuse, and
the National District Attorneys Association; third, as the law now stood, "a
seriously ill child receiving spiritual means alone through prayer according
to the tenets and beliefs of a recognized church or religion, is not subject to
reporting provisions that are applicable to all other children." Amending the
statute by repealing the religious exemption would ensure that all children
have "equal access to health care and that their caretakers are afforded the
same protections and responsibilities regardless of their religious beliefs."
Spokespersons for Child Welfare Services, the Hawaii Medical Association,
and the local chapter of the American Academy of Pediatrics also strongly
supported repeal.[12]

In her testimony before the Senate Judiciary Committee, Nishimura acknowledged that prayer is motivated by "sincere religious beliefs," but she
maintained that the provision exempting some parents of ill children from
child abuse reporting requirements denied "dependent and vulnerable" children the protection they deserved. That children are "deserving of special care

and protection" has long been recognized by the courts and by the codifica-
tion of laws against child abuse and neglect. If a child's illness is not reported
to Child Protective Services, he or she "may never receive necessary medical
attention[,] causing the child unneeded pain and suffering or increased risks
of death or disability." As to the argument that state intervention infringes
on a parent's right to freedom of religion, the U.S. Supreme Court's rulings
in *Wisconsin v. Yoder* (1972) and *Prince v. Massachusetts* (1944) make it clear
that that right must yield "when there is a state interest of sufficient magnitude" and that "the right to practice religion freely does not include liberty to
expose the community or the child to communicable disease or the latter to
ill health or death." For these reasons, Nishimura concluded, the Honolulu
state attorney's office supported the repeal of religious exemptions.[13]

Robert A. Herlinger, a Christian Scientist and church lobbyist, contended
before the Senate committee that there was a "compelling reason" for the
law's accommodating what he called "a religious method of health care." For
more than a century, he asserted, Christian Science has effectively healed
through prayer, and for decades all fifty states have recognized this fact.
Christian Scientists abhor child abuse "under any circumstances," but they
cannot stand by while spiritual healing is "arbitrarily wiped out" under the
guise of protecting children. In fact, Herlinger stated, religious accommodations do not exempt parents from caring for their children but simply
give parents "access to a religious method of health care, in lieu of medical
treatment." Given this context and the twin goals of satisfying the state's
drive to protect children and the constitutional rights of Christian Scientists, Herlinger proposed an amendment to the current accommodation
statute that would allow a "juvenile court [to] determine that medical care
is necessary."[14]

During his Senate testimony Herlinger cited a Minnesota lower court's ruling dismissing manslaughter charges against Kathleen McKown, a Christian
Scientist currently residing in Hawaii whose son died of untreated diabetes.
Herlinger claimed the court's ruling was based on McKown's right to religious freedom. Nishimura quickly countered, explaining that the court had
ruled for McKown because the Minnesota legislature had enacted a religious
exemption to criminal neglect. The Minnesota outcome, she argued, manifested the importance of repealing religious exemptions. Herlinger begged to
differ, but the committee chair, Russell Blair, cut him off, saying it was settled
that the state had a compelling interest to protect children. The committee
sent the bill to the Senate, where it easily won a majority vote.[15]

The effort to repeal did not go as smoothly in the House. The chair of the House Judiciary Committee failed to attend a hearing, and an organization known as Victims of Child Abuse Laws (VOCAL) joined Herlinger in opposing repeal. VOCAL tapped into a sentiment held by some legislators that the Department of Human Services intruded too easily and too often into the lives of families, and therefore the group opposed expanding the reporting requirement. Herlinger played the same card. By extending the reporting requirement to religious parents, he told the committee, "the State could enter the home and intercede between parent and child." Why limit family rights "over some legal language"? he asked. At this point, passage of the repeal bill seemed jeopardized, but during the next two weeks vigorous lobbying by CHILD members and the women's caucus in the legislature led to a unanimous House vote in favor of repeal. Gov. John Waihee signed the bill into law.[16]

The effort to repeal the religious exemption statute in Massachusetts did not achieve success as quickly as those in Maryland, Hawaii, and South Dakota. Four months after the Twitchells' manslaughter conviction Nathan Talbot, the omnipresent church spokesperson, published an op-ed piece in the *Washington Post* in which he claimed that the issues raised in the Twitchells' trial remained unsettled. He sought to reframe the church's argument for spiritual healing in a way that would draw into the campaign a broad coalition of religious groups, skeptics of modern medicine, and opponents of big government. He contended that secular acrimony aimed generally at religious minorities and spiritual healing in particular and the modern intrusive state combined to drive an effort to protect and expand "medical dogma" despite "in-hospital tragedies and continuing pronouncements on the current 'crisis' in the medical care system." According to Talbot, this unholy alliance led state legislatures to dismiss evidence demonstrating that prayer had healed many children of "life-threatening conditions" and to enact laws restricting reliance on spiritual healing in the care of children. These laws had increased the government's role in sustaining what Talbot dismissively called "medical orthodoxy" and fostered the growth of the "massive bureaucratization of health care." In fact, Talbot implied, these circumstances place both secular and religious parents in an untenable situation in regard to the health of their children.[17]

The struggle to determine if the Christian Science Church's effort to form a broad coalition to protect spiritual healing in the care of children or the drive by Massachusetts child advocacy groups to enact legislation to restrict that practice would succeed played out in the legislature in the three years after the Twitchells' conviction.

Rep. John McDonough had a compromise bill aimed at amending the state's religious exemption law ready to put before the House, but he was not optimistic about its passage. The Twitchell verdict, he said, might help push through his bill allowing spiritual healing "unless medical care is necessary to protect the child from suffering serious physical harm or illness." Rep. Byron Rushing, whose district included the Mother Church, opposed the bill, casting the debate in terms of religious freedom and avoiding the question of whether saving a child's life overrides the First Amendment. "In order to maintain our understanding of freedom of religion," Rushing said, "you have to allow parents to be able to make religious decisions for their children." Rep. Shannon O'Brien, elected to the House from western Massachusetts in 1986 at the age of twenty-seven, took a conciliatory position. "I don't think anyone in the Legislature wants to tell Christian Scientists they cannot practice their religion," she told the *Boston Herald,* "but there's a very delicate balance between that and the right of a child to live." O'Brien's language was cautious for good reason. Motivated by a particularly brutal incident of child abuse that had occurred in her Easthampton district, O'Brien had introduced a bill criminalizing child abuse. While the Twitchells' trial was playing out, however, language requiring medical care was deleted from O'Brien's bill at the request of the Christian Science Church. This experience drew O'Brien into the fight to repeal the state's religious exemption law.[18]

On July 9, 1990, Jetta Bernier, the executive director of Massachusetts Committee for Children and Youth (MCCY), hoping to take advantage of the momentum provided by the Twitchells' conviction, formally invited a dozen organizations and individuals to join the coalition that had been working since 1986 to reform or repeal religious exemptions laws. There were three items on the agenda: review the range of religious exemptions in state law and the status of current legislation aimed at these exemptions; develop a consensus on future action to reform or repeal religious exemptions; and identify resources within the group which could be mobilized to achieve these goals.[19]

Two weeks later, twenty-one people took seats around a conference table at MCCY's offices at 14 Beacon Street. Among the newcomers were the former prosecutor John Kiernan, who had returned to private practice; Tom Ferrick, the humanist chaplain at Harvard University; Michael Grodin, a professor of health at Boston University; Jonathan Caine, a pediatrician;

Margaret Blood of the Legislative Children's Caucus; and Teresa Whitehurst of the New England Medical Center. Representative McDonough, a member of the House Health Care Committee, averred that H.B. 3519, the current bill to amend the religious exemption statute, should be dropped because in 1986 the legislature had repealed the statutory crime of child neglect. The religious exemption language attached to the neglect statute, however, was retained. Therefore, McDonough explained, there is a religious exemption statute to a child neglect law that doesn't exist. Nevertheless, Bernier countered, the Christian Science Church continues to tout the exemption as a legal alternative to medical care for children and for that reason it should be repealed. The question could not be resolved, and Casanova shifted the group's attention to H.B. 5461, O'Brien's bill criminalizing acts of child abuse and neglect. Ed Brennan, a lobbyist for the American Academy of Pediatrics, thought the bill was unacceptable for a variety of reasons. A study committee was created.[20]

After the meeting, McDonough, Kiernan, and Casanova continued to talk about the best strategy for achieving the goal of requiring all parents to use medical care for seriously ill children. Kiernan convinced the others that although repeal "is the more difficult option politically," "now is the time to push hard for repeal—for a legislative action with clarity." On the basis of this informal agreement, Casanova presented an "Issues Primer" making a case for repeal at the October meeting of the coalition. With minor changes the coalition adopted the primer and the goal of repealing religious exemptions. By the fall the coalition had agreed to call itself the Coalition to Repeal Exemptions to Child Abuse Laws (CRECAL) and had grown to include more than two dozen organizations, including several that had rejected Casanova's earlier invitation. In addition to creating a broader-based, more efficient organization, the repeal effort received good press. Ellen Goodman, the nationally syndicated columnist for the *Boston Globe,* was an early supporter of repeal. She wrote sympathetically about the Twitchells' dilemma but privileged reason: "[The] state must remain neutral between religions, but that doesn't mean it must remain neutral between 'treatments,' as if spiritual healing and science were equal options for curing a bowel obstruction."[21]

Although CRECAL was better organized in 1990 to win legislative approval for repeal of religious exemption laws, neither McDonough's bill nor O'Brien's child abuse bill made it to a floor vote. In January 1991, however, the coalition received unexpected help from the Supreme Judicial Court (SJC). In the summer of 1989 Michael and Zelia McCauley took their eight-year-old daughter, Elisha, to hospital, where, after a series of tests, the physicians diagnosed the child's illness as leukemia and prescribed a treatment plan that would include blood transfusions. Being Jehovah's Witnesses, the McCauleys refused to consent to the use of blood transfusions because they believed that receiving blood or blood products precludes an individual from resurrection and everlasting life after death. Hospital officials sought authority from the court to permit the use of blood. A judge issued an order authorizing the hospital to "provide all reasonable medical care which in their judgment is necessary to preserve the patient's life and health."[22]

The McCauleys appealed, holding that the judge's order was unconstitutional because it violated their parental and religious rights. Writing for a unanimous court, Chief Justice Paul Liacos acknowledged the interest of parents in their relationship with their children "has been deemed fundamental and constitutionally protected." But parents "do not have unlimited rights to make decisions for their children." Parental rights "do not clothe parents with life and death authority over their children." The state, Liacos continued, "acting as *parens patriae,* may protect the well-being of children." Moreover, the right to the free exercise of religion, including parents' interests in the religious upbringing of their children, is not absolute. Parents do not have an "absolute right to refuse medical treatment for their children on religious grounds." Liacos concluded, "When a child's life is at issue, the first and paramount duty is to consult the welfare of the child."[23]

Kiernan immediately recognized the positive implications of the *McCauley* decision. "I believe it will have significant impact upon our efforts," he wrote to Casanova. He thought it would bolster the state's common law parental duty to provide medical care to a seriously ill child. At the same time, Kiernan added, "there is no criminal statute or penalty for parental failure to comply with the court's decisions. Massachusetts law establishes no enforceable legal duty for parents to provide medical care while the child lives. The most insidious aspect of the present legal arrangement is that the penalty for serious medical neglect of a child only attaches after the child's death." Both men understood that this intolerable situation could be remedied only by repealing the Commonwealth's religious exemption statute and by enacting a new child abuse and neglect law requiring parents to provide their seriously ill children with necessary medical care. That became CRECAL's goal for 1991.[24]

In January 1991 Representative McDonough introduced H.B. 2362, "An Act Relative to Neglected Children," which proposed deleting the existing statutory language creating a religious exemption to medical care for children. The expanded CRECAL repeal coalition met on January 29 to mobilize support for the bill. Five subcommittees—religion, medical, child advocacy, criminal justice, and academics—were created and especially important potential individual supporters identified and assigned to a CRECAL member to lobby. Individuals and organizations were asked to send letters to members of the Judiciary Committee pushing them to support repeal. "We believe," the CRECAL letter to its members stated, that H.B. 2362 does not threaten religious freedom and will protect "children's rights."[25]

On March 25 the Judiciary Committee held a hearing on H.B. 2362. Wendy Mariner, of the School of Public Health at Boston University, and Karen Hudner, of the Civil Liberties Union of Massachusetts, spoke about the constitutional issues affecting religious exemption laws. Mariner made two powerful points: There is no "constitutional right to engage in any religious practice that would endanger another person"; nor is freedom of religion "so fragile in this state that children must die to preserve it." Hudner argued that the exemption language—that a child is not suffering from abuse or neglect if he or she is being treated "in accordance with the tenets and practice of a recognized church or religious denomination by a duly accredited practitioner thereof"—violates the establishment clause of the First Amendment "in that it favors certain kinds of religious views over others."[26]

In a hearing room filled with Christian Scientists, the lobbyist Warren Silvernail articulated the church's position. He made five points: first, the language that the bill would eliminate "is an accommodation of a religious practice that involves a whole way of life as well as a highly successful method of treating disease through prayer"; second, if passed, the bill would create "one *standard*" of care, including "decisions for birth control and abortion made solely by a secular medical community"; third, evidence of spiritual healing is massive; fourth, children have a right to the *best* health care, and loving, responsible Christian Science parents believe spiritual treatment is best; fifth, proponents of H.B. 2362 maintain that repealing the state's religious exemption would make it possible for Christian Scientists to provide children with both spiritual and medical treatment, but the two are not compatible. "Please," pleaded Silvernail, "don't take this advantage away from these children."[27]

At the end of April the Judiciary Committee sent H.B. 2362 to the House floor with a favorable report. Looking forward to a vote, CRECAL bombarded House members with a letter, a summary of the issues, and a brochure asking for their support of H.B. 2362. On May 20 the bill went to the House floor for a vote, although owing to sharp differences that had emerged within CRECAL a positive vote seemed unlikely. Therefore, at Casanova's request, Sal DiMasi, the chair of the Judiciary Committee, successfully moved that H.B. 2362 be tabled until June 18. Casanova and Bernier called a special meeting of CRECAL to iron out the differences between prosecutors, child advocates, physicians, and legal organizations who held opposing positions with regard to two child abuse and neglect bills that were in play both separately and in tandem with the religious exemption issue.[28]

District attorneys and law enforcement officials, most of whom had been recruited by Kiernan, supported a bill that included imprisonment for persons who willfully or negligently permitted a child to be seriously injured. (There were two such bills on the table: Rep. James Brett's H.B. 2610 and O'Brien's H.B. 3263. Brett's bill did not include a religious exemption whereas O'Brien's did.) Child advocates, child welfare professionals, and the Civil Liberties Union all argued that children's rights are ultimately best protected by a policy that strongly presumes family integrity. Therefore, they opposed state intervention into family life except in extreme and specific circumstances.[29]

Because the breach between the two groups within CRECAL could not be closed in one daylong discussion, Bernier and the House leadership brokered a deal among legislative proponents and opponents of the repeal bill (H.B. 2362). The repeal bill was sent to the Committee on Third Reading, a move that allowed up to forty-five days to discharge the bill for a final House vote. The agreement to move the repeal bill forward was one element of a more comprehensive agreement that linked the future of H.B. 2362 to House action on Brett's child abuse and neglect bill. Opponents of repeal obtained agreement that the Brett bill, or a revised child abuse and neglect bill, would be released first by the Committee on Third Reading for a final House debate and vote. The Christian Science Church would then be given the opportunity on the House floor to amend the Brett bill or a revised bill with a new exemption. CRECAL assumed the language of a new religious exemption would follow the wording included in the O'Brien bill. Under that provision Christian Scientists would be exempted from providing children with necessary medical care unless it had been ordered by a court.[30]

Bernier gave the CRECAL members their marching orders: defeat the more permissive religious exemption amendment in the O'Brien bill and make a major effort to revise Brett's bill so that it is acceptable to both prosecutors and child advocates. This could be accomplished by defining acts of child abuse more narrowly and by including a medical neglect provision—

without a religious exemption—that would establish a statutory duty for all parents to obtain medical attention for their seriously ill children.[31]

Work to arrive at a revised child abuse and neglect bill continued into the fall legislative session, but without success. CRECAL did manage to prevent O'Brien's bill containing a religious exemption provision from being reported to the House floor. For this reason, as per the agreement reached in the summer of 1991, on December 4 the repeal bill was released to the House floor for a vote. Fearful the repeal bill would lose, Representative DiMasi and the House leadership determined that the vote was to recommit. Making his maiden legislative speech, Douglas Stoddart, a Republican representative from the suburbs, brought the bill to the floor and spoke in favor of it, that is, not to recommit. House members booed him and then voted 98–50 to recommit, killing the bill for the year.[32]

The effort to enact a law requiring all parents to provide medical care for seriously ill children began again in the spring of 1992. This time around CRECAL decided to drop its narrow focus on repeal in favor of passing a child abuse and neglect law without a religious exemption. Specifically, the coalition embraced O'Brien's revised bill, "Prohibiting Certain Acts Against Children" (H.B. 5597), after she agreed to excise its religious exemption language. At a meeting in May that included Plymouth District Attorney William C. O'Malley, Bernier, and Brennan it was agreed that the bill's definition of bodily injury would be limited in order to address the concerns of pediatricians and child welfare advocates. When H.B. 5597 reached the House floor on June 8, Rep. Joseph B. McIntyre, the chair of the Committee on Criminal Justice, amended the bill to include the agreed-upon language. The bill was passed by voice vote without any attempt by its opponents or the Christian Science Church to include a religious exemption provision.[33]

CRECAL's surprising victory in the House was tempered for two reasons. First, a number of child advocacy groups left the coalition because they could not support criminalizing child abuse and neglect; second, the Christian Science Church had mobilized its members in each senatorial district to lobby for an amendment to H.B. 5597. The proposed amendment would exempt parents from responsibility for a child's "serious physical injury" if the injury was caused by a religiously motivated parent's failure to provide necessary or emergency medical care. In its letter to senators the church put it this way: "Christian Scientists are not asking for exemptions for responsibility for child abuse. We are asking to be allowed to use a system of treatment that is Biblically-based and has proved effective in healing for almost a century."[34]

O'Brien's House bill set off a flurry of parliamentary maneuvers in the Senate. On June 22, with only three other senators present, Sen. Linda J. Melconian attached a religious exemption amendment to H.B. 5597. Sen. Ed Burke moved reconsideration when more senators appeared in the chamber, but Sen. Lucile Hicks blocked the vote. She opposed the bill because it held responsible any person who "permits serious physical injury to a child," a clause she feared could penalize battered women. A week later an attempt to reconsider Melconian's amendment failed 17–13. That meant the amended version went to a third reading and that a second attempt to reconsider could not occur until the Senate's next calendar session following the summer recess.[35]

With CRECAL's strong support, on November 16 Sen. Paul White led a second effort to reconsider Melconian's amendment to exempt Christian Science parents from providing medical care to seriously injured children. Christian Scientists and a cluster of CRECAL members rushed to lobby every senator and his or her staff. Casanova, for example, spoke more than once with the aide of the Republican senator Henri Rauschenbach, who said the senator had received more than one hundred letters from Christian Scientists, with whom he wanted to maintain good relations. But, the aide added, Rauschenbach is reasonable, and he has kids. He abstained on the vote to reconsider. Likewise, Casanova came away from a long conversation with Sen. Patricia McGovern's aide believing the senator would vote to reconsider, but in fact she voted against. Just enough senators did vote to reconsider, however, and a vote to accept or reject Melconian's amendment was scheduled tentatively for November 30.[36]

Within days of the affirmative vote to reconsider, Senator Melconian asked to meet with CRECAL to discuss H.B. 5597 and specifically the issues of religious exemption and battered women. Present at the State House meeting were Melconian, Senator Hicks, Maryanne Mulligan, representing Mass. Law Reform, Silvernail, a representative from Sen. Paul White's office, Kiernan, and Brennan. Melconian said she hoped a compromise could be reached on the divisive issues and a consensus established so that a child abuse and neglect bill could be passed during the current legislative session. Hicks expressed her concern about the issue of battered women, saying she opposed the clause "permitting another to" commit abuse in H.B. 5597 and insisting it be deleted. At this point Silvernail joined the conversation, pledging the church's support for deleting the "permitting" clauses. The remainder of the two-hour meeting focused on the religious exemption issue. "It is clear," Brennan's report on the meeting to Bernier stated, "that no compromise can be reached on this issue." He did add, however, that Melconian asked both sides to discuss whether some form of "rebuttable presumption" could be created which would satisfy the concerns of both sides. If a compromise could not be worked out, Melconian vowed she would do whatever she could to kill the bill. Brennan's report closed with a warning note: "My biggest fear, even if we have the votes to win on the religious exemption issue, we could face a situation in which the senators who support the battered women's groups join with the senators supporting the Christian Science Church who together could have sufficient votes to delete" the bill's religious exemption language.[37]

While negotiations between proponents and opponents of the child abuse and neglect bill went on behind closed doors, the Boston press voiced its opinions. The conservative columnist Jeff Jacoby of the *Boston Herald* branded Senator Melconian's proposed expansion of the spiritual healing exemption "dangerously misguided." "As a rule," Jacoby wrote, "parents should be given the broadest latitude in caring for their children. But not so broad that it paralyzes society from attempting to save the Robyn Twitchells." A week later Bella English of the *Boston Globe,* a friend of CRECAL, made known her opinion of the O'Brien bill. Massachusetts, she began, is one of the few states that does not have a law criminalizing child abuse. "You wouldn't think anyone would object to a bill that protects innocent children from danger or death," but a religious exemption has been slipped into O'Brien's bill. "If you want Massachusetts to join the rest of the civilized world in protecting our children—and if you believe certain parents [battered women] shouldn't be immune from the law," English concluded, "call your senator today. For some kids it could be a matter of life or death." Paul Reid, writing for the *Boston TAB,* was all for the bill criminalizing child abuse and against religious exemptions, but he condemned English and all those who believed the answers would come from "the state alone." A small sample of people from the greater Boston area were divided over whether Christian Scientists should be exempted from the law requiring parents to seek medical care for their children. A sixty-six-year-old Dorchester resident, Walter Isles, said, "It should be up to them" to choose prayer or a doctor, while Priscilla Doucette, fifty-five, said, "We have to protect the children." Cindy Thomas, thirty-three, and Dennis Krysiak, forty-two, agreed that children "need some protection" and "should be checked out by doctors until they are old enough to decide for themselves."[38]

On December 1 Brennan met with Melconian and Silvernail. The church put forward another compromise amendment. Drawn in part from a New

York statute, the proposal provided for an affirmative defense as opposed
to an exemption. In any prosecution for "willfully or negligently permitting
serious physical injury to a child based upon an alleged failure to provide
proper medical care or treatment to the child, the proposal read, it is an affirmative defense that the person having care of such child provided or caused
the child to be treated . . . solely by spiritual means through prayer." The CRE-
CAL coalition flatly rejected the proposed compromise, recognizing that the
addition of the word "willfully" made prosecution substantially more difficult and undermined a considerable number of other statutes and regulations meant to protect children.[39]

On November 2, 1992, running in part on the positive publicity she had
gained by sponsoring the child abuse and neglect bill, Shannon O'Brien won
a Senate seat, trouncing her Republican opponent by a two-to-one margin.
On January 4 Senator O'Brien asked for consideration of H.B. 5597, the bill
she had shepherded through the House. A brief debate followed. At 3:14 p.m.,
in response to a call for the question, the bill passed by a vote of 23–7. However, the legislative year expired before any further action could be taken.
Although deeply disappointed that time had run out, CRECAL at last had
something positive on which to build. The coalition had won favorable votes
in the House and Senate for a child abuse and neglect bill without a religious
exemption; it had outmaneuvered the Christian Science Church despite a
large disparity in financial resources and manpower; and O'Brien's election
to the Senate put her in a position to ensure that the child abuse and neglect
bill became law.[40]

A few weeks after O'Brien's election to the Senate, the SJC agreed to review
the Twitchells' manslaughter conviction. Following Judge Hamlin's denial of
a defense motion for a new trial, the Twitchells' trial lawyers and Suffolk District Attorney Ralph C. Martin urged the SJC to examine the case. Both sides
said the case gave rise to consequential legal issues bearing on the responsibilities of parents who practiced spiritual healing. Briefs were filed in April
1993. Steven M. Umin, a former clerk for U.S. Supreme Court Justice Potter
Stewart and a Washington attorney with more than two decades of experience in health care law, and Kevin J. Hasson, also a member of the bar of the
District of Columbia, represented the Twitchells before the SJC.[41]

As the losing party, the Twitchells bore the heavy burden of arguing that
the state had not made a case for conviction, that they had not received a fair
trial, and that the trial judge had misinterpreted the law. Umin's brief posed
two key questions: "Should There Have Been a Twitchell Trial At All; and Did

the Twitchells Get a Fair Trial?" His legal arguments answered these questions in the negative.[42]

Before their case came to trial, Umin reminded the court, the Twitchells had filed a motion to dismiss, contending that the Commonwealth could not establish that the couple had a "*legal duty* to provide Robyn with conventional medical care." Proof of that duty is essential, Umin wrote, because Massachusetts case law makes clear an omission cannot be the basis for a manslaughter charge unless it is an "omission where there is a duty to act." In simple terms, "not doing something does not amount to an 'omission' unless there is a duty to do it." Neither at common law nor by statute does Massachusetts impose a duty to provide medical care on parents who rely on spiritual treatment, he continued. The spiritual treatment amendment added to the state law defining proper physical care a parent must provide a child, Umin argued, "recognizes the 'right' of parents to rely upon remedial treatment by spiritual means alone."[43]

However, Umin continued, the trial court rejected this "plain reading" of the statute, denied the motion to dismiss, and erroneously instructed the jury "by performing a skin graft that added terms the Legislature had not chosen to the simple language of the spiritual treatment provision." The language Judge Hamlin added to the amendment permitting spiritual treatment restricts its use to situations "when nothing more is necessary" to protect the health of a child. "This crabbed view of the scope of the provision later translated into a charge to the jurors" essentially mandates a verdict against the Twitchells. In other words, Umin added in a footnote, "if the trial court's view of the provision were accepted, the provision would exist merely to humor Christian Scientists, a condescending purpose not reasonably attributable to the Legislature."[44]

In addition to criticizing Judge Hamlin's alleged erroneous ruling, Umin blasted the prosecutor Kiernan's "extensive and sarcastic questioning of Christian Science witnesses" for violating the commands of the First and Fourteenth Amendments and Massachusetts law. The prosecutor's closing argument administered the coup de grâce by telling the jury the Twitchells' beliefs were not "rational, not those of orthodox Christian Scientists and that the significance of [the jury's] verdict was that it will be a bellwether. It will announce the standard that when a child is in this condition that you must call a doctor." This argument, Umin emphasized, "urging the jury to decide whether Christian Science is 'rational' or 'real'—posed precisely the questions the First Amendment forbids."[45]

Finally, Umin focused on the issue of fair warning, that is, sufficient statutory notification that particular behavior constitutes a crime. To conclude that the law gave the Twitchells fair warning requires "total immersion in a world of unreality." Nothing in the common law or the statutory history of the spiritual treatment provision could have prepared the couple for what they first learned in court during a manslaughter prosecution. It's not just that the Twitchells had no inkling that their right to practice spiritual treatment was limited, the "critical fact is that the law gave them no clue that any limitation existed." The law denied the Twitchells due process "by affirmatively misleading them while denying them fair warning." For these reasons, Umin concluded, the Twitchells' manslaughter conviction should be reversed.[46]

After a careful review of the Twitchells' behavior leading to Robyn's death, Martin, appointed to the office of Suffolk district attorney by Gov. William Weld in 1992, as well as the brief prepared by Assistant District Attorney Marcy Cass, drew a stark contrast between the state's "fundamental interest of the highest order in protecting the right of children to live" and the Twitchells' assertion of their First Amendment right of religious freedom and the statutory religious exemption they claimed precluded their prosecution for manslaughter. To carry out its duty to protect children, the Commonwealth argued, the state has a wide range of powers for "limiting parental freedom and authority in matters affecting the child's welfare," including regulating the "familial relationship," compelling "affirmative action" to protect the child's well-being, and enforcing its criminal statutes against parents whose "religious practice results in the death of their child." The Twitchells' wanton and reckless conduct and their indifference to or disregard of probable harmful consequences breached their parental duty by failing to provide their seriously ill infant son with medical care. In fact, the parents' conduct during Robyn's illness made it clear they were aware of the severity of his illness but nevertheless continued to rely only on spiritual treatment. Confronted with similar circumstances, reasonable parents would have consulted a physician and Robyn's "life could have been saved by medical treatment."[47]

The Commonwealth's brief assaulted the Twitchells' assertion that their First Amendment right of religious freedom allowed them to treat Robyn's illness with prayer. On the contrary, parents cannot disobey otherwise valid laws enacted for society's health and welfare under the guise of religious conviction. "Parents may be free to become martyrs for themselves," Cass paraphrased *Prince v. Massachusetts* (1944), "but they are not free to make martyrs of their children. Free religious practice ends where the sacrifice of innocent children like Robyn Twitchell begins."[48]

Similarly, Cass argued, the Twitchells cannot take refuge in the state's statutory religious exemption (G.L. chap. 273, sec. 1). The law violates the constitutional prohibition against legislation respecting an establishment of religion. It exempts only "recognized churches," effectively giving credence to "a particular religion and practice, that of healing by prayer alone." The statutory exemption also violates the constitutional guarantee of equal protection. It creates one standard of behavior for parents who profess a particular religious belief and another standard for those who hold different religious beliefs or no belief. The law also creates a group of children who "will never be protected from their parents' religious beliefs, through no fault or choice of their own. Equal protection should not be denied to innocent children, whether under the label of religious freedom or otherwise." Cass insisted it would be absurd to profess that a religious exemption statute insulated the Twitchells from conviction for involuntary manslaughter "where their failure to provide life-saving medical care endangered and ultimately took their son's life."[49]

Finally, and contrary to the defendants' claim, the Commonwealth's brief stressed that the jury was fully informed about the statutory religious exemption. Defense counsel referred to the exemption in her opening statement, and David Twitchell testified that he knew about it and clearly explained his understanding of the law. Judge Hamlin's instructions to the jury also referred to the exemption and explained its relevance: "The defendants' contrary contention is belied by the facts." Therefore, the Twitchells' conviction should be affirmed.[50]

In keeping with the SJC's usual schedule, the court heard oral argument in *Commonwealth v. Twitchell* on Tuesday morning, May 4, 1993. A court officer called the court to order, and the seven black-robed justices entered the courtroom and took their seats behind the bench, the chief justice at the center and the others arranged around him by seniority: the most senior on the chief justice's right hand, the next on his immediate left, and so on. At the time of the *Twitchell* case, the justices were, from the viewpoint of someone facing them and looking from left to right, the fifty-four-year-old John M. Greaney, elevated to the SJC in 1989 from the Appeals Court; Joseph R. Nolan, appointed to the court in 1981 by the conservative Democratic governor Edward J. King; Herbert P. Wilkins, appointed by Gov. Frank Sargent and the longest-serving justice, his tenure stretching back to 1972; Chief Justice Paul J. Liacos, a law professor at Boston University when Gov. Michael Dukakis appointed him to the SJC in 1976 and a man whose deep commitment to individual rights nearly cost him elevation to chief justice in 1989; Ruth

Abrams, the first woman on the court; the sixty-five-year-old social conservative Francis P. O'Connor, also appointed by Governor King; and Neil L. Lynch, the third of King's appointments and the most conservative member of the court.

According to the SJC's protocol for oral argument, each party is allowed fifteen minutes. The clerk uses a timer equipped with three lights, green signaling fourteen minutes had passed, yellow indicating one minute remained, and red signifying the end of the allotted time. Umin, who spoke first, made three points: prosecution of the couple amounted to an unconstitutional attack on their right to religious freedom; further, it violated the statutory religious exemption provision allowing parents to rely solely on spiritual healing as "remedial treatment" for their children; and the trial judge had denied the Twitchells a fair trial by preventing the jury from hearing evidence of the widespread recognition Christian Science healing has received and by permitting the prosecutor to ridicule the religious beliefs of Christian Scientists. Cass rebutted Umin's three arguments with three of her own: the Twitchells' constitutional argument was invalid because a parent's right to "free religious practice ends where the life of a child" is at stake; the state's religious accommodation provision is part of a law dealing with family neglect and support, and the protection it affords to parents who practice spiritual healing cannot be transferred to the law pertaining to the crime of manslaughter; the questioning of witnesses about their religious beliefs was not designed to demean Christian Science but to rebut the Twitchells' claim that they acted reasonably by relying solely on spiritual healing to treat their seriously ill child.[51]

In early April 1993, several months before the SJC was expected to hand down its Twitchell decision, Governor Weld filed a bill to make child abuse a felony punishable by up to twenty years in prison. "The fact is," the governor said at a news conference, "in this state we punish cruelty to animals more severely than many forms of cruelty to children." Depending on the seriousness of the physical injury, the governor's bill would impose stiff penalties on persons who inflict or "wantonly and recklessly" permit physical injuries to a child. Shortly after the governor's announcement, Senator O'Brien filed a bill similar to the governor's. Within days the Christian Science Church distributed to legislators an information sheet denouncing O'Brien's bill. The church charged that the bill's "bodily injury" language was too broad and violated the First Amendment's free exercise clause. In the view of the church, the remedy for these shortcomings was an "affirmative defense" amendment.[52]

Some child welfare advocates and the Civil Liberties Union of Massachusetts also criticized the bill. David Liederman, the executive director of the Child Welfare League of America, said, "There is no evidence that criminalization makes any difference for kids. It might make the governor and a few others feel good, but it doesn't help kids." Anne Donnelly, the executive director of the National Committee for the Prevention of Child Abuse, agreed. People who abuse their children have very complex problems, and tougher criminal penalties are not "uppermost in their minds." Other critics contended the legislation would have a disproportionate impact on minorities and the poor. Geline Williams, the chief of the Family Protection Unit of the Plymouth County district attorney's office and a CRECAL participant, responded that she and others invested in deterring abuse agreed that punishment is not the sole answer. Eric Maxwell of the Civil Liberties Union wrote, "Government should not be a force to further weaken the already besieged institution of family. . . . [The O'Brien bill] is a draconian solution to a problem requiring sensitivity and finesse." Under this proposal, he continued, everyone who has care of a child would be open to charges of criminal misconduct for spanking that child or for causing an injury while roughhousing. The bill must be defeated, concluded Maxwell.[53]

As the House vote on O'Brien's bill approached, proponents made a last effort to persuade legislators. Writing for CRECAL, Bernier asked the representatives to defeat the religious exemption and the affirmative defense amendment attached to S.B. 219. "Such an exemption," Bernier wrote, "would flagrantly and without justification expose helpless children to unnecessary suffering, disability, and death." A child's life cannot depend on the "success or failure of prayers when life-saving medical care is available." The church believes medicine and prayer cannot be combined and that prayer alone can heal childhood illness, she remarked, but everyone remembers the tragic death of Robyn Twitchell. "We urge you to *vote no on the Church's amendment*. It is a life and death matter for children."[54]

On May 12, 1993, the House made child abuse a felony and rejected an amendment that exempted parents who denied their children medical treatment because of religious belief. On the floor of the House, Representative McDonough said it was fine for him to choose not to see a doctor for a broken arm, but if his three-year-old daughter broke her arm and he refused to treat it medically, the state should step in. Representative Rushing argued that it's difficult to give people rights contrary to societal norms, "but that is what freedom of religion is all about." The lawmakers voted 97–55 against the amendment and sent the bill to the Senate on a voice vote.[55]

Within days after the House passed S.B. 219 Silvernail delivered a packet of materials to every senator's office. The information sheet made the usual arguments: the bill was contrary to the First Amendment and threatened Christian Scientists' way of life. The church also maintained that the bill gave district attorneys "broad and sweeping" definitions of bodily injury that required medical treatment, a provision that jeopardized not only those who use spiritual treatment but also "ethnic and racial minorities whose norms of child care differ from the majority['s]." Attached to the information sheet were several pages of healing testimonies from Christian Scientists. A couple in California told of adopting an unwanted, badly handicapped infant who overcame through prayer "a damaged heart and a serious bone condition." A woman from California reported that her eleven-year-old daughter ran into the street and was hit by a car. A hospital X-ray revealed multiple factures but rather than wait several hours for a doctor to set the bones, the mother and daughter returned home and prayed. Five days later, the child's mother said, the broken bones had healed completely.[56]

On August 11, during the legislature's summer recess and more than seven years after Robyn's death, the SJC handed down its decision on David and Ginger Twitchell's appeal of their conviction for involuntary manslaughter. Justice Wilkins, writing for the majority, signaled the outcome in his first four paragraphs, which can be summarized as follows: Evidence warranted the jury in finding Robyn was in considerable pain from a bowel obstruction for which parents who did not rely on spiritual healing would have sought medical treatment. It is true that Robyn's condition ebbed and flowed, giving the Twitchells hope that spiritual treatment would lead to a cure, but parents have a duty to provide a child with medical care, and therefore the jury was correct in finding that the Twitchells acted "wantonly and recklessly" in failing to provide Robyn with that care. The spiritual healing provision in chapter 273, sec. 1, did not protect the parents from a charge of manslaughter. However, Wilkins added, "special circumstances in this case"—that is, Massachusetts Attorney General Bellotti's statement from 1975 about the 1971 amendment to the child support law (see chapter 5)—would justify a jury's finding that the Twitchells "reasonably believed they could rely on spiritual treatment without fear of criminal prosecution." Because the jury did not hear this affirmative defense, "a substantial risk of a miscarriage of justice" occurred, and therefore the judgments must be reversed.[57]

Wilkins then turned to a detailed analysis of the law. He accepted the Commonwealth's argument that the Twitchells could be found guilty of involuntary manslaughter because their failure to seek medical care for Robyn involved such "a high degree of likelihood that substantial harm will result" to him as to constitute wanton and reckless behavior. He acknowledged that a charge of involuntary manslaughter based on an omission to act could be proved only if the defendant had a duty to act and did not do so. Citing *Commonwealth v. Hall* (1948), a case in which an unwed mother intentionally starved her infant to death, Wilkins found in the common law of homicide a parental duty to provide care. The Commonwealth also recognized in *Commonwealth v. Gallison* (1981), Wilkins added, a common law duty to provide medical services for a child, the breach of which may lead to a charge of involuntary manslaughter.[58]

Wilkins rejected the Twitchells' position that the spiritual treatment statute precluded a charge of involuntary manslaughter against a parent. The religious exemption provision, he pointed out, related to child support and physical care, not to criminal conduct. "It is unlikely," he wrote, that in placing the spiritual treatment amendment in a section of the law regarding a parent's "natural obligations of [child] support" the legislature also intended to change the law of homicide. In fact, a Christian Science spokesperson told the legislative committee amending the child support statute in 1971 that the church sought a spiritual treatment amendment "to make it clear that Christian Scientists, in providing their children with Christian Science treatment and care, are not violating *this* law." The church was eager to have legal protection against the "possibility of being considered neglectful by any individual in authority who may misunderstand our methods."[59]

The distinction between a parent's neglect to provide support and a willful failure to provide necessary and proper physical care to a child and involuntary manslaughter is clear. Wanton and reckless conduct, with which the Twitchells were charged, does not involve a willful intention to cause the resulting harm. Conviction for involuntary manslaughter, Wilkins pointed out, does not require proof of willfulness. Hence the spiritual treatment provision does not apply to involuntary manslaughter.[60]

Finally, Wilkins focused on the issue of fair warning. The rules of due process require that a criminal statute define the offense precisely so that an ordinary person can understand what conduct is prohibited and so that its vagueness does not invite arbitrary enforcement. The defendants avowed that they were denied fair warning because they were misled by the attorney general's 1975 opinion in response to a question from the Office of Children asking "whether parents who fail to provide medical services to children on the basis of religious beliefs will be subject to prosecution for such a failure." The attorney general's answer, subsequently published in *Legal Rights and Obligations of Christian Scientists in Massachusetts,* focused on a parent's negligent failures and omitted any reference to wanton and reckless behavior that could lead to homicide charges. "A reasonable person not trained in the law," Wilkins contended, might fairly read the attorney general's comments as barring prosecution under any circumstances. And because *Legal Rights* contained the misleading statement and was known to the Twitchells, Judge Hamlin should have admitted the handbook into evidence. The attorney general's unclear opinion deprived the defendants of fair warning and the withholding of the Christian Science rights handbook from the jury "created a substantial risk of a miscarriage of justice." For these intertwined reasons the verdicts must be set aside.[61]

The court's decision gave rise, unsurprisingly, to a range of responses. "It's going to be nice to get back to living a normal life," David Twitchell told a *Boston Globe* reporter. He said that meeting the terms of his court-ordered probation, including medical checkups, had been a burden and confused his children. A spokesman for the Christian Science Church expressed relief that the Twitchells' conviction had been overturned but declined to comment on the broader aspects of the decision. Steven Gottschalk, a Christian Science scholar, said the Twitchell case had "profoundly affected the church and rightly so." Some parents, he opined, were frightened and discouraged, while others remained committed to spiritual healing. A compromise must be reached, said Gottschalk, "to ensure the rights of Christian Scientists and fulfill the state's demands to protect children." Speaking for a cluster of children's advocacy groups, Bernier vowed to work "to remove [religious] exemption entirely." District Attorney Martin praised the SJC's decision as an "unparalleled victory for children in this state." The SJC, Martin added, also made it clear that the Twitchell jury was warranted in finding the couple was "wanton and reckless in failing to provide medical care for their son."[62]

About a month after the SJC's decision, Martin announced he would not retry the Twitchells. Rather, he called upon the legislature to repeal the section of Massachusetts law stipulating that a child is not neglected if he or she is being treated only by spiritual means. The SJC's opinion, said Martin, makes it very clear that all parents, regardless of their religious beliefs, have a duty to furnish medical care to their children, "the breach of which can properly be the basis for a manslaughter prosecution." Martin encouraged the legislature to repeal the religious exemption provision added to the child abuse bill currently before the legislature. Finally, the district attorney asked the legislature to enact a law including Christian Science nurses and practitioners as "mandated reporters of potential abuse and neglect."[63]

In early October, before the Committee on Third Reading released the child abuse bill to the Senate for a final vote, O'Brien engaged in one more round of negotiations with three key interest groups. First, to win support from Senator Hicks and those who wanted to afford some protection to battered women who might find themselves unable to protect a child from abuse by a companion, O'Brien agreed to substitute a wanton and reckless standard (that is, when a person with no intent to cause harm acts so unreasonably that he knows or should know it is highly probable harm will result) for a willful standard (that is, a premeditated, deliberate act done with evil intent) and lowered the criminal penalties in the permitting sections. Second, Kiernan, acting for O'Brien, won approval from the Massachusetts District Attorneys Association for deleting the willful standard in favor of wanton and reckless. Third, to satisfy those who believed the definition of "bodily injury" was too broad and that the penalties attached to abusive conduct were too severe, O'Brien agreed to change the language from "serious bodily injury" to "substantial bodily injury" and to reduce the years of imprisonment upon conviction by roughly half. Substituting "substantial" for "serious" responded fairly to Christian Scientists' complaint that the law's intent was to destroy their religion by requiring parents to seek medical care for minor illnesses or injuries. However, there was no compromise on religious exemption. CRE-CAL lobbied intensely to convince legislators not to permit the church's affirmative defense amendment to be added to the bill.[64]

Other voices, too, competed for attention. A few days before the Senate vote on S.B. 219, Silvernail told the *Globe,* "Spiritual treatment is a right, a right we've been using responsibly." If the O'Brien bill had been law when the Twitchells were tried, he added, they would have been sentenced to twenty years' imprisonment for acting on their religious belief that spiritual healing could save Robyn's life. Sen. Brian McDonald, a co-sponsor of a religious exemption amendment, found Silvernail's argument persuasive. "We want to make sure," McDonald said, "we protect children, but also provide protection for Christian Scientists to practice their religion." An editorial in the *Globe* embraced O'Brien's child abuse and neglect bill and soft-pedaled the Christian Scientists' preoccupations.[65]

The O'Brien bill came to the Senate floor for a vote at a sparsely attended session on October 18. The debate focused on an amendment exempting

Christian Science parents from criminal prosecution if a child were provided with "health care solely by spiritual means through prayer in accordance with a religious method of healing," unless the parent failed to carry out "medical treatment for such child ordered by a court." Sen. Brian Lees shouted, "Who is to say what we think is the standard or the norm in treating illness and it's the right way to go?" Sen. Marian Walsh, speaking against the amendment, noted that the 1971 exemption "already has created 'great turmoil' and doubt among Christian Scientists about their legal obligations to their children." We can't become religious police, she insisted, "but we can't decide there will be one exception. We are here to look at a standard that [every] child is entitled to." In a series of lightning-quick moves orchestrated by the Senate leaders, the religious exemption amendment to O'Brien's bill went down to defeat. The chair then quickly called for a vote on O'Brien's bill. Almost without pause the chair announced, "The ayes have it." O'Brien then rose in the chamber and offered a new amendment to repeal chapter 273, section 1, of the General Statutes, the existing religious statute. With a bang of the gavel, the chair declared the ayes had it.[66]

Bernier hailed the Senate vote as a "major victory on several counts." It gives prosecutors "a tool to punish the most egregious cases of child abuse" and makes clear that all parents have a duty to provide medical care to a seriously ill child. But the real winners, she added, are the children of religious parents who now have a legal right to medical care.[67]

The bill went to a conference committee to rectify a handful of minor differences between the House and Senate versions. On November 17 the House adopted the conference committee report and rejected an exemption for parents who deny children medical care for religious reasons. Six weeks later the Senate gave final approval to the bill defining and penalizing child abuse and repealing protection for spiritual healing. In April Governor William Weld had proposed a similar bill to deal with cases of child abuse and signaled his support for repealing the religious exemption law. These early signals fueled the expectation that Weld would sign the O'Brien bill.[68]

On Friday afternoon, December 10, Weld dropped a bombshell by returning the child abuse bill to the House for a "minor amendment." "I strongly agree with and support the intent of S.B. 219 which would codify child abuse as the distinct and brutal crime that it obviously is," he wrote, but repealing the religious exemption law was "unnecessary to achieve the objectives of the child abuse legislation." The governor's move pleased Christian Scientists but stunned lawmakers, child advocates, and district attorneys alike. A spokesman for the Christian Science Church "praised the governor for his action," and an editorial in the *Christian Science Monitor* titled "Prayer Is Not Criminal" explained that "prayer is not just instead of treatment, or in support of treatment: Prayer *is* treatment. And in the case of even young children," the editorial astonishingly asserted, "it is a decision generally made with their active consultation to a degree not widely appreciated." In her widely read column in the *Boston Globe,* however, Bella English labeled Weld a "flip-flopper." What happened between April, when Weld supported repeal of the religious exemption, and December, when he objected to doing just that? English asked. "If I were a betting person," she wrote, "I'd say that Weld has caved in to some heavy-duty lobbying by high-level Republican officials in the Christian Science Church." She pressed the legislature to "send this bill back promptly, as is" and demanded that the governor, "a father of five," sign the bill into law.[69]

Just after lunch on Tuesday, December 14, 1993, the House took up the governor's amendment for a religious exemption, and a handful of House members rose to speak. Representative Rushing was the first to rise to his feet. In a long, rambling speech, Rushing, a Democrat, recommended to the House that it support the Republican governor's amendment. "When most people practice your religion," he said, "it's easy to believe in freedom of religion. But the reason why we have freedom of religion enshrined in our bill of rights is because there are people who believe things we find it very difficult to believe. And that is who needs the protection." Representatives McIntyre, a Democrat, and Stoddart, a Republican, countered Rushing's plea for un-bounded religious freedom with a dose of reality. Both men spoke of the need to protect children. Stoddart, whose earlier speech in favor of repealing the exemption had elicited boos from his colleagues, now told a more receptive audience what a majority had concluded after more than three years of debate: "It's duplicitous to argue this is really a case of religious freedom because nobody in this chamber is saying that grownups or parents cannot practice any religion they want. We are all in agreement that people can practice the religion of their choice. The objection that we in the majority have is that we don't believe that four-year-old children can make a rational decision about their choice of religion. Until the child reaches the age of eighteen, let's not talk about religious freedom."

Representative McDonough, whom Casanova had contacted shortly after Robyn's death and who first had brought the argument for repeal of the religious exemption provision to the House, framed his speech around two words, "symbol" and "comfort," used by members supporting the governor's amendment. It's true, he said, that, given the court's ruling, "the current faith healing exemption is nothing more than a symbol," but it's a "misleading and dangerous" symbol. In full-page ads published in Boston newspapers during the Twitchells' trial the Christian Science Church had claimed that "the couple was acting in accordance with Massachusetts Law." The "church knew better," McDonough stated, "but most people reading that ad did not." He said the legislators have an obligation to the public and to Christian Science Church members to clear up that ambiguity by rejecting the governor's exemption provision. It's also true, he continued, that the comfort an exemption may provide is "misleading and dangerous." If an adult chooses not to have medical treatment for an illness, that's "none of anyone's business," but "a different standard comes into play when we're talking about children." Closing in dramatic fashion, McDonough asked the House to reject the governor's amendment: "We do it for ourselves; we do it for the children; we do it also for the people who belong to these churches, so that they can have very clear guidance."[70]

At this point, the assistant majority leader, Rep. Emanuel G. Serra, recognized a call for the question and ordered a roll call vote. He reminded members who were in favor of the governor's amendment to vote yes and those opposed to vote no. The House members had four minutes to vote by means of an electric roll call machine. The majority floor leader announced the tally: 66 yeas and 83 nays. The governor's amendment was rejected. The Senate followed the next evening, voting 21–11 against allowing the religious exemption provision to remain a law. On December 28 Governor Weld signed into law "An Act Prohibiting Certain Acts Against Children," and although he made no mention of religious exemption, the new law repealed that provision.[71]

After a seven-year battle Massachusetts had adopted a law making child abuse and neglect a felony without religious accommodation and repealed an existing law exempting parents who relied on spiritual healing alone to treat a child's serious illness. At its peak, the campaign to repeal included more than twenty-five health, child advocacy, and law enforcement groups. Working openly and publicly, the reformers achieved their goal of ensuring equal legal access to medical care for all children.

Despite the institution's wealth, media access, discipline, and well-oiled, successful lobbying machine, the Christian Science Church was defeated in its attempt to retain the state's two-decade-old law exempting Christian Science parents from providing medical care to their children. The defeat was owing largely to the inability of the church's leadership to act convincingly outside a century-old, carefully constructed ideological cocoon. Confronted with the unnecessary death of a child, the church failed to show genuine compassion for the young victim, insisting instead on the validity of the law said to shield from punishment parents who used only prayer to treat their seriously ill child, the alleged shortcomings of medical care, the intrusiveness of government, and the curious argument that Christian Science children did not need to be protected by law because most of them would not suffer serious injury or death.[72]

The SJC and the legislature rejected the church's arguments. Working separately but eventually standing on common ground, the SJC and the legislature embraced the argument that all parents had a common law duty to provide medical care for a child and that a parent's failure to act to relieve suffering or prevent death could be found to be wanton and reckless behavior leading to a charge of involuntary manslaughter. The legislature followed the court's lead by enacting a tough child abuse law that incorporated the wanton and reckless standard without a religious exemption and by separately repealing the spiritual treatment provision (sec. 1) that had been orphaned following a 1986 amendment, a change that arguably gave the spiritual treatment provision a broader application.

The successful campaign in Massachusetts to repeal the state's religious accommodation statutes ended the practice of allowing children to die unnecessarily in the name of religious freedom. Child advocacy groups hoped that victory would help strike down religious exemption statutes across the nation.

Conclusion: Religious Freedom and the Public Good

T HE STATE-BY-STATE BATTLE to repeal religious exemption laws waged by children's advocates continued into the twenty-first century, more than one hundred years after the first reported American case of a child dying because its religious parents withheld medical care and years after the "child cases" captured public attention. It was a struggle made more difficult by the erroneous assumption that the practices of religious groups necessarily coincided with the public good; by the claim of conservative legal scholars to have discovered historic roots for constitutionally mandated religious exemptions from laws that were neutral in their general application but were said to infringe on religious conduct; and by congressional passage in 1993 of the Religious Freedom Restoration Act (RFRA). The aim of RFRA was to override the U.S. Supreme Court's ruling in *Employment Division v. Smith* (1990), which held that an individual's religious beliefs did not excuse him or her from complying with a generally applicable, neutral law. The struggle did not end when the court swatted down RFRA in 1997. Congress reenacted a federal-law-only version of RFRA, more than a dozen states enacted laws similar to the RFRA, and all but a handful of states kept their existing religious exemption statutes on the books, demonstrating that a small, well-financed, cohesive religious group could successfully pursue its agenda despite the court's ruling.[1]

The unnecessary death in 2001 of a thirteen-year-old Colorado girl whose parents belonged to a church that believed illnesses and injuries should be treated exclusively with prayer rather than medical care highlighted once again the problem of defining the relationship between the state and religious groups that argue they have a constitutional right to be excused from obeying laws that other citizens are required to obey. Fearful that children's advocates in Colorado and elsewhere might succeed in repealing religious exemption statutes that gave license to this argument, the Christian Science Church joined other religious groups to wage a campaign for a constitutional amendment that would "restore protection for religious rights in America."[2]

On a handful of occasions between 1963 and 1990 the Supreme Court crossed the clear line it had drawn in *Reynolds v. U.S.* (1879) separating constitutional protection for religious belief from unprotected religious conduct. Adell Sherbert, a Seventh-day Adventist, was fired from her job in a South Carolina textile mill and denied unemployment compensation because she refused to work on Saturday, the Sabbath day of her faith. She claimed the state's ruling infringed on her First Amendment right to the free exercise of religion, an argument contrary to *Reynolds*. Justice William Brennan wrote for the majority in *Sherbert v. Verner* (1963), finding that the state had not offered a compelling state interest for denying Sherbert unemployment compensation and reversing the state court's decision affirming the unemployment commission's denial of benefits. "Our holding today," Brennan wrote, "is that South Carolina may not constitutionally apply the eligibility provisions so as to constrain a worker to abandon his religious convictions respecting the day of rest." In dissent, Justice John Marshall Harlan recoiled at the court's conclusion that a state "is constitutionally *compelled* to carve out an exception to its general rule of eligibility," and he predicted "disturbing implications for the future."[3]

Some legal scholars joined Harlan in criticizing the court's departure from one of its oldest constitutional principles. But in *Wisconsin v. Yoder* (1972) the court succumbed to nostalgia for an old-fashioned, simple lifestyle and applied a *Sherbert*-like analysis to rule that the state had failed to demonstrate a compelling interest as to why Amish children should be required to abide by Wisconsin's generally applicable, neutral school attendance law. The Amish argued that enforcement of Wisconsin's compulsory high school attendance law violated the parents' traditional liberty interest with respect to the upbringing of their children, as well as their rights under the First Amendment's free exercise clause, and endangered the group's ancient, deeply held religious commitment to a way of life emphasizing separation from worldly society (see chapter 1). Although the court stressed the historical uniqueness of the Amish, other religious groups, including Christian Scientists, also lay claim to a history linking belief and action, a "way of life," that they argued should be protected by the First Amendment.[4]

Prompted by that cluster of religious groups, conservative legal scholars strongly supported the Supreme Court's new interpretation of the free exercise clause permitting challenges to neutral, generally applicable laws impinging on religious conduct. In 1990, however, when the court returned to the *Reynolds* distinction in *Employment Division v. Smith*, conservatives exploded. Frederick M. Gedicks, a professor at Brigham Young University School of Law, grudgingly admitted that the court's earlier rulings had advanced a conservative religious agenda, but the *Smith* decision, he asserted, showed the court's true beliefs. "The mistake of religious conservatives," Gedicks wrote in the *Christian Science Monitor*, "has been their uncritical assumption that secular conservatives are consistently libertarian when it comes to religious free exercise." In fact, he stated, the "conservative bloc on the Supreme Court is statist with respect to religious freedom, meaning it rarely stands on the side of believers against the government." Religious freedom, Gedicks charged, "now exists at the sufferance of Congress and the state legislators," a situation he found intolerable.[5]

Michael McConnell of the University of Chicago Law School also criticized *Smith*. He claimed to have uncovered evidence suggesting that the framers of the Constitution substituted the phrase "free exercise" for "rights of conscience" in order to be certain the First Amendment protected religiously motivated conduct. Furthermore, he concluded that, read against the historical backdrop he had sketched out, the free exercise clause was intended to support constitutionally mandated religious exemptions. "The *Sherbert* decision," he wrote in what appeared to be a call to action, "created the potential for challenges by religious groups and individual believers to a wide range of laws that conflict with the tenets of their faith, because such laws impose penalties . . . for engaging in religious motivated conduct." Although conservative activists heaped praise on McConnell's argument, the law professor Philip A. Hamburger pointed out that McConnell had not cited a single instance in which a late eighteenth-century American had written that an individual's right to the free exercise of religion included a "general right of peaceable, religious exemption from civil laws."[6]

The conservative law professor Douglas Laycock brushed aside Hamburger's criticism and sought to bolster McConnell's general argument. Rather than merely crediting the influence of eighteenth-century American evangelicals for the view that religious conduct was an integral and protected feature of the free exercise clause, Laycock argued that the Reformation provided the Constitution's framers with "the most salient example of the evil to be avoided," namely, government "interfering in religious matters for reasons of state." Therefore, they sought to curb the state's power to regulate religious behavior. Much has changed since the Reformation, Laycock wrote, but a constant is that the "state punishes people for disapproved religious practices." Too many people today have misread this crucial piece of our history, he maintained, and don't realize that the state has been and still is responsible for much of the persecution of religious people. We have come a long way from the Reformation, Laycock acknowledged, but the state's "evil" role "has remained the same."[7]

This antistate ideology rooted in opposition to the court's *Smith* decision catapulted Laycock into the role of leader of a broad coalition responsible for drafting and winning passage of the RFRA in 1993. Testifying before Congress, Laycock convincingly argued that the court's decision in *Smith* was an aberration. He and a group of lawyers representing more than fifty religious and secular interest groups persuaded Congress that it was accepted free exercise doctrine to subject every law at every level of government to strict scrutiny. Specifically, government may not substantially burden a person's free exercise of religion even by enforcing a neutral, generally applicable law unless it demonstrated that "application of the burden" advanced "a compelling government interest" and was the "least restrictive means" of doing so.[8]

The law professor and historian Marci A. Hamilton rebutted Laycock's assertion. The "Supreme Court," she wrote, "had never even broached, let alone reached" the position that the free exercise clause required that every law be subjected to strict scrutiny. Rather, the court's *Smith* decision encourages religious groups "to go to the legislatures for relief from particular laws imposing particular burdens on religious practice" and there negotiate an exemption as long as it adheres to the "no harm" rule. Under RFRA "every law was to be subject to strict scrutiny, whether neutral and generally applicable or not," and free exercise trumped even criminal acts, including child abuse laws.[9]

The RFRA sailed through Congress. The House passed the measure by voice vote, and the Senate approved the bill 97–3. The *New York Times* uncritically applauded RFRA, joining the chorus of religious groups and civil libertarians who argued that the *Smith* decision "threw away decades of precedent and watered down the religious liberty of all Americans." By passing the RFRA, the *Times* concluded with a swipe at the court, "Congress asserts its own interest in protecting religious liberty, a welcome antidote to the official insensitivity to religion the Court spawned in 1990." On November 16,

1993, President Bill Clinton signed RFRA, hailing the new law as holding the government "to a very high level of proof before it interferes with someone's free exercise of religion."[10]

Four years later, in *City of Boerne v. Flores*, the Supreme Court struck down RFRA. Its decision turned on two fundamental points: Congress exaggerated its Fourteenth Amendment enforcement powers, and it violated the Constitution's separation of powers doctrine. Writing for the majority, Justice Anthony Kennedy acknowledged that Congress had broad powers under the Fourteenth Amendment's enforcement clause, the rationale for the legislation. However, Congress may only enforce, not define, a person's right to life, liberty, and property. After identifying unconstitutional behavior, Congress may propose a remedy commensurate with the violation, but RFRA "cannot be considered remedial or preventive legislation," Kennedy wrote, "if those terms have any meaning." No evidence was presented to Congress or to the court of a "pattern of religious discrimination in this country." The proponents of the RFRA had spoken only anecdotally of "incidental burdens." Justice Kennedy ended his opinion with a short history lesson. Our national experience, he wrote, "teaches that the Constitution is preserved best when each part of the government respects both the Constitution and the proper actions and determinations of the other branches." The courts "retain the power, as they have since *Marbury v. Madison*, to determine if Congress has exceeded its authority under the Constitution." In fact, the court found that Congress had overstepped its constitutional limits when it enacted RFRA and therefore ruled the act unconstitutional.[11]

Speaking in the same hyperbolic terms he had used before Congress and the Supreme Court, Laycock told a reporter that the *Boerne* ruling "unilaterally asserted the Court's power to contract our liberties and to deprive Congress of its power to protect those liberties." Hamilton, the counsel for the city of Boerne, fired back. "The high-pitched responses of many religious groups that we now face a grave danger that religious liberty will no longer be protected," she wrote, "is simply not so." RFRA sought "a radical shift in the constitutional standard to be applied to religious practice." The Constitution's framers were keenly aware that religion could be both "tyrannized and tyrannical," she wrote, and for that reason the Constitution separated church and state and the *Boerne* court ruled as it did.[12]

After the Supreme Court's holding that RFRA's requirement that all laws be subject to strict scrutiny was unconstitutional, the Christian Science Church joined a chorus of disappointed religious groups bemoaning the government's alleged war on religion. At the church's annual meeting in 1994, Virginia Harris, the chairman of the board of directors, charged the government with conducting an "unconstitutional" attack on the church. She gave as an example the Minnesota civil case stemming from the death of twelve-year-old Ian Lundman, whose Christian Science mother and stepfather, as we have seen, withheld medical care from the boy. A trial jury found Ian's mother and stepfather and the Christian Science Church jointly liable for the boy's death. It also awarded Doug Lundman, Ian's father, nine million dollars in punitive damages to be paid by the church. Harris implied that the "real motive" behind the Minnesota court's judgment was the government's effort to restrict religious freedom.[13]

The options considered by the church-led coalition included a constitutional amendment, pursuit of legal cases that could eventually reach the Supreme Court and result in the overturning of *Boerne,* fifty "mini-RFRAs," and a new federal law that met the Supreme Court's objections. Laycock proposed urging Congress to pass a law requiring a "high level of protection for religious observances as a condition of receiving federal money." Other lawyers propounded a narrowly written law tied to Congress's power to regulate interstate commerce.

In the end, the coalition chose to work state by state. Proponents of state RFRAs relied heavily on anecdotes to show how pervasive antireligious mischief had become since *Boerne* had crippled the RFRA. They told legislative committees about a Muslim firefighter who was forced to shave his beard, about a Jewish man who was required to take off his skullcap in a courtroom, and about dozens of churches that were denied building permits in commercial zones. This scattergun strategy succeeded in Connecticut, Florida, and Alabama, but by the time the Texas legislature took up the issue a chorus of critics—city officials, prosecutors, pediatricians, and private property advocates—were contending that the proposed law could blunt law enforcement's efforts to prosecute criminals and spur lawsuits by property owners. Pediatricians testified that "more parents could claim religious reasons for denying medical care for their children," and land-use advocates spoke about the chaos RFRA would cause with regard to zoning laws. The Pennsylvania legislature stripped a number of proposed exemptions from its version of RFRA, including mandatory reporting of child abuse. Children's advocates led successful opposition to state RFRAs in Maryland and California. To date, thirteen states have passed RFRA-like laws.[14]

In 2001, four years after the *Boerne* decision and two years into Bill Owens's first term as governor of Colorado, during which time he had witnessed the medically untreated deaths of four children, Owens seized the opportunity to push for repeal of the state's religious exemption law. Thirteen-year-old Amanda Bates died on February 5, 2001, of complications from medically untreated diabetes. Amanda was the second of Randy and Colleen Bates's twelve children to die without medical care, their son Gerald Bates having died at home at the age of three months in 1997. Randy, thirty-eight, and Colleen, thirty-six, were members of the General Assembly of the Church of the First Born. Since 1974 eleven other children of First Born parents had either died or were stillborn when medical treatment was withheld from them. Parents were convicted in only three cases. Of the approximately 25,000 members of the First Born church in the United States, about 285 families in six congregations lived in Colorado. The church bases its belief in faith healing on the book of James 5:15: "Is one of you ill? He should send for the elders of the congregation to pray over him and anoint him with oil in the name of the Lord. The prayer offered in faith will save the sick man, the Lord will raise him from his bed." If a sick person died, First Born members believed it was God's will. The dead were said to be asleep until Judgment Day, when they would awaken and join the Lord and their families in heaven.[15]

Amanda Bates died at a Denver hospital. She had been flown there after someone at the Bateses' home in western Colorado called 911 to report an unattended death. Paramedics arrived at the Bateses' small, brown house on a weed-filled lot strewn with rusted cars shortly after 8 a.m. Amanda was not breathing. The emergency technicians were able to revive her, and with artificial support she clung to life for several hours. The next day her body was returned to her hometown, where the coroner of Mesa County, Dr. Rob Kurtzman, performed an autopsy. He determined that Amanda's death had resulted from untreated diabetes and a massive infection that spread throughout her lower body and turned to gangrene. Her illness could have been easily recognized and treated, Kurtzman stated, and her life saved with the simplest medical intervention. Opening the door to the possible prosecution of Amanda's parents, he classified the girl's death as a homicide, ruling that she died as a direct result of the withholding of medical treatment. Kurtzman acknowledged, however, that existing Colorado law made a successful prosecution problematic.[16]

By coincidence two Colorado legislators had introduced a bill to eliminate the state's religious exemption provision just days before Amanda's death. The exemption stated that parents or guardians who withheld medical care on religious grounds could not be held liable for harm to a child as long as the faith-healing treatments used were recognized by the Internal Revenue Service and by major insurers. Only Christian Science treatments fit the law's criteria for exemption from a charge of child abuse, but Peter Weir, the executive director of the Colorado District Attorneys Council, stated that the exemption had "a chilling effect on prosecution" of all faith-healing groups. Governor Owens, state prosecutors, and child advocacy groups supported the newly introduced bill striking the exemption. The powerful lobby of the Christian Science Church opposed the proponents of equal protection for all children.[17]

The exemption had been reluctantly added to legislation sponsored by then–state senator Owens in 1989. Owens was attempting to tighten an earlier Colorado law that gave blanket immunity to parents who denied medical treatment on religious grounds unless the child was in imminent danger of dying. Colorado, like most other states, added a religious exemption provision to their child neglect and abuse statute because in 1974 HEW required states that sought federal funds for child abuse prevention programs to add an accommodation statute recognizing spiritual healing as legitimate care. The department dropped that regulation in 1983, but the state-initiated law stayed on the books. Six years later Owens tried to strike the exemption. The Christian Science Church successfully mobilized to retain an exemption in a form privileging Christian Scientists. To save the bill Owens agreed to add the exemption. "That was the price he had to pay to get it passed," Owens's spokesman said. Amanda's death in 2001 gave Owens, a rising Republican star whose election campaign emphasized family values, another opportunity to strike the exemption.[18]

Less than a week after Amanda's death, the *Denver Post,* Colorado's largest newspaper, and a cluster of vocal parents joined Governor Owens's campaign to repeal the Christian Science exemption. An editorial in the *Post* titled "Unholy Neglect" blasted people "who claim to be religious" and at the same time "watch the torturous deaths of their own offspring." Worse, the editorial went on, Colorado law permits this behavior if the child is receiving "a recognized method of religious healing." This "gaping hole, big enough for many children's caskets to slide through, is the law's failure to define that 'recognized method.'" Christian Scientists, not unexpectedly, opposed the legislature's effort to repeal the exemption. The *Post* cheered the reform: "It's high time the state send a strong, clear message that all children will be protected under the law."[19]

Chuck Green, a columnist for the *Post,* followed up his paper's editorial with an angry, commonsense argument. If you leave your child in a closed car on a hot day, Green pointed out, the child will die, and the parent will be charged with a criminal offense. If you leave you child home alone and the child is "trapped in a fire," that's a criminal offense. What's the difference, he asked, when Amanda's parents watched her die and offered only prayer? Colorado law is so murky there may be no penalty for the parents. Her parents were given a choice: "Unlock the doors and let your child breathe life, or withhold Amanda's diabetes medications and let her die. There's little difference, except in the eyes of the law—and in this case the law is an ass."[20]

Readers of the *Post* weighed in as the repeal bill moved through the legislature. "Our lawmakers are reportedly locked in a struggle over ending state tolerance for child abuse by faith healers," John Fleming wrote. "Faith healing is pure superstition." Freedom of religion, he went on, means no one should interfere with people's beliefs, "but it sure doesn't mean that proper medical care may be withheld." A Denver resident, Ted Kramer, applauded the legislators who stood for repeal and "against homicide of children by faith healers." Christian Scientists argue that spiritual healing is widely used, Kramer continued. "The fault is not in using spiritual healing, but using it at the exclusion of proven medical treatment." Freedom of religion includes a parent's right to make "life and death decisions such as Amanda Bates' family made," wrote Thomas B. Coberly, a member of the Christian Science Church. "The state must not second guess their religious faith."[21]

A committee of the Colorado House of Representatives heard testimony from both children's advocates and a Christian Science spokesman in the week before the House debate over the bill to repeal that section of the state's law allowing treatment by spiritual means. Kurtzman spoke first, telling the committee that Amanda Bates's slow death was so painful he couldn't bear to give lawmakers the details during public testimony. The former Christian Scientist and president of CHILD, Rita Swan, recounted the unnecessary death of her son Matthew and said, "Parents simply should not have the legal right to let children die regardless of their church's power." Robert Doughtie, a Christian Science practitioner, testified against the bill. There are "millions of people in this country and around the world," he told the legislators, "who practice spiritual healing. We're disappointed that society accepts only one possible solution to the healing of physical ills."[22]

The House of Representatives narrowly passed the repeal measure following an emotional debate in which religiously conservative Republicans and moderate Republicans lined up on opposite sides. The Republican Gayle

Berry told House members that in the days leading up to her death Amanda suffered from gangrene of the genitals and buttocks and swelling of the brain. "Her brain was swelling. It had no place to go but down the spinal cord," Berry said, causing some House members to gasp. The conservative Republican Shawn Mitchell brushed aside Berry's story as an attempt to sway people's emotions. The fact is, Mitchell declared, the bill violates the First Amendment's freedom of religion and would not stop parents who have a strong belief about faith healing. Besides, he added, parents whose children die under such circumstances are subject to prosecution. "It's great parents can be prosecuted," Berry shot back, "but the child is just as dead." Moderates in the House predicted that the Democratic-controlled Senate would also pass the bill and that Governor Owens would sign it into law.[23]

Two weeks after the House passed the repeal bill, Mesa County District Attorney Frank Daniels filed charges against Randy and Colleen Bates. They were arraigned for criminally negligent homicide, reckless manslaughter, reckless child abuse resulting in death, and criminally negligent child abuse resulting in death. Daniels acknowledged that although the current law contained a loophole exempting Christian Scientists, it "muddies the law and makes it difficult to prosecute any cases." Under current law, Daniels said, "Colorado has been endorsing a life-threatening practice. My hope is the law is changed."[24]

Just days after the trial court heard preliminary motions, the Senate health committee held a hearing on the repeal bill. Ruth Aponte, a lobbyist for the Colorado chapter of the American Academy of Pediatricians (AAP), was among those calling for passage of the bill removing the legal exemption that shielded parents from prosecution under the child abuse statutes when they failed to provide medical care for children. A Christian Science lobbyist shocked members of the committee by announcing that the church agreed with the proposed repeal. "We support removing religious accommodation," Tom Dennison, an attorney and member of the Christian Science Church told the senators. But there was a catch. The church intended to introduce an amendment that would eliminate "medical" care as the exclusive way to care for a sick child and replace it with "health" care, a word Christian Scientists believed would permit their brand of spiritual healing. "Parents should be able to choose how to care for their child as long as it's proper," Dennison stated. Jan Carey, a spokesperson for the Interfaith Alliance, saw the subterfuge: "We believe that martyring children because of the parents' belief systems is child abuse."[25]

As had happened in the House, moderate Republican senators bolted from their party line and declared they were voting to repeal the state provision exempting religious parents from providing medical care to their children. "I'm stepping back and looking at this as a dad," Sen. Ron Teck told his colleagues. "These kids who are dying shouldn't be dying. We've got to encourage these parents to take their children to the doctor." The Republican floor leader, Sen. John Andrews, and nine of his colleagues said the bill clashed with religious freedom and was not likely to be effective. The bill passed the Senate by a vote of 25–10. On April 17 Governor Owens signed into law the bill precluding the use of faith healing under the state's child abuse law when used in place of medicine for a child in danger in dying. Colorado thus became the sixth state to eliminate religious exemptions.[26]

A day after the legislature sent the bill to Governor Owens, Randy and Colleen Bates sat at the defendant's table in a Mesa County courtroom charged with being criminally liable for the death of their daughter Amanda. Members of the First Born Church sat in quiet support in the rear of the courtroom. Five months later, under the terms of a plea agreement, the couple acknowledged the likelihood of a conviction at trial but did not plead guilty. In November, Judge Amanda Bailey ordered the parents to each do thirteen hundred hours of community service, one hundred hours for each year of their daughter's life. She also ordered the Bateses to provide medical insurance for their remaining twelve children and to take them to a doctor whenever necessary.[27]

Neither the Bateses' conviction nor the half dozen others won earlier by prosecutors against Christian Science parents ended the long struggle between the church and state over medical neglect laws. Similarly, the Colorado legislature's repeal of its religious exemption provision meant that as of 2006 forty-four states still had laws exempting Christian Scientists who relied on spiritual healing from prosecution for child abuse. In short, the central question that had roiled the country in the 1980s and 1990s remained hotly contested: Do Christian Scientists have a right to exemption from a generally applicable, neutral law designed to protect children from harm because the law is said to impinge on their religious freedom? An analysis of the building blocks that influenced the framers of the Constitution and on which the U.S. Supreme Court built *Smith* and *Boerne* gives an unequivocal answer: Historical and legal evidence does not support the unfettered free exercise of religion.

When a child of Christian Science parents dies of a medically treatable illness for which the parents provided only spiritual treatment, they and their church routinely raise a defense based on the First Amendment right of free exercise of religion, even when manslaughter charges are brought. Such a strategy manifests the distinction between those parents who are held accountable to the generally applicable, neutral law prohibiting child abuse and those religious parents who are exempted from the law and therefore are not held accountable for the harm they inflict on their medically untreated ill child. This unconscionable division undermines the rule of law and violates the principle of do no harm. The distinction also implies that ill-informed legislators too often confuse religious liberty and license.[28]

The Founding Framers assimilated the no-harm rule, as articulated by the seventeenth-century English political philosopher John Locke. He argued for a robust right of religious conscience, but he also insisted that that right carried with it an obligation to abide by laws enacted to advance the public good. A religious believer who violated the law undermined the rule of law to which all citizens must adhere. Thomas Jefferson, as I noted in the introduction, echoed Locke: Freedom of belief and "free argument and debate" were essential human rights, but when those "principles break out into overt acts against peace and good order," it is the "rightful purpose of civil government, for its officers to interfere." Jefferson made the same point when he wrote to James Madison suggesting the need for "retouching" the Constitution but warning that rights, including freedom of religion, had the capacity to "do evil." Specifically, Jefferson wrote, "the declaration that religious faith shall be unpunished, does not give impunity to criminal acts" dictated by religious belief. The centuries-old rule of do no harm is at the heart of the rule the Supreme Court has spelled out in *Reynolds, Prince, Smith,* and *Boerne,* namely, religious groups are subject to generally applicable, neutral laws.[29]

Some specific religious-based exemptions, including oath taking in court and military service, had long been accommodated. And it's also true that all state constitutions had free exercise clauses and that all the states protected at least some religious conduct. However, writing for the majority in *Boerne,* Justice Antonin Scalia took aim at those who insisted that the court's *Smith* decision deviated from eighteenth-century commentators who allegedly advocated religious exemptions to general laws. First, he highlighted Locke's oft-cited definition of freedom as "the right to 'to do only what was not lawfully prohibited.'" Next, he marshaled a wealth of historical evidence to demonstrate convincingly that eighteenth-century state constitutions permitted the free exercise of religion only so long as it did not violate general laws governing conduct. In short, Scalia concluded, there was no historical or jurisprudential evidence to sustain the contemporary conservative argument that government was waging a war on religion or that "radical courts have attempted to gut our religious freedom."[30]

Historical evidence and the Supreme Court's major free exercise decisions make it manifest that the rule of law applies equally to religious groups and to all others. Christian Scientists, however, have argued that the law should not infringe on their religious conduct in regard to the spiritual treatment of children's serious illness unless the state can demonstrate a compelling interest. The law prohibiting child abuse rests on a compelling interest, namely, the state's centuries-old right to protect children. To declare that the withholding of medical care from a seriously ill child trumps the law prohibiting child abuse asks the public to believe that spiritual healing can do no harm. In fact, as we've seen, reliance on spiritual treatment alone has caused numerous children's deaths. Accommodating such religious conduct violates the no-harm rule and is inconsistent with the public good. When legislators succumb to Christian Science lobbyists who advocate a special religious interest or who privilege harmful religious conduct, they are guilty of undermining the very religious freedom they claim to be protecting.

Notes

Introduction

1. The Christian Science parents of three additional children who died from untreated illnesses were not prosecuted. Stephen Gottschalk, "Spiritual Healing on Trial: A Christian Scientist Reports," *Christian Century*, June 22–29, 1988, 602. *Freedom and Responsibility: Christian Science Healing for Children* (Boston: First Church of Christ, Scientist, 1989).

2. Comment, "Christian Science and Medical Practitioners," *Journal of the American Medical Association* 33 (1899): 1049; Rennie B. Schoepflin, *Christian Science on Trial: Religious Healing in America* (Baltimore: Johns Hopkins University Press, 2003), 183–89; *In re First Church of Christ, Scientist*, 205 Pa. 543, 551 (1903) the Pennsylvania Supreme Court affirmed a lower court decision denying a Christian Science Church a charter of incorporation because the church allowed "incompetent persons" to "attempt the cure and healing of disease." Catherine Cookson, *Regulating Religion: The Courts and the Free Exercise Clause* (New York: Oxford University Press, 2001) 150; "Death Due to Faith Cure," *New York Times*, June 24, 1899; "How Faith Curists Heal," *New York Times*, December 19, 1899; "Dean J. Osgood's Death Was Hastened by Christian Science Methods," *New York Times*, August 15, 1900; "Killed by Christian Science," *New York Times*, May 30, 1901; A. M. Bellwald, *Christian Science and the Catholic Faith* (New York: Macmillan, 1922) 9, 191.

3. Mary Baker Eddy, *Science and Health, with Key to the Scriptures* (Boston: First Church of Christ, Scientist, 1994), 167. Rodney Stark, "The Rise and Fall of Christian Science," *Journal of Contemporary Religion* 13 (1998): 210–11.

4. Stark, "Rise and Fall of Christian Science," 209; Vincent DeFrancis and Carroll L. Lucht, *Child Abuse Legislation in the 1970s* (Denver: American Humane Association Children's Division, 1974), as quoted in Lynne Curry, *The DeShaney Case: Child Abuse, Family Rights, and the Dilemma of State Intervention* (Lawrence: University Press of Kansas, 2007), 55–56.

5. The National Academy of Sciences, *Understanding Child Abuse and Neglect*, 1995, 78, www.nap.edu; Vincent De Francis, *Child Protective Services in the United States: Reporting a National Survey* (Denver: Children's Division, American Humane Association, 1956), as quoted in John E. B. Myers, "A Short History of Child Protection in America," *Family Law Quarterly* 42 (Fall 2008): 454–61. Three of the Christian Science couples in this book divorced: Laurie Walker in 1981, Kathy and Doug Lundman in 1984, and Mark and Susan Rippberger in 1996.

6. *Walker v. Superior Court*, 47 al. 3d 112 (1988); *State of Minnesota v. McKowan*, 475 N.W. 2d 63 (1991); *Hermansons v. State of Florida*, 604 So. 2d 775 (1992). See also chapter 6, "Repeal of Religious Exemptions."

7. The Christian Science Church was not alone in its opposition to perceived state interfer-

ence with religion. From roughly 1962 to 1997 a majority of American religious groups united in accusing the U.S. Supreme Court of waging war against religious freedom. *Engel v. Vitale,* 370 U.S. 421 (1962); *Abington School District v. Schempp,* 374 U.S. 203 (1963); Josephine Ripley, "High Court Ruling on School Prayer Finds U.S. Ready," *Christian Science Monitor,* June 18, 1963. Stephen L. Carter, *The Culture of Disbelief: How American Law and Politics Trivialize Religious Devotion* (New York: Anchor Books, 1993). Marci A. Hamilton, *God vs. the Gavel: Religion and the Rule of Law* (New York: Cambridge University Press, 2005), 6. For repeal, see generally chapter 6.

8. Edward Dolnick, "Murder by Faith," *In Health,* January/February 1990, 62–63. Kevin Delaney, "We Thought Our Faith Could Save Our Son," *Redbook,* January 1987, 105–6. John Carroll Lathrop, a Christian Science practitioner, defined his work, in "Christian Scientist Held for Manslaughter," *New York Times,* October 24, 1902.

9. The Supreme Court of Michigan granted an appeal, *The Rev. Ralph Brown, Personal Representative of the Estate of Matthew Swan, Deceased v. Jeanne Laitner, June Ahern and the First Church of Christ, Scientist,* 432 Mich. 855 (1988) and then denied the appeal, Judge Charles L. Levin dissenting, *Brown v. Laitner,* 432 Mich. 861 (1989). www.childrenshealthcare.org.

10. Associated Press, "Christian Scientists Convicted in Daughter's Death," *Miami Herald,* April 19, 1989; Nathan Talbot, "The Position of the Christian Science Church," *New England Journal of Medicine* 309 (1983): 1641–44; Eddy, *Science and Health,* 14–16, 468.

11. Eddy, *Science and Health,* x; Rennie B. Schoepflin, "Christian Science Healing," in *Other Healers: Unorthodox Medicine in America,* ed. Norman Gevitz, 193–96 (Baltimore: Johns Hopkins University Press, 1988). Eddy, *Science and Health,* 110, 146, 168, 108. There is a huge and contentious literature about how much of Eddy's Christian Science was original. For a brief analysis, see R. Laurence Moore, "The Occult Connection: Mormonism, Christian Science, and Spiritualism," in *The Occult in America: New Historical Perspectives,* ed. Howard Kerr and Charles Crow, 145–47 (Urbana: University of Illinois Press, 1983).

12. Alfie Kohn, "Mind Over Matter," *New England Monthly* (March 1988): 60; Stark, "Rise and Fall of Christian Science," 200, 204; Mary Baker Eddy, *Manual of the Mother Church* (Boston: First Church of Christ, Scientist, 1895), 25–26, 30, 33.

13. Paul Starr, *The Social Transformation of American Medicine* (New York: Basic Books, 1982), 105–6; Eddy, *Science and Health,* 161; For a contemporary response to Eddy's argument, see W. A. Purrington, "Eddyism before the Law," *Albany Law Journal* 62 (1900–1901): 358–62.

14. Eddy, *Science and Health,* 167.

15. Schoepflin, *Christian Science on Trial,* 146–50. The U.S. Supreme Court affirmed the state's use of its police power to establish criteria for a medical license in *Dent v. West Virginia,* 129 U.S. 114 (1889).

16. *Prince v. Massachusetts,* 321 U.S. 158, 170 (1944).

17. *Regina v. Wagstaff,* 10 Cox C.C. 530 (1868). Shawn Francis Peters, *When Prayer Fails: Faith Healing, Children and the Law* (New York: Oxford University Press, 2008), 53–61.

18. *Regina v. Senior,* 1 Q.B. Div. 283, 19 Cox C.C. 219 (1899). C. C. Cawley, "Criminal Liability in Faith Healing," *Minnesota Law Review* 39 (1954–55): 30, 54–55.

19. Cawley, "Criminal Liability in Faith Healing," 55–56; Peters, *When Prayer Fails,* 58.

20. Sec. 289 New York Penal Code as cited in *People v. Pierson,* 176 N.Y. 201, 209 (1903).

21. *People v. Pierson,* 176 N.Y. 201, 210–12; John Alexander Dowie, an Australian who preached that the devil caused disease, moved his ministry to Chicago in 1890 and founded the Christian Catholic Church there; Peters, *When Prayer Fails,* 71–73; Haight did not cite *Reynolds v. U.S.,* 98 U.S. 245 (1879), but he did cite *Regina v. Senior,* 1 Q.B. 283.

22. Schoepflin, *Christian Science on Trial,* 190. "Topics of the Times: Christian Science in Action," *New York Times,* May 6, 1920. Curry, *The DeShaney Case,* 46, 50–52.

23. C. Henry Kempe, Frederic N. Silverman, Brandt F. Steele, William Droegemuller, and Henry K. Silver, "The Battered Child Syndrome," *Journal of the American Medical Association* 181 (1962): 17–24. See also Ray E. Helfer and Ruth Kempe, *The Battered Child* (Chicago:

University of Chicago Press, 1968); Barbara J. Nelson, *Making an Issue of Child Abuse: Political Agenda Setting for Social Problems* (Chicago: University of Chicago Press, 1984), 2–3, 63; Curry, *The DeShaney Case*, 53, 56; Robert M. Press, "New Allies Fight Child Abuse: Federal Funds, Better Reporting, *Christian Science Monitor*, February 14, 1974. CAPTA 42 U.S.C. sec. 5101 (1982; Sup. 1987). 45 C.F.R. 1340. 1–2 (b)(1).

24. 45 C.F.R. 1340. 1–2(b)(1). Eric W. Treene, "Note: Prayer-Treatment Exceptions to Child Abuse and Neglect Statutes, Manslaughter Prosecutions, and Due Process of Law," *Harvard Journal of Legislation* 30 (1993): 143–45. Christine A. Clark, "Religious Accommodation and Criminal Liability," *Florida State University Law Review* 17 (1990): 559, 560n5.

25. The church reported 268,915 members in 1936, whereas in 1990 members may have numbered no more than 106,000, Stark, "Rise and Fall of Christian Science," 191–92. Kohn, "Mind Over Matter," 96; Mark Larabee, "One Denomination Labors Tirelessly," *Oregonian*, November 30, 1998.

26. *Reynolds v. U.S.*, 98 U.S. 145, 164.

27. Hamilton, *God vs. the Gavel*, 207–8, quoting John Locke, *Two Treatises of Government* sec. 6; *Reynolds v. U.S.*, 98 U.S. 145, 164; Richard A. Epstein, "The Harm Principle—And How It Grew," *University of Toronto Law Journal* 45 (1995): 369, 371, 417.

28. *Reynolds v. U.S.*, 98 U.S. 145; *Cantwell v. Connecticut*, 310 U.S. 296 (1940); *Prince v. Massachusetts*, 321 U.S. 158.

29. *Sherbert v. Verner*, 374 U.S. 398 (1963); *Wisconsin v. Yoder*, 406 U.S. 205 (1972).

30. Curtis J. Sitomer, "Healing and Free Exercise of Religion," *Christian Science Monitor*, May 28, 1991; Douglas's dissent, in Yoder, 406 U.S. 205, 241, 245.

31. David N. Williams, "Christian Science and the Care of Children: The Constitutional Issues," *Freedom and Responsibility: Christian Science Healing for Children* (Boston: First Church of Christ, Scientist, 1989), 66–68, 70.

32. *Employment Division v. Smith*, 494 U.S. 872, 885 (1990), quoting *Lyng v. Northwest Indian Cemetery Protective Association*, 485 U.S. 439, 451 (1988); *Employment Division v. Smith*, 494 U.S. 872, 878–79; *Reynolds v. U.S.*, 98 U.S. 145, 166–67.

33. Howard Varinsky, Jury and Trial Consultant, Report of a Survey of 400 jury-eligible adults, in Arizona Superior Court, *Maricopa County v. John and Catherine King*, December 1988, vol. 3, Exhibit D; *Walker v. California Superior Court*, 47 Cal. 3d 112, 140 (1988); William Carlsen, "Christian Science Case: A Ruling on Religious Freedom," *San Francisco Chronicle*, November 11, 1988; Nat Hentoff, "The Death of a Christian Science Child," *Washington Post*, December 3, 1988.

34. Christian Scientists distinguish their demonstrative prayer from the intercessory prayer made by other religions. A large scientific study of intercessory prayer offered by strangers found it had no effect on the recovery of heart patients. Benedict Carey, "Long-Awaited Medical Study Questions the Power of Prayer," *New York Times*, March 31, 2006.

1. Amy Hermanson

1. Christine Evans, "Was Ill Child's Death A Murder? Sarasota Trial Tests Law That Guards Parents' Religious Rights," *Miami Herald*, April 10, 1989, and Edward Dolnick, "Murder by Faith," *Washington Post*, September 25, 1990, provide details about the employee and family meetings; Chris Hermanson's remark to her friend, Jeffrey Good, "Dead Girl's Parents Had Medical Care, Neighbor Testifies," *St. Petersburg Times*, April 14, 1989; Jeffrey Good, "Dying for Their Beliefs, Christian Science Parents on Trial in Girl's Death," *St. Petersburg Times*, April 9, 1989; *William Hermanson and Christine Hermanson v. State of Florida*, Court of Appeal of Florida, Second District, 570 So. 2d 322, 324 (1990).

2. Good, "Dying for Their Beliefs," for teachers' and Perino's remarks about Amy's health. June R. McHugh, the director of Rohr Academy, is quoted in the same article as saying to Christine Hermanson that her daughter seemed to be suffering from "a physical ailment";

Christine said the "situation was being handled." Gary Christman, a storeowner next to Hermanson's music academy, said he noticed dramatic changes in Amy's appearance four to six weeks before her death. *William Hermanson and Christine Hermanson v. State of Florida,* 604 So. 2d 775, 777–78 (1992), Discretionary Review of Decision of the District Court of Appeal of Florida, Second District, Brief of Respondent, 17–18.

3. Rennie B. Schoepflin, "Christian Science Healing," in *Other Healers: Unorthodox Medicine in America,* ed. Norman Gevitz, 201–2 (Baltimore: Johns Hopkins University Press, 1988). The Massachusetts Metaphysical College, dedicated to training Christian Science practitioners, was chartered in 1881.

4. Mary Baker Eddy, *Science and Health, with Key to the Scriptures* (Boston: First Church of Christ, Scientist, 1971), 412, 417, 157; Robert Peel, *Spiritual Healing in a Scientific Age* (New York: Harper and Row, 1987).

5. *Hermanson v. State,* Court of Appeal of Florida, 570 So. 2d 322, 326.

6. William James, *The Varieties of Religious Experience: A Study in Human Nature* (New York: Penguin Books, 1985), 107, quoted the aphorisms of the mind cure movement to highlight its message of agency: "Pessimism leads to weakness. Optimism leads to power"; Schoepflin, "Christian Science Healing," 193–94. Later in life Eddy attacked mesmerism and "bath, diet, exercise, air" as anti-Christian, Catherine L. Albanese, *A Republic of the Mind and Spirit: A Cultural History of American Metaphysical Religion* (New Haven: Yale University Press, 2007), 293.

7. Anne Harrington, *The Cure Within: A History of Mind-Body Medicine* (New York: W. W. Norton, 2008), 112–14. Christian Science's fundamental texts are the Bible and *Science and Health.*

8. Eddy, *Science and Health,* 482–83; Peel, *Spiritual Healing,* 47–50, 54–100; Stephen Gottschalk, "Spiritual Healing on Trial: A Christian Scientist Reports," *Christian Century,* June 22–29, 1988, 602. Christian Science requires a physician at childbirth and permits a physician to set broken bones, administer an anesthetic for severe pain, and allows dental care and "mechanical" aids such as eyeglasses. Richard A. Hughes, "The Death of Children by Faith-Based Medical Neglect," *Journal of Law and Religion* 20 (2004–5): 247, 248 n10.

9. Hughes, "Death of Children," 327; Evans, "Was Ill Child's Death a Murder?"; *Hermanson v. State,* Supreme Court of Florida 604 So. 2d 775, 778–79.

10. The court erroneously credited Sellers with completing a "three and one-half year training course" and compared her duties with those "performed by a licensed practical nurse." A licensed practical nurse is required to take courses in biology, physiology, and chemistry and to pass an exam administered by the state board of nursing. None of these prerequisites apply to Christian Science nurses. *Hermanson v. State,* Court of Appeal of Florida, 570 So. 322, 327; Evans, "Was Ill Child's Death a Murder?"

11. Associated Press, "Diabetic Girl, 7, Dies Untreated," *Miami Herald,* November 14, 1986; Associated Press, "Christian Scientists Face Murder Charge in Diabetes Death of Daughter," November 13, 1986. Before Amy's death Bill had planned to become a practitioner; *Hermanson v. State,* Court of Appeal of Florida, 570 So. 2d 322, 325–26; "Bill Hermanson," www.linkedin.com.

12. Associated Press, "Diabetic Girl, 7, Dies Untreated."

13. Nelson, *Making an Issue of Child* Abuse, 42–43 (rediscovery), 99–101 (Biaggi and Mondale), 112–17 (CAPTA bill passes and Nixon signs it).

14. 42 U.S.C. sec.5101 (1982 & Supp. 1987); 45 C.F.R. 1340.1–2(b)(1). Fla. Stat. 415.503(7)(f) (1975); Fla. Stat. Ann. secs. 39.01(30)(b), (45,) 984.03(37). CAPTA was amended and reauthorized several times. The 1978 act did not include a spiritual healing exemption, but HEW included a religious exemption in the regulations issued with the reauthorization. In 1983 the Department of Health and Human Services (HHS) issued new regulations that read as follows: "States are free to recognize or not to recognize a religious exemption without that choice having any effect on eligibility for a state child abuse grant." 48 Fed. Reg. 3697–3700

(1983). A 1996 amendment specified that nothing in the act could be construed as establishing a federal requirement that a parent provide medical care that is contrary to the religious beliefs of the parent. 42 U.S.C. sec. 5106i; Rita Swan to Judge Vaughn R. Walker, November 19, 1992 (Kenneth Casanova, Boston, personal papers, photocopies in author's possession), in which Swan points out that "religious exemptions discourage reporting" (Casanova Papers); in Rita Swan to Bev Schroeder, March 12, 1994 (Casanova Papers), Swan asked Sen. Tom Harkin to block the attempt of the Christian Science Church to stop HHS from requiring states to change their religious exemption statutes.

15. Charles E. Anderson, "When Faith Healing Fails," *ABA Journal*, July 1989, 22; for the spiritual treatment proviso, Section 415.503 (7) (f) Flr. Statutes 1985. The statute was originally passed in 1975 and moved to a different statutory section in 1985; *Wisconsin v. Yoder*, 406 U.S. 205 (1972).

16. Whitaker's argument rested on Section 827.04 (1)–(2) Flr. Statutes 1985 defining felony child abuse and Section 782.04 (4) Flr. Statutes 1985 stipulating that the "killing of a human being while engaged in the commission of child abuse constitutes murder in the third degree." United Press International, "Parents: We Can't Be Charged, Religious Freedom an Issue in Death," *Miami Herald*, April 19, 1988.

17. *Hermanson v. State*, Court of Appeal of Florida, 570 So. 2d 322, 325, 327–28; the Court of Appeal disagreed with Dakan's ruling and dismissed the charge of manslaughter, ibid., 328; Thomas C. Tobin, "Christian Scientist Parents to Be Tried in Child's Death," *St. Petersburg Times*, June 18, 1988.

18. *Hermanson v. Circuit Court of the Twelfth Judicial Circuit*, Supreme Court of Florida, 537 So. 2d 569. (November 30, 1988); Hermanson v. Circuit Court of Twelfth Judicial Circuit, Court of Appeal of Florida, Second District, 536 So. 2d 248 (December 1, 1988); Justice Kennedy's ruling, Jay Pitts, "Trial of Christian Science Couple Delayed," *St. Petersburg Times*, December 6, 1988.

19. Jeffrey Good, "Jury Choice Difficult in Parents' Trial," *St. Petersburg Times*, April 11, 1989; Jeffrey Good, "Case Is about Abuse, Not Belief, State Says," *St. Petersburg Times*, April 13, 1989; Deborah Sharp, "Beliefs Lead to Charges: Florida Says Girl's Death Was Murder," *USA Today*, April 12, 1989.

20. Good, "Case Is about Abuse."

21. Ena Naunton, "When Spiritual Healing Fails the Body," *Miami Herald*, April 14, 1989.

22. Ibid.

23. Rita Swan, "Matthew, You Cannot Be Sick," *Dublin Review* 37 (Winter 2009–10), www.dublinreview. Swan wrote this essay two years after her son's death, but it wasn't published until 2009; Lori Miller Kase, "Swan's Way: One Woman's Crusade against Spiritual Healing," *American Health*, July–August, 1992, 16–18; Roger Rosenblatt, "A Woman at Christmas," *Life Magazine*, December 1990; Mark Larabee, "Parents Turn Grief into a Mission: Change the Law," *Oregonian*, November 28, 1998; Dolnick, "Murder by Faith."

24. Larabee, "Parents Turn Grief into a Mission: Change the Law"; Rosenblatt, "A Woman at Christmas."

25. Kase, "Swan's Way," 16; Associated Press, "Christian Scientists Convicted in Daughter's Death," *Miami Herald*, April 19, 1989.

26. Caroline Fraser, "Suffering Children and the Christian Science Church," Atlantic Online, April 1995, www.theatlantic.com; *New England Monthly*, March 1998, www.alfiecohn.org; www.community.seattletimes.newsource.com, June 10, 1990; Dolnick, "Murder by Faith"; Associated Press, "Christian Scientists Convicted in Daughter's Death."

27. *Hermanson v. State*, Court of Appeal of Florida, 570 So. 2d 322, 326; *Hermanson v. State*, Supreme Court of Florida, 604 So. 2d 775, 779 (1992).

28. Good, "Dead Girl's Parents Had Medical Care"; Associated Press, "On Trial State Rests in Christian Science Case," *Miami Herald*, April 15, 1989.

29. Good, "Dead Girl's Parents Had Medical Care."

30. Associated Press, "On Trial State Rests in Christian Science Case"; Dolnick, "Murder by Faith."

31. Associated Press, "On Trial State Rests in Christian Science Case"; Jeffrey Good, "Evidence Rejected in Parents' Trial," *St. Petersburg Times,* April 15, 1989.

32. Jeffrey Good, "Defense Rests Case in Silence: Parents Don't Discuss Denying Medical Help," *St. Petersburg Times,* April 18, 1989.

33. Associated Press, "Christian Scientists Convicted in Daughter's Death"; New York Times Regional Newspapers, "Religion Rejected as Murder Defense," *New York Times,* April 20, 1989; Jeffrey Good, "Christian Scientists Guilty in Girl's Death: Parents Relied on Prayer, Not Medicine," *St. Petersburg Times,* April 19, 1989.

34. Hermanson v. State of Florida, Discretionary Review of Decision of the District Court of Appeal of Florida, Second District, Brief of Respondent, Robert Butterworth, Attorney General, 15.

35. Good, "Christian Scientists Guilty in Girl's Death"; Jeanne Pugh, "The Christian Scientists' Prescription: Basic to Healing for Christian Scientists Is Faith in Becoming One with the Mind That Is God," *St. Petersburg Times,* April 19, and May 6, 1989.

36. Good, "Christian Scientists Guilty in Girl's Death"; Anderson, "When Faith Healing Fails," 22.

37. Associated Press, "Christian Scientist Has Compassion for Jurors," *Miami Herald,* April 21, 1989.

38. Staff, "Dead Child vs. the Law," *Miami Herald,* April 21, 1989; Editorial, "A Child's Right to Live," *St. Petersburg Times,* April 20, 1989; City Edition, "A Trial's Aftermath: Framers Say Law Shouldn't Cover Deaths," *St. Petersburg Times,* April 21, 1989.

39. Jeffrey Good, "Parents Convicted of Child's Death Go Free," *St. Petersburg Times,* July 1, 1989. Good reported that Christian Scientists in Florida had contributed "more than $250,000" to the Hermansons' legal defense fund. Judge Dakan denied the Hermansons' motion to defer their probation pending their appeal's outcome, Dail Willis, "Couple Must Give Children Medical Care," *St. Petersburg Times,* September 1, 1989.

40. *Hermanson v. State,* Court of Appeal of Florida, 570 So. 2d 322 (1990), 325. The spiritual treatment proviso, section 415.503 (7) (f) Flr. Statutes 1985. The appeal court ruled that Judge Dakan's reliance on *Bradley v. State,* 79 Fla. 651 (1920), as a basis for dismissing the Hermansons' manslaughter charge was erroneous because of the many changes in child abuse laws since *Bradley.* Ibid., 328n3.

41. *Hermanson v. State,* Court of Appeal of Florida, 570 So. 2d 325.

42. Ibid., 329, 330–31.

43. Ibid., 331.

44. *Reynolds v. U.S.* 98 U.S. 145 (1879); Sarah Berringer Gordon, *The Mormon Question: Polygamy and Constitutional Conflict in Nineteenth-Century America* (Chapel Hill: University of North Carolina Press, 2002).

45. *Reynolds v. U.S.* 98 U.S. 145, 162, 164, 167; *Davis v. Beason,* 133 U.S. 333 (1889).

46. *Davis v. Beason,* 133 U.S. 333; Marci Hamilton, *God vs. the Gavel: Religion and the Rule of Law* (New York: Cambridge University Press, 2005), traces Jefferson's argument for a "no harm" principle to John Locke's *A Letter Concerning Toleration* and *Two Treatises of Government,* 207–8.

47. *Prince v. Massachusetts,* 321 U.S. 158, 163 (1944).

48. Ibid., 164–67; *Meyer v. Nebraska,* 262 U.S. 390 (1923); *Pierce v. Society of Sisters,* 268 U.S. 510 (1925).

49. *Prince v. Massachusetts,* 321 U.S. 158, 168, 170. Justice Jackson's dissent argued that the state had failed to prove the child's well-being was endangered by her religiously motivated street work. He also maintained Simmons was engaged in "genuine religious, rather than commercial activity," 171.

50. Hamilton, *God vs. the Gavel,* 212.

51. *Sherbert v. Verner*, 374 U.S. 398, 400, 404, 406, 407 (1963).

52. Shawn Francis Peters, *The Yoder Case: Religious Freedom, Education, and Parental Rights* (Lawrence: University Press of Kansas, 2003), 1–4.

53. *Wisconsin v. Yoder*, 406 U.S. 205, 207, 210, 211.

54. Ibid., 220, 230.

55. David N. Williams, "Christian Science and the Care of Children: The Constitutional Issues," *Church and State*, September 1989, 69–71. In State of Arizona v. John King and Catherine King, State's Response to Defendants' Motion for Reconsideration, April 14, 1989, vol. 6, 18, the prosecution argued it was not settled law that *Yoder* applied to criminal prosecution.

56. *Employment Division v. Smith*, 494 U.S. 872, 878–79 (1990).

57. *Hermanson v. State*, Court of Appeal of Florida, 570 So. 2d, 322, 332;; *Nash v. United States*, 229 U.S. 373, 377 (1913).

58. Ibid., 336–37.

59. Ibid., 337. *William Hermanson and Christine Hermanson v. State of Florida*, Court of Appeal of Florida, Second District, 1990 Fla. App. LEXIS 8891 (1990).

60. *Hermanson v. State*, Supreme Court of Florida, 604 So. 2d 775, 780–81, 782; *United States v. Cardiff*, 344 U.S. 174 (1952); *Linville v. State*, 359 So. 2d 450 (Fla. 1978); Chad M. Oldfather, "Appellate Courts, Historical Facts, and the Civil–Criminal Distinction," *Vanderbilt Law Review* 57 (2004): 437, 455–56, distinguishes a trial court proceeding from an appellant court by noting, "Written text triggers a different process than oral language, one that is considerably more amenable to logic and abstraction."

61. Karen Branch, "Court Overturns Parents' Convictions In Girl's Death," *Miami Herald*, July 3, 1992; Jennifer L. Stevenson, "Freedom of Religion? It Has Always Fostered Questions," *St. Petersburg Times*, December 1, 1991.

2. Shauntay Walker, Seth Glaser, and Natalie Rippberger

1. Meningitis is an "inflammation of the meninges, the membranes surrounding the brain and spinal column. The infection may be viral or bacterial; bacterial meningitis is generally far more serious and life threatening than viral meningitis, but bacterial meningitis is treatable with antibiotics. The infection of the meningitis surrounding the brain and spinal column leads to inflammation and swelling of the brain, and resulting pressure against the cranium and damage to the brain itself. Adult patients report that the disease is an 'excruciating illness," *People v. Rippberger*, 231 Cal. App. 3d 1667, 1677 (1991); Jane Brody, a health columnist, reports that bacteria meningitis strikes 1 person in 100,000 in the United States each year, "Lowering the Risk of Bacterial Meningitis," *New York Times*, September 4, 2001; Moshe Arditi et al., "Three-Year Multi-center Surveillance of Pneumococcal Meningitis in Children," *Pediatrics* 102 (November 1998): 1087–97, reports that 14 (7.7 percent) of 180 medically treated children died from the disease.

2. *California Penal Code* (1st ed., 1872), section 270; *California Statutes 1925*, chapter 325, section 1, 544; *California Statutes 1976*, chapter 673, section 1, 1661; *Walker v. Superior Court*, 47 Cal. 3d 112 (1988). The 1976 amendment breezed through the California legislature by votes of 59–0 in the Assembly and 28–1 in the Senate. Gov. Jerry Brown signed the measure into law, *Sacramento Bee*, August 18, 1985; in the 1970s states were required to enact an exemption statute to qualify for federal child abuse funds. 42 U.S.C. sec. 5101 (1982 and Supp. 1987).

3. Herb Michelson, "Prayer Healing—When Is It Legal? Laws Bounced Back and Forth," *Sacramento Bee*, August 18, 1985.

4. *Walker v. Superior Court*, 47 Cal. 3d 112, 127, 128, 128n7.

5. Mary Baker Eddy, *Science and Health, with Key to the Scriptures* (Boston: First Church of Christ, Scientist, 1971), 482–83; DeWitt John, *The Christian Science Way of Life* (Englewood Cliffs, N.J.: Prentice Hall, 1962), 18.

6. Janna C. Merrick, "Christian Science Healing of Minor Children: Spiritual Exemption

Statutes, First Amendment Rights, and Fair Notice," *Issues in Law and Medicine* 10 (December 1994): 321–42; William Franklin Simpson, "Comparative Longevity in a College Cohort of Christian Scientists," *Journal of the American Medical Association* 262 (September 1989): 1657–58; Simpson's study compared the graduating classes from Principia College, a Christian Science institution, and those of the College of Liberal Arts, University of Kansas, from 1934 to 1983 and concluded that the graduates of Principia College had "a significantly higher death rate than the control population," 1657; Rita Swan, "When Faith Fails Children," *Humanist*, November 2000, www.thehumanist.org.

7. Eddy, *Science and Health*, 412, 468, 9–15.

8. California juvenile court proceedings and records are closed to the public. www .co.dakota.mn.us. I have relied on *In re Eric B.*, 189 Cal. App. 3d 996 (1987).

9. *In re Eric B.*, 189 Cal. 3d 996. In its petition to the court the Office of Child Abuse cited California Welfare and Institutions Code section 300 (a): "Any person under the age of 18 years who comes within any of the following descriptions is within the jurisdiction of the juvenile court which may adjudge that person to be a dependent child of the court: (a) Who is in need of proper and effective parental care or control and has no parent or guardian, or has no parent or guardian willing to exercise or capable of exercising care or control, or has no parent, guardian or custodian actually exercising care or control." The Contra Costa Juvenile Court assumed jurisdiction over Eric and in August 1984 continued his status as a dependent child.

10. *In re Eric B.*, 189 Cal. App. 3d 996, 1001, 1002.

11. Ibid., 1004–6.

12. Ibid., 1006–7.

13. Martha Shirk, "Christian Science Practitioner Expelled," *St. Louis Post Dispatch*, November 3, 1993.

14. Martin Halstuk, "Religious Freedom Collides with Medical Care," *San Francisco Chronicle*, April 25, 1988; Walker v. Superior Court, Petition to the Supreme Court of the United States for Writ of Certiorari, Response in Opposition, 4–5. *Sacramento Bee*, March 21, 22, 1984. Walker's father, Lawrence Stutsman, praised Laurie's "strong will" and hoped she "won't have to stand trial"; she isn't a "danger to anyone else," he said. *San Francisco Chronicle*, April 25, 1988.

15. Bee Metro Staff, "Woman Surrenders in Death of Daughter," *Sacramento Bee*, March 23, 1984; Denny Walsh, "Mother's Conviction Thrown Out: Judges Rules Spiritual Healing Laws Contrary to Fair Trial," *Sacramento Bee*, January 4, 1997; Rita Swan, "Christian Science Mom Convicted of Manslaughter," *Children's Healthcare Is a Legal Duty*, no. 2 (1990): 7; child endangerment, California Penal Code section 273a and California Penal Code section 192 (b) define involuntary manslaughter. *Walker v. Superior Court*, 47 Cal. 3d 112, 118–20.

16. Wayne Wilson, "Trial for Mother Ordered in Girl's Meningitis Death," *Sacramento Bee*, September 29, 1984.

17. United Press International, "Prayer Fails to Cure Child, Parents May Be Charged," *Santa Monica Evening Outlook*, March 30, 1984; Rita Swan, "California Judge Acquits Christian Science Couple," *Children's Healthcare Is a Legal Duty*, no. 1 (1990): 16–17.

18. Richard J. Brenneman, *Deadly Blessings: Faith Healing on Trial* (Buffalo: Prometheus Books, 1990), 36, 39–40, 51, 56, 64, 65–66; Brenneman, a self-described "former Christian Scientist" and journalist, gained access to the investigative notes of the Santa Monica police. Eddy, *Science and Health*, 42, 44; Jesus's resurrection, Eddy writes, was scientific proof that God is life, and life is deathless.

19. Associated Press, "Practitioner, Couple Indicted in Tot's Death," *Santa Monica Evening Outlook*, June 22, 1984.

20. Associated Press, "Christian Science Couple Ordered to Stand Trial in Son's Death," *Santa Monica Evening Outlook*, February 28, 1985; Swan, *Children's Healthcare Is a Legal Duty*, no. 1 (1990): 18.

21. Associated Press, "Christian Science Couple Arraigned on Murder Charges in Their Son's Death," *Santa Monica Evening Outlook*, March 13, 1985.

22. *People v. Rippberger*, 231 Cal. App. 3d 1667, 1674–75; Rita Swan, "Christian Scientists Guilty in Daughter's Death," *Children's Healthcare Is a Legal Duty*, no. 3 (1989): 1–12.

23. George Snyder, "Parents Face Charges in Death of Infant," *San Francisco Chronicle*, March 14, 1985.

24. Ibid.

25. George Snyder, "Touchy Christian Science Case Begins," *San Francisco Chronicle*, May 31, 1985; George Snyder, "Christian Science Parents on Trial in Child's Death," *San Francisco Chronicle*, July 13, 1985; Rita Swan, "Christian Science Parents Withdraw Appeal of Conviction," *Children's Healthcare Is a Legal Duty*, no. 4 (1991): 7, identifies Mackenroth as a member of the Christian Science Church.

26. O'Mara is described in Wade Chow, "Trials, But Mostly Tribulations," www.legalaffairs. org; Wilson, "Trial for Mother Ordered," *Sacramento Bee*, September 29, 1984; Dale Vargas, "Christian Scientist Must Stand Trial in Child's Death," *Sacramento Bee*, June 1, 1990; California Penal Code, section 270, defines child neglect.

27. Walker v. Superior Court of Sacramento County, Petition to the Supreme Court of the United States for Writ of Certiorari, Appendix C, Statement of Decision on Motion to Dismiss Charges, December 18, 1984, A77, A79–A80, A82, A83, A90–A92.

28. *Walker v. Superior Court*, 47 Cal. 3d 112, 119.

29. Michelson, "Prayer Healing—When Is It Legal?"

30. Ibid.

31. Faizah Alim, "Mother Charged in Death Claims Law Protects Her," *Sacramento Bee*, October 26, 1985.

32. *Walker v. Superior Court*, 47 Cal. 3d 112, 119; *Walker v. Superior Court*, 194 Cal. App. 3d 1090; 222 Cal. Rptr. 87 (1986).

33. *Walker v. Superior Court*, 222 Cal. Rptr. 87, 89, 90, 94.

34. Ibid., 94, 96.

35. Of the five judges who voted to hear Walker, only Mosk and Broussard remained in 1988; Times Wire Services, "Justices to Hear Faith-Healing Cases Fatal to 2," *Los Angeles Times*, March 28, 1986; the California Supreme Court stayed the Rippbergers' trial pending the outcome of its ruling on Walker's appeal; John Culver, "The Transformation of the California Supreme Court, 1977–1997," *Albany Law Review* 61:5 (Summer 1998): 1461, 1463, 1464, 1466–67.

36. *Walker v. Superior Court*, 47 Cal. 3d 112, 119–20, 142; Van de Kamp's biography: www.nndb.com; his brief is cited, *Walker v. Superior Court*, 47 Cal. 3d 112, 132–34. Christopher's biography, www.omm.com/warrenchristopher; his brief is cited, *Walker v. Superior Court*, 47 Cal. 3d 112, 140; *Prince v. Massachusetts*, 321 U.S. 158 (1944).

37. Philip Hager, "Prayer Healing Will Face Court Test in Girl's Death," *Los Angeles Times*, March 6, 1988; Philip Hager, "Prosecutor Seeks Trial for Christian Scientists," *Los Angeles Times*, March 9, 1988.

38. Germaine LaBerge, Oral History Interview with Honorable Stanley Mosk, Justice of the California Supreme Court, February 18, March 11, April 2, May 27, June 22, 1998, 31–32.

39. Peter Schrag, "The Case of Laurie Walker," *Sacramento Bee*, March 23, 1988.

40. Times Wire Services, "Justices to Hear Faith-Healing Cases."

41. Letters to the Editor, "Girl's Death," *Los Angeles Times*, March 30, 1988.

42. Walker v. Superior Court, 47 Cal. 3d 112; LaBerge, Oral History Interview with Mosk, ii, 13–14, 16, 17.

43. *Walker v. Superior Court*, 47 Cal. 3d 112.

44. *Walker v. Superior Court*, 47 Cal. 3d 112, 121–22, 126, 127, 129, 135, 137, 138; *People v. Arnold*, 66 Cal. 2d 438, 452 (1967) ruled that the phrase "other remedial care does not sanction unorthodox substitutes for 'medical attendance,'" but sanctioned prayer "in addition to rather than in lieu of the responsibility to furnish medical attendance."

45. *Walker v. Superior Court,* 47 Cal. 3d 112, 139–40; *Wisconsin v. Yoder,* 406 U.S. 205 (1972); *Prince v. Massachusetts,* 321 U.S. 158, 170, 166–67.

46. *Walker v. Superior Court,* 47 Cal. 3d 112, 140.

47. Ibid., 141–42. For Holmes's quote, see *Nash v. U.S.,* 229 U.S. 373, 377 (1913).

48. *Walker v. Superior Court,* 47 Cal. 3d 112, 145; Mosk explained that the court found section 270 did not provide a defense against charges of felony child endangerment and manslaughter, and he therefore decided not to take up the establishment clause question. But he thought that since it had been raised and briefed, the issue should be addressed so as to provide guidance to the legislature. The quotation is from *Epperson v. Arkansas,* 393 U.S. 97, 103–4 (1968).

49. *Walker v. Superior Court,* 47 Cal. 3d 112, 146–52. On February 2, 1989, the court also dismissed the Rippbergers' petition for appeal, vacated the stay, and the Court of Appeal returned the case to the trial court; *Rippberger v. Superior Court of the County of Sonoma,* Supreme Court of California, 1989 Cal. LEXIS 578; *People v. Rippberger,* 231 Cal. App. 3d 1667.

50. Claire Cooper, "Trial OK'D for Mom in Prayer-Cure Death," *Sacramento Bee,* November 11, 1988; William Carlsen, "Christian Science Case: A Ruling on Religious Freedom," *San Francisco Chronicle,* November 11, 1988; Marjie Lundstrom, "Death of Child Now Court Test of Faith," *Sacramento Bee,* June 18, 1989; Editorial, "Church and State (Cont.)," *Los Angeles Times,* November 17, 1988; speaking at the Mother Church in Boston, Talbot put a positive spin on the California court's decision. The court "did not say the parents violated the law," he said. "It simply said that a jury would need to make this determination." Curtis J. Sitomer, "California High Court Orders Trial for Christian Science Parent," *Christian Science Monitor,* November 14, 1988.

51. Tamara Jones, "Child Deaths Put Faith on Trial," *Los Angeles Times,* June 27, 1989; Lundstrom, "Death of Child Now Court Test of Faith."

52. George Snyder, "Christian Science Parents on Trial in Child's Death," *San Francisco Chronicle,* July 13, 1989.

53. *People v. Rippberger,* 231 Cal. App. 3d 1667, 1675.

54. Ibid., 1676, 1677.

55. Ibid., 1677.

56. Ibid., 1677–78.

57. Ibid., 1679; "George Snyder, "Trial of Christian Scientists: Father's Tearful Testimony on Baby's Death," *San Francisco Chronicle,* July 28, 1989.

58. George Snyder, "Christian Scientist Case: Accused Father True to Faith," *San Francisco Chronicle,* July 29, 1989.

59. Associated Press, "Christian Science Couple Found Innocent on Involuntary Manslaughter," *San Francisco Chronicle,* August 4, 1989; George Snyder, "Christian Scientists: Mixed Verdict for Pair in Their Child's Death," August 5, 1989; Editorial, "Speaking for Children," *Christian Science Monitor,* August 17, 1989.

60. Curtis J. Sitomer, "California Couple Sentenced in Spiritual Case," *Christian Science Monitor,* November 6, 1989; News, "North Bay: Probation Upheld in Child's Death," *San Francisco Chronicle,* January 17, 1990.

61. *People v. Rippberger,* 231 Cal. 3d 1667, 1688–89; on September 18, 1991, the Rippbergers withdrew their petition to the California Supreme Court for a review of their conviction on felony child endangerment; the Ventura County Superior Court granted Susan Middleton-Rippberger's petition for divorce from Mark Rippberger on July 7, 1996. www.ventura.courts .ca.gov.

62. Associated Press, "Christian Scientists Acquitted in Death of 15-Month-Old Son," *Los Angeles Daily News,* February 18, 1990.

63. David Parrish, "Parents Cleared in Tot's Death: Religious Beliefs and Child Care-Law," *Los Angeles Daily News,* February 17, 1990.

64. Marjie Lundstrom, "Prayer-Healing Case on Way to Trial," *Sacramento Bee,* June 20, 1989.

65. Rita Swan, "California Legislature Rejects Christian Science Bill," *Children's Healthcare Care Is a Legal Duty,* no. 1 (1990): 7–10.

66. Ibid.

67. Ibid. California's religious exemption laws remain in force. Calif. Penal Code 11165.2(b).

68. Vargas, "Christian Scientist Must Stand Trial in Child's Death"; Swan, "Christian Science Mom Convicted," 6.

69. Wayne Wilson, "Mom Guilty in 1984 Prayer-Healing Death," *Sacramento Bee,* June 22, 1990.

70. Wayne Wilson, "Christian Scientist Mother Spared Jail in Daughter's Death," *Sacramento Bee,* July 28, 1990.

71. Rita Swan, "Conviction of California Christian Scientist Upheld," *Children's Healthcare Is a Legal Duty,* no. 3 (1992): 1–3.

72. Walsh, "Mother's Conviction Thrown Out."

3. Ian Lundman

1. Hennepin County, Minnesota, Divorce Records, Sept. 13, 1984, Case No. 27-FA-000114776, District Court, Fourth Judicial District, Family Court Division, Hennepin County, In Re Marriage of Douglass Grant Lundman and Kathleen Stuart Lundman, October 10, 1984, 3, 4; McKown v. Lundman, Petition for Writ of Certiorari, October 1995, 2–3, cert. denied. Douglass was a full-time student and unemployed at the time of the divorce proceedings whereas Kathleen was employed by the Minnesota Orchestral Association, Margaret Zack, "Case of Boy's Death Will Decide Whether Religion Can Preclude Medical Aid," *Star Tribune,* September 9, 1991; Margaret Zack, "Father Testifies in Case of Boy's Death, Mother Had Chosen Spiritual Healing," *Star Tribune,* July 31, 1993; Margaret Zack, "$5.2 Million Awarded to Dead Boy's Family, Christian Science Practices at Issue in Suit," *Star Tribune,* August 19, 1993.

2. Kathleen and Bill McKown were married on June 8, 1986, Hennepin County Marriage Records; Zack, "Case of Boy's Death"; Zack, "$5.2 Million Awarded to Dead Boy's Family"; Rita Swan, *Children's Healthcare Is a Legal Duty,* no. 1 (1992): 2; Zack, "Case of Boy's Death," noted that the McKowns had moved to Hawaii.

3. In 1971 Doug graduated from Principia College, a college for Christian Scientists in Elsah, Illinois, and later received a bachelor's degree in fine arts and a bachelor's degree in architecture from the University of Minnesota, www.linkedin.com; Lundman v. First Church of Christ, Scientist and James Van Horn, Cross-Petition for a Writ of Certiorari, in the Supreme Court of the United States, October 1995, 5; Lundman's career path, www.douglasslundman.info; *Douglass Lundman v. Kathleen McKown, and others,* Court of Appeals of Minnesota, 530 N.W.2d 807, 832 (1995).

4. Zack, "Case of Boy's Death"; Kathy disputed Doug's version of the telephone conversation. In re the Marriage of Douglass Grant Lundman and Kathleen Stuart Lundman, No. 114776, 1989, slip op at 5 (Minn. Dist. Ct. June 5, 1989), as cited in Janna C. Merrick, "Christian Science Healing of Minor Children: Spiritual Exemption Statutes," *Issues in Law and Medicine* 10 (1994): 321–42. Because death is not a reality according to Christian Scientists, they do not use the word *death,* but rather *passing.* See Mary Baker Eddy, *Science and Health, with Key to the Scriptures* (Boston: First Church of Christ, Scientist, 1994), 427:26, "The dream of death must be mastered by Mind here or hereafter. Thought will waken from its own material declaration, 'I am dead,' to catch this trumpet-word of Truth, 'There is no death'"; Mary Thomas Burke, Jane Chauvin, Judith G. Mirantis, "Death is the belief in death. There is no death as humans are immortal spirit. After that which we *call* 'death,' spiritual development toward Truth continues until all evil, or 'error' destroys itself." *Religious and Spiritual Issues in Counseling* (New York: Brunner-Routledge, 2005), 261.

5. Medical treatment for DKA involves intravenous fluids and insulin; with timely treatment, mortality is less than 5 percent. *State of Minnesota v. Kathleen Rita McKown, William Lisle McKown, and Mario Victor Tosto,* 461 N.W.2d 720, 721 (1990 Minn. App.).

6. *Lundman v. McKown,* 530 N.W.2d 807, 813–15, 821. David Shaffer, "Faith-healing Brings Charges in Boy's Death," *St. Paul Pioneer Press,* October 12, 1989; M. S. Eledrisi, M. S. Alshanti, M. F. Shah, B. Brolosy, and N. Jaha, "Overview of the Diagnosis and Management of Diabetic Ketoacidosis," *American Journal of Medical Science* 331:5 (May 2006): 243–51. Margaret Zack, "Religion an Issue as Trial Starts in Boy's Death," *Star Tribune,* July 20, 1993; Aaron Epstein, "Supreme Court Allows $1.5 Million Judgment against Religious Group," *St. Paul Pioneer Press,* January 23, 1996.

7. Laurence C. Nolan and Lynn D. Wardle, *Fundamental Principles of Family Law* (Buffalo: William S. Hein, 2006), 538–39; second degree manslaughter is defined, Sec. 5 Minn. Stat. sec. 609.205 (1988); amended 1989 Minn. ALS 290; and child neglect, Minn. Stat. sec. 609.378, (1989); 1989 Minn. ALS 282; David Shaffer, "Faith Healing Issue Centers on Risk of Death for Children," *St. Paul Pioneer Press,* October 12, 1989; State of Minnesota v. Kathleen Riga [*sic*] McKown, William Lisle McKown, Mario Victor Tosto, Order to Dismiss and Memorandum, County of Hennepin, District Court, Fourth Judicial District, April 2, 1990.

8. Farrell's description is from "Jim [Klobuchar] on Gene," *News Brief,* a newsletter of Lawyers Concerned for Lawyers, a group of recovering chemically dependent lawyers and judges that Farrell helped found in 1976. www.mnlcl.org; on March 27, 1990, the state accepted Tosto's motion to dismiss. Order to Dismiss and Memorandum, 1, 4.

9. Order to Dismiss and Memorandum, 8; Jim George, "Dismissal Sought in Death of Boy, 11," *St. Paul Pioneer Press,* January 1, 1990.

10. Order to Dismiss and Memorandum, 5, 8; David Shaffer, "Medical Help Was Needed, Prosecutor Argues," *St. Paul Pioneer Press,* March 27, 1990.

11. Order to Dismiss and Memorandum, 4–9. "In pari materia" is the legal term for Farrell's argument that Minnesota's child neglect and manslaughter laws had a common purpose and must therefore be read and applied together, *Black's Law Dictionary* (St. Paul: West, 1991), 544; Lawrence J. Goodrich, "Case against Christian Scientists Dismissed," *Christian Science Monitor,* April 5, 1990.

12. David Shaffer, "Christian Science Couple Cleared in Faith-Healing Death," *St. Paul Pioneer Press,* April 3; David Shaffer, "Dismissal of Manslaughter Charges in Faith-Healing Case to Be Appealed," *St. Paul Pioneer Press,* April 6, 1990.

13. Jim George, "Appeals Court Gets Christian Science Case," *St. Paul Pioneer Press,* July 12, 1990.

14. Ibid.

15. Judge Gardebring noted that the circumstances surrounding Ian Lundman's death were unlikely to occur again because one month after the boy's death the legislature passed a law making "practitioners of healing arts" mandated reporters "if lack of medical care may cause imminent and serious danger to the child's health." Minn. Stat. sec. 626.556 (Supp. 1989); 1989 Minn. ALS 282. However, in March 1991 at a Senate Judiciary Committee hearing Van Horn stated that Christian Science practitioners had no obligation to report sick children to child welfare services. Rita Swan, *Children's Healthcare Is a Legal Duty,* no. 4 (1992): 6. *State of Minnesota v. McKown,* Court of Appeals, 461 N.W.2d 720, 722–23, 724 (1990).

16. David Shaffer, "Prosecutor Asks Christian Science Case Be Reinstated," *St. Paul Pioneer Press,* April 5, 1990; Associated Press, "Bill Would Block Protection for 'Spiritual Treatment,' " *St. Paul Pioneer,* March 12, 1991; Spear's statement is quoted in Judge Farrell's Order to Dismiss and Memorandum, April 2, 1990, 7.

17. Swan, *Children's Healthcare Is a Legal Duty,* no. 4 (1992): 6–7. Maria Alena Castle and Steven D. Peterson, "Faith-Healing Exemption Serves to Endanger Children," *St. Paul Pioneer Press,* March 24, 1992. In April 1994, by a vote of 103–30, the House passed a bill stipulating a criminal penalty for parents who withheld medical care from a child. The Senate failed to

act. Political Briefing, "Bill Would Penalize Faith-Healing Parents," *St. Paul Pioneer Press,* April 15, 1994.

18. Castle and Peterson, "Faith-Healing Exemption."

19. *State of Minnesota v. Kathleen Rita McKown, William Lisle McKown and Mario Victor Tosto,* Supreme Court of Minnesota, 475 N.W.2d 63, 67–69 (1991 Minn.); Lydia Villalva Lijo, "Christian Science Couple Can't Be Charged," *St. Paul Pioneer Press,* September 20, 1991; Appointed to the Minnesota Supreme Court in 1991, Justice Gardebring did not participate in the decision because she had ruled on the case while on the Appeals Court. "Esther Faces Life: Reflections from the Hon. Esther M. Tomljanovich," *Hennepin Lawyer: Official Publication of the Hennepin County Bar Association,* August 24, 1991.

20. Obituary, M. Jeanne Coyne, *Star Tribune,* August 6, 1998; *State of Minnesota v. McKown,* 475 N.W.2d 63, 70.

21. *State of Minnesota v. McKown,* 475 N.W.2d 63, 69–71.

22. Ibid., 71.

23. Margaret Zack, "Court Rules for Pair Who Let Son Die, Christian Scientists Followed Law, Ruling Says," September 20, 1991, *Star Tribune; State of Minnesota v. McKown,* 475 N.W.2d 63, 69. Richardson's comment paraphrased *Prince v. Massachusetts,* 321 U.S. 804 (1944); Lijo, "Couple Can't Be Charged"; the U.S. Supreme Court denied certiorari, *State of Minnesota v. McKown,* 502 U.S. 1036 (1992).

24. Lydia Villalva Lijo, "Father Sues Church Members for Son's Death," *St. Paul Pioneer Press,* May 2, 1991; Swan, *Children's Healthcare Is a Legal Duty,* no. 1 (1991): 13.

25. Susan Bridge, *Monitoring the News: The Brilliant Launch and the Sudden Collapse of the Monitor Channel* (London: M. E. Sharpe, 1998), 42, 120. Paul Hemp, "Church Enters Tough Industry with Missionary Zeal," *Boston Globe,* March 24, 1991; Caroline Fraser, "Suffering Children and the Christian Science Church," *Atlantic Monthly,* April 1995, www.rickcross.com.

26. Joan Vennochi, "Judgment Day," *Boston Globe,* September 27, 1991; James L. Franklin, "Christian Science Church Defends Publishing Book Linked to Bequest," *Boston Globe,* October 13, 1991; Franklin, "Science Church to Cut Workers, Shut Cable TV," *Boston Globe,* June 5, 1992.

27. Margaret Zack, "Judge Allows Father to Sue in Death of Boy Who Was Denied Medical Care," *Star Tribune,* December 6, 1991; www.martindale.com; Douglass Lundman was appointed trustee of Ian's estate in April 1991; Order and Memorandum on Plaintiff's Motion to Amend Complaint to Add Punitive Damages, June 30, 1993, 1–8.

28. Zack, "Religion an Issue." When Kaster completed his opening the defense moved for a mistrial, arguing that his statement sought to put the defendants' religious beliefs on trial. Judge Rice denied the motion, ibid.

29. Margaret Zack, "Lawyer Says Woman Held Lifelong Belief in Spiritual Healing," *Star Tribune,* July 21, 1993; Patrick Sweeney, "Christian Science Mom Believed Prayer Would Cure Son, Attorney Says," *St. Paul Pioneer Press,* July 21, 1993; in an article in *Minnesota Lawyer* on June 9, 2003, about an increase in the number of settlements and verdicts for the plaintiff in wrongful death cases, Kaster attributed his success in the Lundman case, in part, to "the defense's 'remarkable' strategy of blaming the father for the death of his own son when the father wasn't even in town."

30. Zack, "Case of Boy's Death."

31. State of Minnesota v. Kathleen R. McKown, Petition for Writ of Certiorari, in the Supreme Court of the United States, October Term 1991, Brief of Amicus Curiae, Affidavit of Kathleen McKown, A-1. A common skin infection occurring among preschool children, impetigo is usually treated with soap and water. Common warts are caused by a virus and typically disappear on their own within a few months. *Lundman v. McKown,* 530 N.W.2d 807, 830. Jim George, "Mother Recalls Final Hours of Prayer for Dying Son, 11," *St. Paul Pioneer Press,* July 27, 1993; Zack, "$5.2 Million Awarded to Dead Boy's Family." Ian was not a church member; the standard age of admission to the Christian Science Church is twelve.

32. Margaret Zack, "Mother Didn't Realize Spiritual Healing Was Failing, Says Lawyer," *Star Tribune*, August 18, 1993.

33. The jury also found Doug Lundman not negligent. Zack, "$5.2 Million Awarded to Dead Boy's Family"; Patrick Sweeney, "$5 Million Verdict Returned: Christian Science Church, Mother Held Responsible in Boy's Death," *St. Paul Pioneer Press*, August 19, 1993; Kevin Diaz, "Jury to Look at Punitive Damages for Father in Prayer Healing Case," *Star Tribune*, August 21, 1993; Associated Press, "Christian Scientists Found Liable in Death," *New York Times*, August 19, 1993.

34. Diaz, "Jury to Look at Punitive Damages"; Margaret Zack, "Jury Deliberates without Verdict, Weighing Punitive Damages in Christian Science Case," *Star Tribune*, August 25, 1993; Margaret Zack, "Father Gets Additional $9 Million in Son's Death, Christian Science Is Likely to Appeal," *Star Tribune*, August 26, 1993; Patrick Sweeney, "Christian Scientists Take Verdict Seriously: Jury Considers Whether to Order Punitive Damages," *St. Paul Pioneer Press*, August 25, 1993; Associated Press, "Church Told to Pay More in a Death," *New York Times*, August 27, 1993; Elaine Woo, "Warren Christopher Dies at 85," *Los Angeles Times*, March 20, 2011.

35. Zack, "Father Gets Additional $9 Million"; Associated Press, "Church Told To Pay More."

36. Patrick Sweeney, "Activist Pleased That Jury Set Punitive Damages: But She's Unsure If Church Will Alter Its Views," *St. Paul Pioneer Press*, August 26, 1993; Margaret Zack, "Ethicists Hail Verdict In Boy's Death," *Star Tribune*, August 20, 1993, includes remarks by Warren Christopher; Stephen L. Carter, "The Power of Prayer Denied," *Christian Science Monitor*, February 7, 1996.

37. Associated Press, "Church Told to Pay More"; Zack, "Ethicists Hail Verdict In Boy's Death."

38. Doug Grow, "Victory over Christian Science Church Gives No Solace to Father," *Star Tribune*, September 3, 1993; Zack, "Ethicists Hail Verdict In Boy's Death."

39. Grow, "No Solace to Father."

40. Ibid.

41. Margaret Zack, "Defendants to Ask to Pay Less in Boy's Death," *Star Tribune*, October 13, 1993; Patrick Sweeney, "Judge Lowers Money Award in Christian Science Case," *St. Paul Pioneer Press*, March 18, 1994.

42. "News Item" from the Minnesota Judicial Branch. www.mncourts.gov, June 7, 2000. *Lundman v. McKown*, 530 N.W.2d 807 (1995).

43. *Lundman v. McKown*, 530 N.W.2d 807, 816–17. The court also held the church was not liable for $150,000 in compensatory damages.

44. Ibid., 817–18. The legal principle that brings the state into direct conflict with religious views is *parens patriae*, literally "parent of the country," an English common law term that recognizes the state's right to care for those that cannot care for themselves.

45. Ibid., 818–19.

46. Ibid., 819–20.

47. Ibid., 820.

48. Ibid., 820–21.

49. Ibid., 822 (emphasis added by Davies). In 1992 the Christian Science Church canceled its training programs for nurses. Perhaps prompted by Judge Davies's ruling holding Lamb partially responsible for Ian Lundman's death, the *Christian Science Journal* announced in November 1991 that each member of the church must be responsible for "self-government" and therefore preparation for nursing will be an "individual activity." Nurses continued to be listed in the *Journal*, but such a listing did not indicate an official church connection, merely a self-advertisement.

50. Ibid., 822–23.

51. Ibid., 826–28; in 1998 a divided California court ruled that neither the Christian Science

Church nor the Christian Science grandmother who was babysitting twelve-year Andrew Wantland had a duty of care to the boy, who died of juvenile diabetes. *Gayle Quigley v. First Church of Christ, Scientist and Ruth Wantland,* 65 Cal. App. 4th 1027 (1998).

52. *Lundman v. McKown,* 530 N.W.2d 807, 822, 823–26; Patrick Sweeney, "Ruling Says Church Not Liable in Boy's Death: But Court States Parents Must Seek Care," *St. Paul Pioneer Press,* April 4, 1995; Kevin Duchschere, "Damages against Christian Science Church Are Dropped," *Star Tribune,* April 4, 1995.

53. Sweeney, "Church Not Liable In Boy's Death"; Swan, *Children's Healthcare Is a Legal Duty,* no. 3 (1996): 12; Stephen L. Carter, "The Power of Prayer Denied."

54. Margaret Zack, "State High Court Won't Hear Appeal of Suit Against Church," *Star Tribune,* June 4, 1995; *McKown v. Lundman,* 516 U.S. 1099 (1996) cert. denied. Linda Greenhouse, "Christian Scientists Rebuffed in Ruling by Supreme Court," *New York Times,* January 23, 1996.

4. Ashley King

1. State of Arizona v. John Harold King and Catherine Justine King Superior Court of Arizona, Maricopa County, Adult Probation Department, Vol. 8, Merrie E. Bronson to Judge Ronald Reinstein, September 10, 1989; Marc A. Cosenza to Judge Ronald Reinstein, September 8, 1989; Janice Shepherd to The Honorable Judge Ronald Reinstein, September 7, 1989. Vol. 6, Response to the State's Reply Regarding State's Motion to Compel, May 3, 1989, Pupil Progress Report, 1986–87, Scottsdale Public Schools, Cherokee Elementary School; Arizona Department of Education, Certificate of Achievement in Reading, June 3, 1987; Vol. 8, State v. Catherine King, Presentence Investigation, 8.

2. State of Arizona v. John Harold King and Catherine King, Superior Court of Arizona, Maricopa County, Adult Probation Department, John King, Presentence Investigation, Vol. 8:1, 8; William T. King to Max Bessler, Adult Probation Department, September 7, 1989, Vol. 8; Catherine King, Presentence Investigation, Vol. 8:1, 8, 9.

3. Elizabeth Ashley King was born in San Francisco on January 28, 1976; Charlene P. Craig, CPS, phone conversation with Douglas, Temporary Custody Notice, Progress Notes, May 5, 1988, Vol. 1:11; Vol. 3:14–17; State of Arizona v. Catherine King, Presentence Investigation, Defendant's Statement, September 22, 1989, Vol. 8:8; King listed some "beautiful healings": she became "gravely ill" as a toddler, but a practitioner prayed for her through the night, and her good health returned in the morning; her teeth were straightened through prayer; she was kicked in the stomach by a horse and didn't think she was going to live, but Christian Science treatment immediately eased the pain, and four days later there was no evidence of the accident; she healed her husband's deafness; Arizona v. Catherine King, Presentence Investigation, Defendant's Statement, September 22, 1989, 9–10.

4. Arizona v. Catherine King, Presentence Investigation, Defendant's Statement, September 22, 1989, 10–11.

5. In the Superior Court of the State of Arizona In and For the County of Maricopa, Proceedings Before the 100th Maricopa County Grand Jury, In Re: John Harold King and Catherine King, Phoenix, Arizona, August 3, 1988, Testimony of Paradise Valley Detective Edwin A. Boehm, based on his interview with Tammy Vandenberg, Vol. 1:18–20. The Grand Jury Reporter mistakenly spelled the detective's name as Baime.

6. State of Arizona v. Catherine King, Presentence Investigation, Defendant's Statement, September 22, 1989, Vol. 8:10–11; Craig, Progress Notes, Vol. 3:4.

7. Craig, Progress Notes, Vol. 3:4; Craig cited A.R.S. [Arizona Revised Statutes] 13-3623, "Child Abuse." Proceedings Before the 100th Maricopa County Grand Jury, In Re: John Harold King and Catherine King, Phoenix, Arizona, August 3, 1988, Vol. 1:10; State of Arizona v. John Harold King, Presentence Investigation, September 22, 1989, Vol. 8:1.

8. Proceedings Before the 100th Maricopa County Grand Jury, In Re: John Harold King and Catherine King, Phoenix, Arizona, August 3, 1988, Vol. 1:11; State of Arizona v. John Harold King, Presentence Investigation, September 22, 1989, Vol. 8:1; Craig, Progress Notes, Vol. 3:7–8.

9. Craig, Progress Notes, Vol. 3:9–10, 14–15; Boehm testified before the grand jury that Douglas told him Ashley was bedridden sometime in December, a statement that contradict-ed Catherine King's memory. Proceedings Before the 100th Maricopa Grand Jury: In Re John Harold King and Catherine King, Phoenix, Arizona, August 3, 1988, Vol. 1:42; for Douglas's remarks, Craig, Progress Notes, Vol. 1:14–15.

10. Craig, Progress Notes, Vol. 3:16–20.

11. Craig, Progress Notes, Vol. 1:13, 30; Vol. 3:21.

12. State of Arizona v. John Harold King, Presentence Investigation, September 22, 1989, Vol. 8:2; Charlene Craig, Progress Notes, May 6, 1988, Vol. 1:1, Vol. 3:22.

13. State of Arizona v. John Harold King, Presentence Investigation, September 22, 1989, Vol. 8:2–3; Proceedings Before the 100th Maricopa County Grand Jury, In Re: John Harold King and Catherine King, Phoenix, Arizona, August 3, 1988, Vol. 1:33–34; if the tumor has not spread to the lungs, long-term survival rates are very high. www.ncbi.nlm.nih.

14. State of Arizona v. John Harold King, Presentence Investigation, September 22, 1989, Vol. 8:3–4; Charlene Craig, Statement of Interested Parties, Vol. 8:5; Charlene Craig, Progress Notes, May 6, 1988, Vol. 1:2. A.R.S. 8-821, "Taking into temporary custody"; Proceedings Be-fore the 100th Maricopa County Grand Jury, In Re: John Harold King and Catherine King, Phoenix, Arizona, August 3, 1988, Vol. 1:37; Catherine King to Mrs. Smith, May 27, 1988, Vol. 6.

15. Craig, Progress Notes, Vol. 3:27, 22, 28–29; Proceedings Before the 100th Maricopa County Grand Jury, In Re: John Harold King and Catherine King, Phoenix, Arizona, Vol. 1:33–35.

16. Craig, Progress Notes, 29–30; on May 11, when hospital nurses bathed and washed her hair, Ashley said she had not been bathed or had her hair washed since January, Craig, Prog-ress Notes, Vol. 3:41–42.

17. Presentence Investigation, September 22, 1989, Vol. 8:3; Craig, Progress Notes, Vol. 3:31.

18. Presentence Investigation, Catherine Justine King, September 22, 1989, Vol. 8:3; Craig, Progress Notes, May 9, 1988, Vol. 3:34–35.

19. Craig, Progress Notes, Vol. 3:34–36.

20. Proceedings Before the 100th Maricopa County Grand Jury, In Re: John Harold King and Catherine King, Phoenix, Arizona, August 3, 1988, Vol. 1:44–45.

21. Craig, Progress Notes, Vol. 3:43–44; Exhibit 2, State v. King, Motion for Reconsidera-tion, Interview with Dr. James Joy by Robert Hooker, defendant's attorney, March 29, 1989, Vol. 5:11, 12, 13, 16, 18; on the same day Hooker interviewed Joy, the psychiatrist was inter-viewed by Deputy District Attorney for Maricopa County K. C. Scull, to whom Joy gave op-posite answers to two of the three key questions posed by Hooker: Joy didn't know if Ashley was in pain or if she had a means for controlling pain; he also believed Catherine King "had a strong influence on the child," Vol. 5:9, 11; A.R.S. 13-3623, F: 2 defines "child" as an "individual under eighteen years of age." When an "individual is less than 18 years a parent, guardian, or other person *in loco parentis* must consent for the minor's health care." A.R.S. 1-215.

22. Craig, Progress Notes, Vol. 3:37–38, 41–42; Proceedings Before the 100th Maricopa Grand Jury, In Re: John Harold King and Catherine King, August 3, 1988, Vol. 1:37–38; Joy told Hooker the nursing unit "was polarized against the parents and towards the child," Exhibit 2, State v, King, Interview with Dr. James Joy by Robert Hooker, Vol. 5:19.

23. Craig, Progress Notes, Vol. 3:44–45; Exhibit 2, State v. King, Interview with Dr. James Joy, by Robert Hooker, Vol. 5:6–7; the term *consecration* does not signify a status, as King's use implied. See www.spirituality.com, Mary Baker Eddy, *Science and Health, with Key to the Scriptures* (Boston: First Church of Christ, Science, 1994), 688:18, 28:9, 3:12, 388:1; Catherine

King may have privileged the last citation: "Through the uplifting and consecrated power" Christian martyrs "obtained a victory over the corporeal senses, a victory which [Christian] Science alone can explain"; Mary Baker Eddy, *Manual of the Mother Church* (Boston: First Church of Christ, Science, 1911), 35, article IV, sec. 3, states that children who are approved by a church official may become church members at the age of twelve years; Ashley turned twelve on January 28, 1988, when she was a patient at Upward View; Presentence Investigation, Catherine Justine King, September 22, 1989, Vol. 8:11.

24. Craig, Progress Notes, Vol. 3:45, 47; Carol Sowers, "Prayer to Supersede Hospital Treatment For Ailing Girl," *Arizona Republic,* May 13, 1988.

25. Craig, Progress Notes, Vol. 3:51; "Girl, 12, Dies of Bone Cancer Despite Prayers," *Phoenix Gazette,* June 7, 1988; "Parents Face Charges for Not Having Child Treated," *Prescott Courier,* August 10, 1988.

26. In *Parham v. J.R.,* 442 U.S. 584, 603 (1979), Chief Justice Warren Burger echoed Anglo-American law when he stated that children were "simply not able to make sound judgments concerning many decisions. Parents can and must make those judgments"; Presentence Investigation, Catherine Justine King, September 22, 1989, Vol. 8:12; Kent Greenfield, "The Sweat Lodge Guru Guilty Verdict: Recognizing the Deadly Influence of Authority," www .huffingtonpost.com, June 24, 2011.

27. Interview with R.N. [registered nurse] Esther Muñoz, conducted by Ruth Smith of O'Connor, Cavanaugh, April 12, 1989, Vol. 7:2–5, 20–21, 25, 23, 24–25, 27–29, 45, 13, 2.

28. Interview with R.N. Esther Muñoz, April 12, 1989, Vol. 7:54, 57–59; State v. Catherine King, Presentence Investigation, October 4, 1989, Vol. 8:12.

29. State of Arizona v. John Harold King and Catherine Justine King, "A True Bill," August 3, 1988, Vol. 1:1–2; Brent Whiting, "2 Indicted in Death of Ill Daughter," *Arizona Republic,* August 10, 1988; Brent Whiting, "Collins Assailed by Lawyer," *Arizona Republic,* August 17, 1988; "'Ignorance, Bigotry' behind Case," *Mohave Daily Miner,* August 17, 1988.

30. "Woman's Sentence Is Birth Control," *New York Times,* May 26, 1988; Tamar Jacoby, "Is Sterilization the Answer?," *Newsweek,* August 8, 1988; Editorial, "Pregnancy Ban: Look, Ma, No Abuse," *Arizona Republic,* May 27, 1988, cheered Forster's sentence; under pressure, Judge Budzyn reversed the order, "Birth Control Order Is Overturned," *New York Times,* September 3, 1988.

31. *Arizona Rules of Criminal Procedure,* Rule 10.1 and 10.2; Defendants Kings' Motion for Change of Judge for Cause, Vol. 1:2; at the time of his death in April 2008, www.legacy .com, Hooker was the director of the Tucson Public Defenders office. He told his staff he wanted them "to stand up to the prosecutors," www.pimacountybar.org; "The Arizona Eagle," April 4, 2008, http:dpaterson.blogspot.com; Defendants Kings' Motion for Change of Judge for Cause, August 26, 1988, Vol. 1:1–2; State's Response to Defendant's Motion for Change of Judge, August 31, 1988, Vol. 1:1–4; Honorable Thomas W. O'Toole, Granting Change of Judge, September 14, 1988, Vol. 1:2–3; Notice of Change of Judge, September 26, 1988, Vol. 1:18; Reassignment on Notice of Change of Judge, Vol. 1:6. www.ncstl.org/education. www .phoenixnewtimes.com, September 25, 2007.

32. Arizona Rules of Criminal Procedure, 12.9; *U.S. v. Dionisio,* 410 U.S. 1, 93 (1973); A.R.S 8-546 (B). Motion to Dismiss or, in the Alternative, to Remand For a New Determination of Probable Cause, September 19, 1988, Vol. 1:4–14; This motion was signed by Attorney Glenda E. Edmunds, a member of the firm O'Connor, Cavanagh, representing John and Catherine King.

33. Response to Motion to Dismiss, October 3, 1988, Vol. 1:2–3, 3–5, 6–7.

34. Reply in Support of Motion to Dismiss or, in the Alternative, to Remand for a New Determination of Probable Cause, October 14, 1988, Vol. 1:5–6, 7.

35. State of Arizona v. John and Catherine King, Superior Court of Arizona, Maricopa County, October 24, 1988; Judge Reinstein Order Denying the Motion to Dismiss and Granting the Motion to Remand, Vol. 2:22–25.

36. Robert J. Hooker to K. C. Scull, October 31, 1988, Arizona v. John and Catherine King, Vol. 3; E. Nathan Schaye, "In Memoriam: Robert Hooker, April 9, 2008"; Arizona Attorneys for Criminal Justice hosted Popko's seminar in Tucson on April 10, 1987, and his article, "Arizona's County Grand Jury: The Empty Promise of Independence," *Arizona Law Review* 29 (1987): 667, appeared the same year.

37. Proceedings Before the 102nd Maricopa County Grand Jury, November 3, 15, 1988, Vol. 2; Indictment(s) of Catherine and John King, Arizona Superior Court, Maricopa County, December 6, 1988, Vol. 2:17–18; Defendants Motion to Dismiss or, in the Alternative, to Remand for a New Determination of Probable Cause, January 20, 1989, Vol. 2:5, 12, 29, 35, 45; There is a legal literature arguing children's right to give informed consent, including W. Waddington, "Consent to Medical Care for Minors: The Legal Framework," in *Children's Competence to Consent,* ed. Gary B. Melton, et. al. (New York: Plenum Press, 1983), and Robert Batey, "The Rights of Adolescents," *William and Mary Law Review* 23 (1982): 363, 384, urges the "abandonment of a monolithic view of childhood" and recognition that some children are "capable of making decisions for themselves." Hooker retained Howard Varinsky, a jury and trial consultant, who prepared a report showing that 60.1 percent of a random sample of four hundred Maricopa County residents over the age of eighteen said a Christian Science child did not have the capacity to make a decision as to his or her best treatment for a life-threatening illness, and 49.5 percent thought Christian Science parents should be held responsible for a child's death, Arizona v. John and Catherine King, Vol. 3, Exhibit D.

38. Response to Motion to Dismiss and/or Remand, February 3, 1989, Vol. 4:3, 10, 5, 7, 4, 25, 27, 29.

39. Reply in Support of Motion to Dismiss, or in the Alternative, to Remand for a New Determination of Probable Cause, February 17, 1989, Vol. 4:6–7, 16–17; *In the Matter of the Appeal in Cochise County Juvenile Action,* No. 5666-J, 133 Arizona 157 (1982); *Commonwealth v. Barnhart,* 345 Pa. Super. 10; 497 A.2d. 616 (1985); *Prince v. Massachusetts,* 321 U.S. 158 (1944).

40. Reply in Support of Motion to Dismiss or, in the Alternative, to Remand for a New Determination of Probable Cause, February 17, 1989, Vol. 4:7, 15, 19; *In the Matter of the Appeal in Cochise County Juvenile Action,* No. 5666-J, 133 Arizona 157, 158 (1982).

41. Response to Motion to Dismiss and/or Remand, February 3, 1989, Vol. 4:15–16; *Commonwealth v. Barnhart,* 345 Pa. Super. 10; 497 A.2nd 416, 620, 622); Daniel J. Kearney, "Parental Failure to Provide Child with Medical Assistance Based on Religious Belief Causing Child's Death—Involuntary Manslaughter in Pennsylvania," *Dickinson Law Review* 90 (1985–86): 861; Reply in Support of Motion to Dismiss or Remand, February 17, 1989, Vol. 4:20, 21.

42. Response to Motion to Dismiss and/or Remand, February 3, 1989, Vol. 4:17; Reply in Support of Motion to Dismiss or Remand, February 17, 1989, Vol. 4:17, 21–22; in addition to denying the scope of *Prince,* the defense argued that *Rasmussen v. Fleming,* 154 Arizona 200 (1987), a case involving two guardians with differing opinions about a course of action for a seventy-year-old incompetent woman could be read to mean the twelve-year-old Ashley had the right to refuse medical treatment; *Prince v. Massachusetts,* 321 U.S. 158, 166, 169 (1944).

43. The court's decision: Defendants Motion to Dismiss or Remand, March 1, 1989, Vol. 5:14, 15, 18–19, 15, 19, 20–21, 22; Reinstein expressed surprise that the prosecution chose not to cite *Walker v. Superior Court of Sacramento County,* 47 Cal. 3d 112 (1988), and noted that he gave "considerable weight to the decision almost directly on point with this case."

44. Motion for Reconsideration, March 29, 1989, Vol. 5:2, 3, 5, 6, 26–27; Edmonds's argument for the court's supervisory power over a grand jury was drawn from Popko, "Arizona's County Grand Jury."

45. State's Motion to Summarily Deny Defendants' Motion for Reconsideration, April 14, 1989, Vol. 5:2, 3.

46. State's Response to Defendants' Motion for Reconsideration, April 18, 1989, Vol. 6:1–3, 9.

47. State's Response, April 18, 1989, Vol. 6:10–11; A.R.S. 8-546, A.R.S. 13-3623 (B), and A.R.S. 13-3623 (C).

48. State's Response, April 18, 1989, Vol. 6:11–12.

49. Ibid., Vol. 6:20–22.

50. Ibid., Vol. 6:33–34.

51. From the time of Judge Reinstein's appointment to the Kings' case until his order denying reconsideration, the defendants had waived their right to a speedy trial four times. Notice of Waiver of Speedy Trial Rights, April 26, 1989, Vol. 6; during the same period three Motions to Compel Discovery were filed, April 14, 1989, Vol. 6; State of Arizona v. John and Catherine King, Judge Ronald Reinstein, Ruling on Motions, May 5, 1989, Vol. 6:11–12.

52. State v. John and Catherine King, Motion in Limine, June 6, 1989, Vol. 7:1–2; Opposition to Motion in Limine, June 26, 1989, Vol. 7:2–3, 6.

53. Reply to Defendants' Opposition to Motions in Limine, June 30, 1989, Vol. 7:2–4; the Kings responded by citing *Rasmusssen By Mitchell v. Fleming*, 154 Ariz. 200 (1986), a case in which the court held that the guardian of Rasmussen, a seventy-year-old incompetent ward, had the authority to withhold medical care. The appeal court held that the right to refuse medical care was based on the constitutional right to privacy.

54. The Kings petitioned the Arizona Supreme Court to obtain review of the Court of Appeal's decision to decline jurisdiction over Judge Reinstein's denial of defendants' motion to dismiss or remand according to Rule 12.9, John King and Catherine King v. Superior Court of the State of Arizona, August 10, 1989, Vol. 8; Motion for Stay of Trial, August 24, 1989, Vol. 7; Notice of Waiver of Speedy Trial Rights, August 25, 1989, Vol. 7; Response to Defendants' Motion for Stay of Trial, August 28, 1989, Vol. 7; Plea Agreement / Change of Plea, September 1, 1989, Vol. 7:14; Plea Agreement: John King, September 15, 1989, Vol. 8; Plea Agreement: Catherine King, September 15, 1989, Vol. 8.

55. State v. John King, Presentence Investigation, Defendant's Statement, October 14, 1989, Vol. 8:4; Brent Whiting, "Plea Deal Lets Pair Avoid Felony," *Arizona Republic*, September 2, 1989; State v. Catherine King, Presentence Investigation, Defendant's Statement, October 14, 1989, Vol. 8:14.

56. Jan Forrister to Judge Reinstein, September 8, 1989, Vol. 8; Catherine King to Mrs. Smith, May 27, 1988, Vol. 6; in addition to complaining about her treatment Catherine's letters asked recipients to help defray the couple's legal costs. According to a fund-raising letter titled "King Defense Trust Fund," dated April 19, 1989, and signed by Mary-Ed Bol Duniway, reprinted in Rita Swan's *Children's Healthcare Is a Legal Duty*, no. 4 (1989): 4, "Legal preparation costs for the Kings['] appeals were $30,000 to 40,000 per month"; Duniway thanked the people whose contributions had made it possible to pay off $160,000 in legal fees but emphasized that "we are more than $140,000 in arrears."

57. State of Arizona v. John King, Presentence Investigation, Defendant's Statement, October 14, 1989, Vol. 8:4; Whiting, "Plea Deal Lets Pair Avoid Felony." Robert Hooker to Judge Ronald Reinstein, September 22, 1989, Vol. 8.

58. Donna Lane to Judge Reinstein, December 7, 1988, Vol. 2; Anonymous to Judge Reinstein, September 27, 1989, Vol. 8; Michelle Bearden, "A Prescription of Prayer," *Arizona Republic*, May 14, 1988.

59. George Gregg to Max Bessler, September 9, 1989, Vol. 8; Jan Forrister to Judge Reinstein, September 8, 1989, Vol. 8.

60. State of Arizona v. John King: Judgment and Sentence, September 26, 1989, Vol. 8; State of Arizona v. Catherine King: Judgment and Sentence, September 26, 1989, Vol. 8; State v. John King, Judgment and Sentence, September 26, 1989, Vol. 8; State v. Catherine King, Judgment and Sentence, September 26, 1989, Vol. 8; State v. John King, Presentence Investigation, Defendant's Statement, October 14, 1989, Vol. 8:4; Catherine King stated she "could not afford a felony conviction" because she hoped to become an attorney; State v. Catherine King, Presentence Investigation, Defendant's Statement, October 14, 1989, Vol. 8:5; Ronald James Pursley to Katherine [*sic*] King, October 6, 1989, Vol. 8; Pursley to John King, November 2, 1989, Vol. 8; Pursley to Katherine [*sic*] King, November 2, 1989, Vol. 8; Norman L. Helber to

Mary-Ed Duniway, November 15, 1989, Vol. 8; Richard Rodgers to Catherine King, December 14, 1989, Vol. 8; Sandra Tomjann to John King, February 23, 1989, Vol. 8.

61. Catherine King to The Honorable Ronald Reinstein, May 7, 1990, Vol. 8; K. C. Scull to Judge Reinstein, May 17, 1990, Vol. 8; State of Arizona v. John King and Catherine King, Petition for Early Termination of Probation, Denied, May 30, 1990, Vol. 8; State of Arizona v. John King, Motion for Early Termination of Probation, Granted, April 24, 1991, Vol. 8; State of Arizona v. Catherine King, Motion for Early Termination of Probation, Granted, April 24, 1991, Vol. 8.

5. Robyn Twitchell

1. G.L. [General Laws] chap. 273, sec.1. See, generally, Leo Damore, *The "Crime" of Dorothy Sheridan* (New York: McNally and Loften, 1978).

2. Damore, *"Crime" of Dorothy Sheridan,* 296–97.

3. Acts and Resolves, 1971, chap. 762; G.L. chap. 273, sec. 1; during the Twitchell trial Superior Court Judge Sandra Hamlin found "no indication from the plain language of the statute or the legislative history that G.L. c. 273, sec. 1 was amended in 1971 in reaction to a manslaughter prosecution of a mother [Sheridan] for treating her child with Christian Science healing rather than conventional medicine." Memorandum and Order on Defendant's Motion to Dismiss, April 19, 1989, 18n23.

4. Justice Lawrence D. Shubow, "Justice's Report on Inquest Relating to the Death of Robyn Twitchell," Inquest No. 1 of 1986, 23; *Legal Rights and Obligations of Christian Scientists in Massachusetts* (Boston: Christian Science Committee on Publication, 1983), 18–23; "Opinions of the Attorney General of Massachusetts," *Report of the Attorney General* 12, 139–40 (Boston: Commonwealth of Massachusetts, 1975).

5. Mary Baker Eddy, *Science and Health, with Key to the Scriptures* (Boston: First Church of Christ, Scientist, 1994), 109: Stephen Gottschalk, "Spiritual Healing on Trial: A Christian Scientist Reports," *Christian Century,* June 22–29, 1988, 604–5. *Freedom and Responsibility: Christian Science Healing for Children* (Boston: First Church of Christ, Scientist, 1989), 4.

6. Doris Sue Wong, "Twitchell Sought Treatment for Self," *Boston Globe,* June 1, 1990.

7. Shubow, "Report on Inquest," 4–5.

8. Ibid., 6–7.

9. Ibid., 8–9.

10. Judge Shubow noted that thousands of pages of evidence about Christian Science had been introduced and considered as well as a number of scholarly articles countering claims of spiritual healing, including Rita Swan's "Faith Healing, Christian Science and the Medical Care of Children," *New England Journal of Medicine* 309 (December 29, 1983): 1639; Shubow, "Report on Inquest," 9–10; Shubow's report was not made public until July 6, 1990, following the Twitchells' trial.

11. Shubow, "Report on Inquest," 3, 19, 20, 17, 27.

12. Ibid., 28–35.

13. Doris Sue Wong, "Christian Scientists Indicted in Son's Death," *Boston Globe,* April 27, 1988; Commonwealth v. David Twitchell and Ginger Twitchell, Memorandum and Order on Defendants' Motion to Dismiss, 6.

14. Wong, "Christian Scientists Indicted"; Editorial, "Children and Religion," *Boston Herald,* May 5, 1988.

15. Elizabeth Neuffer, "Spiritual Healing: A Debate of Rights, Critics Demand Accountability for Child Deaths," *Boston Globe,* May 22, 1990; *Wisconsin v. Yoder,* 406 U.S. 205 (1972).

16. Commonwealth v. David and Ginger Twitchell, Memorandum and Order on Defendants' Motion to Dismiss, 9–10, 12, 15, 16–17, 24–28.

17. David Twitchell and Ginger Twitchell v. Commonwealth, Memorandum of Decision, May 23, 1989, 1, 20–22; *Commonwealth v. Gallison,* 383 Mass. 659, 665 (1981); Judge Hamlin re-

jected the defendants' argument that Attorney General Bellotti's 1975 opinion barred prosecution, ruling that the "opinion speaks to negligent behavior and does not cover conduct that is wanton and reckless and, therefore, rises to the level of manslaughter," 18; David Twitchell and Ginger Twitchell v. Commonwealth, Memorandum of Decision, Justice Herbert P. Wilkins, May 23, 1989.

18. Kenneth Casanova, "Narrative Statement" (Kenneth Casanova, Boston, personal papers, photocopies in author's possession); Nathan Talbot to Kenneth Casanova, April 11, 1986 (Casanova Papers); Rita Swan to Kenneth Casanova, December 3, 1988 (Casanova Papers).

19. Casanova, "Narrative Statement" (Casanova Papers); Massachusetts House of Representatives, Mr. McDonough of Boston, petition (accompanied by bill, House 4728 of John E. McDonough), An Act to Ensure the Provision of Medically Necessary Care for Children, 1989.

20. Casanova, "List of Organizations" (Casanova Papers).

21. Swan to Massachusetts CHILD Members, March 27, 1989 (Casanova Papers); Bernier to Salvatore DiMasi, May 3, 1989 (Casanova Papers); Edward A. Penn, M.D., President, American Academy of Pediatrics, to Michael LoPresti, Senate Chairman, Joint Legislative Committee on Judiciary, April 21, 1989 (Casanova Papers); Edward J. Brennan, Jr. to Ken Casanova, April 24, 1989 (Casanova Papers); Joseph J. O'Connor, M.D., to Salvatore DiMasi, April 21, 1989 (Casanova Papers); other organizations that joined the coalition to amend included the American Society of Law and Medicine, Larry Gostin to Salvatore DiMasi, May 4, 1989 (Casanova Papers); see also *Journal of the American Medical Society* 264 (1990): 1226, 1233–34.

22. Sheila Decter to Bryon Rushing, May 31, 1989 (Casanova Papers); Rabbi Simeon J. Maslin, "Mysterious Beliefs," *Jewish Exponent,* May 18, 1990, 37, 65.

23. Eli Newberger to Joint Committee on Judiciary, March 27, 1989 (Casanova Papers); Leonard H. Glantz to Salvatore DiMasi, May 1, 1989 (Casanova Papers); Dershowitz is quoted in, David Ollinger, "Christian Science on Trial," *St. Petersburg Times,* June 4, 1989; this article was reprinted and distributed to the Judiciary Committee by Casanova.

24. The following are included in the Casanova Papers: Dear XX, "I am asking your organization or individuals within it to support H.B. 4728," March 4, 1989; Dear [Legislator], "I am following-up our recent telephone conversation," October 9, 1989; Dear [Legislator], "I am enclosing some additional material," August 7, 1989; "United States Supreme Court decisions that children cannot be deprived of necessary medical care," undated; "House Bill 4728 Fact Sheet," 1989; Dear Representative, "I very much want to thank you for your efforts on behalf of H.B. 4728," August 30, 1989; "Positions of Judiciary Committee Members," 1989.

25. Official membership numbers have not been made public since the 1930s; estimates place the number of members from two hundred thousand to five hundred thousand, but the number may be smaller; David Margollick, "Death and Faith, Law and Christian Science," *New York Times,* August 6, 1990; Doris Sue Wong, "Judge Keeps Manslaughter Charge against Christian Science Parents," *Boston Globe,* April 23, 1989; Shubow, "Report on Inquest," 16.

26. "Some Thoughts About the Accommodation of Religious Practices," First Church of Christ, Scientist, Committee on Publication for Massachusetts (1988), 2 (Casanova Papers).

27. "From Your Christian Science Neighbors" (1988), 1–2 (Casanova Papers).

28. "Fact Sheet: Answers to Common Questions about Efforts to Repeal Religious Accommodation Laws," Committee on Publication for Massachusetts, 1990 (Casanova Papers).

29. Adam Gaffin, "Professor Says Religious Freedom at Stake in Christian Science Case," *Middlesex News,* 1988.

30. Robert Mendelsohn, "The People's Doctor," *Columbia Features,* March 10, 1988; Mendelsohn had enormous disdain for the medical profession; in 1979 he called doctors "dishonest, corrupt, unethical, poorly educated, and downright stupid more often than the rest of society." http://whale.to/vaccine.

31. Rita Swan, Dear CHILD Members, March 27, 1989; Professor Wendy K. Mariner of the Boston University School of Public Health and School of Medicine submitted written testi-

mony urging repeal: "It would be to the legislature's credit to repeal it before a court has the opportunity to strike it down as unconstitutional." "Testimony Before the Massachusetts Joint Committee on Judiciary Concerning House Bill 4728," 5 (Casanova Papers).

32. Casanova, "Testimony for 1989, Judiciary Comm. Hearing" (Casanova Papers).

33. Rita Swan, Dear CHILD Members, March 27, 1989.

34. "Member List, Joint Committee on Judiciary, 1989" (Casanova Papers); Casanova, "Summary of 1990," and Casanova to Dear XXX, June 21, 1990; the coalition's spring 1990 bill (H.B. 3519) was sent to the Joint Committee on Health Care; Casanova to Dear XX, March 20, 1990 (Casanova Papers); Renee Loth, "Faith, Science Clash on Child-Neglect Proposal," *Boston Globe,* April 12, 1990; M. E. Malone, "Legislators' Panel Sends Neglect Bill to Court," *Boston Globe,* April 24, 1990.

35. Doris Sue Wong, "Christian Science Couple Ask Court to Quash Statements in Son's Death," *Boston Globe,* December 5, 1989; under questioning during the motion hearings, Nathan Talbot revealed he had visited District Attorney Newman Flanagan's office in an attempt to head off an investigation of Robyn Twitchell's death, Charles Craig, "Church Leader Attempted to 'Head Off' Investigation," *Boston Herald,* February 7, 1989.

36. Alex Beam, "Damage Control," *Boston Globe,* February 9, 1990; "Why Is Prayer Being Prosecuted in Boston?," *Boston Globe,* April 11, 1990; Eddy, *Science and Health,* 142–44.

37. Alan Dershowitz, "Let's Not Sacrifice Kids to Religion," *Boston Herald,* April 16, 1990.

38. Doris Sue Wong, "Twitchell Trial to Test Child-Rearing Law," *Boston Globe,* April 15, 1990; Associated Press, "Trial of Couple in Son's Death Called Attack on Christian Science," *Chicago Tribune,* April 16, 1990.

39. Associated Press, "Trial of Couple in Son's Death," *Chicago Tribune,* April 16, 1990.

40. The *Boston Globe* challenged Judge Hamlin's order closing jury selection; Doris Sue Wong, "Twitchell Jurors to Be Chosen Publicly," *Boston Globe,* April 18, 1990; Charles Craig, "Potential Jurors in Christian Science Case Asked about Beliefs," *Boston Herald,* April 19, 1990; Chris Dickinson, "Inside the Twitchell Trial," *Boston Phoenix,* September 7, 1990.

41. Doris Sue Wong, "A Couple's Faith Is Key as Twitchell Trial Opens," *Boston Globe,* May 5, 1990.

42. Wong, "A Couple's Faith Is Key." Clearly unhappy with Klieman's reference to *Legal Rights,* Judge Hamlin cautioned the jury: "That is not the law of the Commonwealth."

43. Doris Sue Wong, "Twitchell Boy May Have Been Dead Hours Before Help Arrived, Jury Told," *Boston Globe,* May 8, 1990.

44. Doris Sue Wong, "Doctor Testifies in Twitchell Trial That Boy's Illness Was Treatable," *Boston Globe,* May 9, 1990; Doris Sue Wong, "Child's Death Called Preventable 'Catastrophe,'" *Boston Globe,* May 16, 1990; Globe Staff, "Doctor Testifies in Twitchell Case," *Boston Globe,* May 17, 1990; Dr. Johan G. Blickman, a defense witness, rebutted testimony of medical experts for the prosecution by arguing that Robyn suffered an illness that strikes suddenly and that radiology tests can successfully detect the presence in only 15 percent of the people who have it, Doris Sue Wong, "Twitchell Witness Rebuts Experts," *Boston Globe,* June 9, 1990.

45. Doris Sue Wong, "Twitchells Said to Have Discussed Doctor," *Boston Globe,* May 18, 1990; Doris Sue Wong, "Witnesses Testify on Statements Made by Christian Science Couple," *Boston Globe,* May 22, 1990. The defense sought unsuccessfully to suppress Dery's and Power's statements because they provided the foundation for the prosecution's case.

46. Charles Craig, "Christian Scientist Tells Court Church Allows MD Visits," *Boston Herald,* May 11, 1990.

47. Rita Swan, "Twitchell Convicted," *Children's Healthcare Is a Legal Duty,* no. 3 (1990): 12. Charles Craig, "Healer Tried Prayer to Bring Back Dead Child," *Boston Herald,* May 12, 1990.

48. Doris Sue Wong, "Practitioner Describes Sick Child's Last Breath," *Boston Globe,* May 12, 1990.

49. Craig, "Healer Tried Prayer"; Charles Craig, "Twitchell Boy Appeared Cured, Witness Testifies," *Boston Herald,* May 13, 1990.

50. Doris Sue Wong, "Baby Sitters Say Twitchell Boy Appeared Normal," *Boston Globe*, May 30, 1990.

51. Doris Sue Wong, "Accused Father Tells of Son's Death; Twitchell Breaks Down Describing Final Hours," *Boston Globe*, May 31, 1990.

52. Doris Sue Wong, "Twitchell Sought Treatment for Self," *Boston Globe*, June 1, 1990.

53. Doris Sue Wong, "Twitchell Testifies He Believed Spiritual Healing Was Lawful," *Boston Globe*, June 2, 1990; *Commonwealth v. Twitchell*, 416 Mass. 114, 127 (1993); Swan, "Twitchell Convicted," 18.

54. Charles Craig, "Dad: I'd Consider Medicine," *Boston Herald*, June 5, 1990; Doris Sue Wong, "Twitchell Says with 2d Chance, He'd Seek Doctor for Son's Illness," *Boston Globe*, June 5, 1990; Swan reports the church created an 800 telephone number so that church members could access information related to David Twitchell's testimony, Swan, "Twitchell Convicted," 18.

55. Manny Garcia, "Care Might Not Have Saved Boy," *Boston Globe*, June 13, 1990; Amy Callahan, "Doctor Says Boy Had Signs of Injury," *Boston Globe*, June 14, 1990.

56. Swan, "Twitchell Convicted," 21–24; Doris Sue Wong, "Twitchell Boy Moaned," *Boston Globe*, June 28, 1990.

57. Charles Craig, "Deliberations Set in Twitchell Trial," *Boston Herald*, July 2, 1990; Doris Sue Wong, "Twitchell Case Goes to Jury," *Boston Globe*, July 3, 1990; Bella English, "Wronged Rights a Tougher Case," *Boston Globe*, June 25, 1990.

58. Charles Craig, "Twitchells' Fate in Jury's Hands," *Boston Herald*, July 3, 1990; Wong, "Twitchell Case Goes to Jury."

59. Kiernan, "Notes for Closing Argument," Twitchell Trial, 1990" (Casanova Papers).

60. Wong, "Twitchell Case Goes to Jury"; Swan, "Twitchell Convicted," 25.

61. Wong, "Twitchell Case Goes to Jury"; Doris Sue Wong, "Twitchell Jury Twice Asks Judge's Guidance," *Boston Globe*, July 4, 1990.

62. Doris Sue Wong, "Christian Science Couple Convicted in Son's Death," *Boston Globe*, July 5, 1990; Elizabeth Neuffer, "Verdict Seen as Fueling National Debate," *Boston Globe*, July 5, 1990; Charles Craig, "Twitchells Guilty, Convicted of Manslaughter in Son's Death," *Boston Herald*, July 5, 1990; Doris Sue Wong, "Judge Indicates Twitchells Will Get Probation," *Boston Globe*, July 6, 1990. Five weeks after the verdict, a juror named D'Ambrosio regretted her vote to convict and charged Judge Hamlin with bias, Doris Sue Wong, "Juror's Claim of Biased Judge Spurs No Action," *Boston Globe*, August 11, 1990.

63. Wong, "Christian Science Couple Convicted."

64. Craig, "Twitchells Guilty"; Harvey Dickson, "Judge Takes the Hard Line," *Boston Herald*, July 6, 1990.

65. Wong, "Twitchells Will Get Probation."

66. Doris Sue Wong, "Twitchell Sentence: 10 Years' Probation," *Boston Globe*, July 7, 1990.

67. Ellen Goodman, "Healing: Faith vs. Reason," *Boston Globe*, July 12, 1990.

68. Wong, "Twitchells Will Get Probation."

69. Editorial, "The Twitchell Tragedy," *Boston Herald*, July 5, 1990; 6, 1990. Tribe also argues that the belief–action dichotomy on which the prosecution relied is "at best an oversimplification," Laurence Tribe, *American Constitutional Law*, 2d ed. (New York: Foundation Press, 1988), 1184.

70. Neuffer, "Verdict Seen as Fueling Debate"; Alice McQuillan, "Child Rights Leaders Hail Verdict," *Boston Herald*, July 6, 1990.

6. Repeal of Religious Exemptions

1. Arkansas and West Virginia enacted laws that permitted religious belief as an affirmative defense for child abuse and homicide; Ark. Code Ann. sec. 5-10-101(a)(9) 1997; W.VA. Code, sec. 61-8D-2(d) 2004; a 1995 Oregon law (Or. Laws 657 [H.B. 2492]) allowed religious belief as

an affirmative defense against a charge of child abuse as well as manslaughter and homicide. In 1999 Oregon repealed five sections of its religions exemption law, and in 2011 lawmakers removed special legal protection for parents who treat seriously ill children with faith healing rather than providing medical care, but the most serious charge that can be brought against a parent is second-degree manslaughter; Rita Swan, "Victory in Oregon," *Children's Healthcare Is a Legal Duty,* no. 1 (2011): 1–7 (Doug and Rita Swan moved to Salem, Oregon, temporarily in order to help repeal the state's exemption law); and Shawn Marie, "Faith Healing and the Law: Ending Oregon's Double Standard," blog.oregonlive.com; in 1984 the Indiana General Assembly tried but failed to repeal its religious exemption statute. In *Bergmann v. State,* 486 N.E. 2d 653 (Ind. App. 1985), however, the court found religious exemption was a defense only for child neglect, Ind. Code 35-46-1-4, not for the crime of reckless homicide, Ind. Code 35-42-1-5. 1995 Or. Laws 657.

2. Michelle Bearden, "Cases Test Church–State Relationship," *Phoenix Gazette,* May 14, 1988; Jean Heller, "Abuse Laws Still Vague When Faith Is Involved," *St. Petersburg Times,* October 3, 1998.

3. Editorial, "Politics and Spiritual Healing," *Sacramento Bee,* September 2, 1992. Swan testified before legislative committees in Minnesota, South Dakota, Colorado, Maryland, Missouri, Rhode Island, Nebraska, Iowa, and Oregon. www.scienceinmedicine.org.

4. SDCL 26-8A-2 (2): A child whose parent fails to provide proper or necessary subsistence, supervision, education, or medical care for a child's health, guidance, or well-being falls within the legal definition of abused; SDCL 26-8A-3; SDCL 26-8A-4; SDCL 26-8A-2 (4); SDCL 25-7-16 (court may order medical treatment). A similar statute covered disabled adults, SDCL 22-46-4. Rita Swan, "South Dakota Is Number 1!" *Children's Health Care Is a Legal Duty,* no. 1 (1990): 10–13. For the sake of clarity, I use Joni Clark and Joni Cooke throughout, although in 1990 she was known as Joni Cooke Eddy and, after 2000, as Joni Cutler.

5. Rick Ross, "End Times Ministries and Where It All Began," First Coast News, Florida, November 4, 2008, www.rickross.com; Rick Ross, "Sioux Falls Woman Remembers End Times Control," March 10, 2006, www.rickross.com; Charles Meade died on April 10, 2010, at the age of 94; http://groups.google.com.

6. Mark Larabee, "The Battle over Faith and Healing, *The Oregonian,* November 28, 1998.

7. Ibid. Swan, "South Dakota Is Number 1!," 11. Greg Messore, "A Vision of the End of Time," Lake City Reporter, November 18, 1988, www.rickross.com; Mike Lynch, "Baby's Death Caused Mom to Leave Cult," *AAP* [American Academy of Pediatrics] *News,* June 3, 1990, 15.

8. Swan, "South Dakota Is Number 1!," 11–12.

9. Ibid., 12–13; *AAP News,* June 3, 1990, 3. The new law allowed a religious exemption for vaccination.

10. Swan, "South Dakota Is Number 1!," 13: On September 14, 1990, the South Dakota chapter of the American Academy of Pediatrics honored Rita Swan, Geri Smith, and Joni Clark [Cooke Eddy], Rita Swan, "Awards Given for South Dakota Repeal Work," *Children's Healthcare Is a Legal Duty,* no. 4 (1990): 9.

11. CAPTA, 42 U.S.C. 5101; Rita Swan, "Victory in Hawaii," *Children's Healthcare Is a Legal Duty,* no. 1 (1992): 1–2.

12. A 1983 CAPTA regulation left the choice of retaining or repealing religious exemption law to the state. The absence of an exemption no longer barred a state from obtaining federal money for child abuse prevention programs; 45 CFR 1340.2(d); Winona E. Rubin to Honorable Russell Blair, Chairperson, Senate Committee on Judiciary, February 14, 1992 (State of Hawaii Department of Human Services); Judy Lind to Russell Blair, February 13, 1992 (Department of Human Services, Child Welfare Services State Advisory Council); George Starbuck, M.D., to Russell Blair, February 17, 1992 (American Academy of Pediatrics–Hawaii Chapter).

13. Lori Nishimura, RE: S.B. 2883, Relating to Child Abuse, February 18, 1992 (Department of the Prosecuting Attorney).

14. Robert A. Herlinger to Russell Blair, Senate Judiciary Committee, February 18, 1992 (Christian Science Committee on Publication for Hawaii).

15. Swan, "Victory in Hawaii," 1–2; Swan provided legal material to Nishimura; The Court of Appeal cited the trial court's unpublished decision: *State of Minnesota v. Kathleen McKown, and others,* 461 N.W. 2d 720, 722–23.

16. Swan, "Victory in Hawaii," 2; Robert Herlinger to Honorable Wayne Metcalf, Chair, House Judiciary Committee, March 12, 1992 (Christian Science Committee on Publication for Hawaii); Rubin, Nishimura, and Starbuck also testified, and Swan provided guidance and information.

17. Nathan Talbot, "When Some Turn to Prayer," *Washington Post,* November 27, 1990; Rita Swan attempted to respond to Talbot; the *Post* editor Meg Greenfield rejected Swan's article, and Swan wrote her an angry letter, claiming bias, Rita Swan to Meg Greenfield, December 28, 1990 (Casanova Papers).

18. Alice McQuillan, "Twitchell Case Spotlights Plight of Child Advocates," *Boston Herald,* July 8, 1990; Bella English, "A Criminal Omission," *Boston Globe,* October 22, 1992; when, in 1987, two-year-old Laura Lynn Lazarovich was savagely beaten by her parents, O'Brien discovered child abuse was a misdemeanor, Don Aucoin, "Bill Aims to Get Tough on Child Abusers," *Boston Globe,* October 6, 1993; O'Brien's H.B. 5504, "An Act Prohibiting Certain Acts Against Children," 1989; Swan to O'Brien, November 7, 1989, and O'Brien to Swan, November 17, 1989 (Casanova Papers).

19. Jetta Bernier to Advocates for Children, July 9, 1990 (Casanova Papers).

20. Meeting of Child Advocates, Minutes, July 24, 1990 (Casanova Papers).

21. Casanova to Ed Brennan, August 5, 1990 (Casanova Papers); "Coalition to Repeal Exemptions to Child Abuse Laws," Minutes of October 23, 1990, Meeting" (Casanova Papers); "Answer to Twelve Common Questions About Massachusetts' Religious Exemption Law," March 1991 (Casanova Papers); Massachusetts Committee for Children and Youth (Fall/Winter 1990), 1. Some of the child advocacy groups—for example, the Massachusetts Society for the Prevention of Cruelty to Children, the Office of Children, and the Civil Liberties Union of Massachusetts—that earlier had rejected participation now joined CRECAL, "Death by Religious Exemption," Appendix 1 (January 1992); Ellen Goodman, "Healing: Faith vs. Reason," *Boston Globe,* July 12, 1990.

22. *In the Matter of Elisha McCauley,* 409 Mass. 134, 136 (1991).

23. Ibid., 137.

24. Kiernan to Casanova, January 17, 1991 (Casanova Papers); *Death by Religious Exemption: An Advocacy Report on the Need to Repeal Religious Exemptions to Necessary Medical Care for Children* (January 1992), 34–36, masskids.org.

25. House No. 2362, "An Act Relative to Neglected Children," 1991; Coalition to Repeal Exemptions to Child Abuse Laws, "Agenda," January 29, 1991 (Casanova Papers); CRECAL "Assignments," February 6, 1991 (Casanova Papers); Dear xxx, February 5, 1991 (Casanova Papers).

26. Wendy K. Mariner, "Testimony to House Judiciary Committee," March 23, 1991, 4, 8 (Casanova Papers); Karen Hudner, "H.B. 2362," March 25, 1991 (Casanova Papers).

27. Silvernail, "Comments on Public Testimony Offered by Proponents of H.B. 2362," (Casanova Papers).

28. Casanova to Dear XXX, May 1, 1991 (Casanova Papers); Jetta Bernier to CRECAL Members, May 29, 1991 (Casanova Papers); Jetta Bernier, Eileen Ouellette, Ginny Burns to CRECAL Members, June 3, 1991 (Casanova Papers).

29. William C. O'Malley, Massachusetts District Attorneys Association, May 13, 1991 (Casanova Papers); John A. Kiernan to National District Attorneys Association, Official Policy Position: Exemptions from Child Abuse Prosecution, July 14, 1991 (Casanova Papers).

30. Jetta Bernier to CRECAL Members, July 16, 1991, RE: [Brett] House No. 2610 and [O'Brien] House No. 3263.

31. Ibid.

32. Teresa M. Hanafin, "Bill Seeks to Eliminate Faith-Healing Shield: Group Opposes Religious Exemption," *Boston Globe,* December 12, 1991.

33. Geline W. Williams, Assistant District Attorney to Representative Joseph B. McIntyre, June 2, 1992 (Casanova Papers); *Journal of the House,* Monday, June 8, 1992, House No. 5597.

34. Casanova to Dear Senator, June 18, 1992 (Casanova Papers); Casanova to Dear Senator, June 19, 1992 (Casanova Papers); Warren Silvernail to Dear Senator, June 22, 1992 (Casanova Papers).

35. *Senate Calendar,* June 22, 1992, #353, 14, "Senate, 1992, Yeas and Nays," First Reconsideration H.B. 5597, June 22, 1992; motion to reconsider Melconian amendment fails, 17–13; Jetta Bernier to Dear Senator, November 4, 1992. (Casanova Papers).

36. *Senate Calendar,* November 16, 1992, #353, 37; Bernier to Dear Senator, November 18, 1992 (Casanova Papers); Casanova, "Positions of Senators," November 1992, Senate, 1992, 16 Yeas and 15 Nays (Casanova Papers).

37. Edward J. Brennan Jr. to Jetta Bernier, Geline Williams, John Kiernan, Helen Rees, November 20, 1992 (Casanova Papers).

38. Jeff Jacoby, "Spiritual Healing and the Law," *Boston Herald,* November 23, 1992; Bella English, "No Excuses for Child Abuse," *Boston Globe,* November 30, 1992; Paul Reid, "Child Abuse, Religion and the State," *Boston Tab,* December 8, 1992; "Your View," *Boston Herald,* December 27, 1992.

39. Brennan to Bernier, December 2, 1992 (Casanova Papers).

40. *Journal of the Senate,* 1992–93, 1530.

41. Judge Hamlin ruled that the Twitchells had not been denied the right to a fair trial; that her instructions were not biased; and the public charge of bias by two jurors was after-the-fact unhappiness with the verdict, Doris Sue Wong, "Judge Denies Christian Scientists a New Trial in Their Son's Death," *Boston Globe,* October 7, 1992. Commonwealth v. David and Ginger Twitchell, Brief for the Commonwealth on Appeal from the Superior Court Department of the Trial Court, 46, 48, 49.

42. Commonwealth of Massachusetts v. David R. Twitchell and Ginger Twitchell, Brief of Appellants David and Ginger Twitchell.

43. Ibid., 21–22.

44. Ibid., 23–24; Memorandum and Order on Defendants' Motion to Dismiss, 15.

45. Brief of Appellants, 51.

46. Ibid.,, 30–32.

47. Brief for the Commonwealth, 46–48.

48. Ibid., 48.

49. Ibid., 49–50.

50. Ibid., 57–58.

51. Doris Sue Wong, "Twitchells Ask Court to Overturn Conviction," *Boston Globe,* May 5, 1993.

52. Eric Fehrnstrom, "Gov. Proposes Stiffer Child Abuse Penalty," *Boston Herald,* April 3, 1993; Senate No. 219, "An Act Prohibiting Certain Acts Against Children"; "Information for your consideration about S 219, An Act prohibiting certain acts against children" (Casanova Papers); see also the remarks of Victor Westburg, who had replaced Talbot as the manager of the Committee on Publication: M. Victor Westberg, "Church and state: Reliance on God is authorized by the highest power there is, supreme Spirit," *Christian Science Sentinel,* June 28, 1993, 7, "It is man's inalienable right to practice the truth of divine Science to do God's will."

53. Victoria Benning, "Critics: Law Alone Won't End Child Abuse," *Boston Globe,* April 20, 1993; Eric S. Maxwell to Joint Committee on Criminal Justice, 1–3, April 14, 1993 (Casanova Papers).

54. Bernier to Dear Representative, April 21, 1993 (Casanova Papers).

55. Eric Fehrnstrom, "House OKs Bill Making Child Abuse a Felony," *Boston Herald,* May 13, 1993.

56. Committee on Publication, First Church of Christ, Scientist, "Information for your consideration about S 219," May 17, 1993, 1–3, and "Testimonies," B1, B5.

57. *Commonwealth v. David R. Twitchell,* 416 Mass. 114 (1993).

58. Ibid., 117–18; *Commonwealth v. Hall,* 322 Mass. 523, 528 (1948); *Commonwealth v. Gallison,* 383 Mass. 659 (1981).

59. *Commonwealth v. Twitchell,* 416 Mass. 114, 120, 121n9.

60. *Commonwealth v. Twitchell,* 416 Mass. 114, 122.

61. Ibid., 123–27; Wilkins noted that the defense failed to make an argument for admission of *Legal Rights* or ask for a jury instruction. Justice Nolan dissented, accusing the majority of "improperly straining" in concluding that the attorney general's opinion of 1975 might be understood to bar criminal prosecution in any circumstances. Ibid., 131.

62. Tom Coakley, "Christian Science Couple's Conviction in Death Overruled," *Boston Globe,* August 12, 1993; Editorial: "A Message for Christian Scientists," *Boston Globe,* August 13, 1993.

63. News Release, Ralph C. Martin, District Attorney, September 9, 1993 (Casanova Papers).

64. For the changes penciled into S. 219, see Committee on Bills in the Third Reading, October 4, 1993 (Casanova Papers); Bernier to Dear Senator, September 29, 1993 (Casanova Papers).

65. Don Aucoin, "Bill Aims to Get Tough on Child Abusers," *Boston Globe,* October 6, 1993; Editorial, "When Children Are Victims," *Boston Globe,* October 6, 1993.

66. Doris Sue Wong, "Spiritual Healing Provision Vetoed; Mass. Senate Vote Setback for Church," *Boston Globe,* October 19, 1993. Lees wrote an op-ed titled "Protecting Children and Religious Freedom," November 3, 1993, *Christian Science Monitor,* in which he claimed that the "rights Christian Scientists seek are those very rights the Founding Fathers recognized as essential to a free people." "Massachusetts Moves to Criminalize Severe Child Abuse: Becomes Third State to Repeal Religious Exemption," *MCCY* [Massachusetts Committee for Children and Youth] *News* (Winter 1993), 1.

67. "Massachusetts Moves to Criminalize Severe Child Abuse," *MCCY News,* 2.

68. Fehrnstrom, "House OKs Child Abuse Bill"; Herald Staff, "Senate Vote Toughens Penalties for Child Abuse," *Boston Herald,* December 2, 1993.

69. William Weld, Governor, to The Honorable House of Representatives, December 10, 1993 (Casanova Papers); Doris Sue Wong and Dan Aucoin, "Weld Bid on Law Faulted, Critics Hit Stance on 'Religious' Statute," *Boston Globe,* December 11, 1993; "Bay State Governor Vetoes Child-Abuse Bill," *Christian Science Monitor,* December 13, 1993; Bella English "Weld Flip-Flop May Risk Lives," *Boston Globe,* December 15, 1993; Peter Howe and Doris Sue Wong, "Senate OKs $120m Budget," *Boston Globe,* December 16, 1993, reported the Senate's vote overriding Weld's veto.

70. Videotape of House Session, December 14, 1993 (Massachusetts State Archives).

71. *Journal of the House,* December 14, 1993, and *Senate Journal,* 1993, "Yeas and Nays." Doris Sue Wong, "Rebuffed on Abuse Bill, Weld Still Will Sign It," *Boston Globe,* December 23, 1993; William Weld, Governor, to The Honorable Senate and House of Representatives, December 28, 1993 (Casanova Papers); Maryland repealed its religious exemption statute five months after Massachusetts; 1994 Bill Tracking MD H.B. 630, 408th Legislative Session; Dan Casey, " '94 Session: Big Issues Were Too Hot," *The Capital* (Annapolis, Md.), April 10, 1994.

72. Talbot, "When Some Turn to Prayer."

Conclusion: Religious Freedom and the Public Good

1. Michael W. McConnell, "The Origins and Historical Understanding of Free Exercise of Religion," *Harvard Law Review* 103 (May 1990): 1409; Douglas Laycock, "Continuity and Change in the Threat to Religious Liberty: The Reformation Era and the Late Twentieth

Century," *Minnesota Law Review* 80 (1995–96): 1047; Religious Freedom Restoration Act, 42 U.S.C. sec. 2000bb-1 (1993); *Employment Division v. Smith,* 494 U.S. 872 (1990); *City of Boerne v. Flores,* 521 U.S. 507 (1997).

2. Nancy Lofholm, "Faith Healing vs. Kids' Rights, Christian Scientists to Fight Bill Dropping Legal Shield For Parents," *Denver Post,* February 10, 2001; Rodney K. Smith, "Does Obama Really Care about Religious Freedom in America?" *Christian Science Monitor,* February 17, 2012.

3. *Sherbert v. Verner,* 374 U.S. 398, 410, 423, 419 (1963); the Supreme Court applied *Sherbert* to three additional unemployment compensation cases: *Thomas v. Review Board of Indiana Employment Division,* 450 U.S. 707 (1981); *Hobbie v. Unemployment Appeals Commission of Florida,* 480 U.S. 136 (1987); *Frazee v. Illinois Department of Employment,* 489 U.S. 829 (1989).

4. Jonathan A. Weiss, "Privilege, Posture, and Protection: 'Religion' in the Law," *Yale Law Journal* 73 (9164): 593; J. Morris Clark, "Guidelines for the Free Exercise Clause," *Harvard Law Review* 83 (1969): 327; *Wisconsin v. Yoder,* 406 U.S. 205 (1972). A parent's "liberty interest" dates from *Meyer v. Nebraska,* 262 U.S. 390 (1923); Shawn Francis Peters, *The Yoder Case: Religious Freedom, Education, and Parental Rights* (Lawrence: University Press of Kansas 2003).

5. Frederick M. Gedicks, "Religious Conservatives Misjudged the Court," *Christian Science Monitor,* July 18, 1991.

6. *Employment Division v. Smith,* 494 U.S. 872; McConnell, "The Origins and Historical Understanding," 1409, 1481–90, 1511–12, 1412, 1461–62; Philip A. Hamburger, "A Constitutional Right of Religious Exemption: An Historical Perspective," *George Washington Law Review* 60 (1991–92): 915, 917.

7. Laycock, "Continuity and Change," 1047, 1048, 1049, 1102.

8. Douglas Laycock, "Free Exercise and the Religious Freedom Restoration Act," *Fordham Law Review* 62 (1994): 883–904; Religious Freedom Restoration Act, 42 U.S.C. sec. 2000bb-1. (2000).

9. Marci A. Hamilton, *God vs. the Gavel: Religion and the Rule of Law* (New York: Cambridge University Press, 2005), 226.

10. Editorial, "Congress Defends Religious Freedom," *New York Times,* October 25, 1993; Peter Steinfels, "Clinton Signs Law Protecting Religious Practices," *New York Times,* November 17, 1993.

11. *Boerne v. Flores,* 521 U.S. 507, 520, 531, 532, 536. Linda Greenhouse, "Laws Are Urged to Protect Religion," *New York Times,* July 15, 1997; Robert Marquand, "Court Tests Limits of Religious Liberty," *Christian Science Monitor,* February18, 1997; Robert Marquand, "High Court Questions Reach of Religious Liberty," *Christian Science Monitor,* February 20, 1997.

12. Linda Greenhouse, "High Court Voids A Law Expanding Religious Rights," *New York Times,* June 26, 1997. Marci Hamilton, "Religious Reach," *Christian Century,* July 16–23, 1997, 644–45.

13. Lawrence J. Goodrich, "Church to Explain Its Value to World," *Christian Science Monitor,* June 8, 1994.

14. Monitor's View, "Bolstering Religious Freedom," *Christian Science Monitor,* July 21, 1999; Scott Baldauf, "Bolstering the Right to Worship," *Christian Science Monitor,* January 26, 1999; *Texas Civil Practice & Remedies Code Annotated,* sec. 110.010 (New York: Vernon's, 2010); *Pennsylvania Consolidated Statutes Annotated,* sec. 2406 (b) (New York: Westlaw, 2004); Hamilton, *God vs. the Gavel,* 181–83.

15. Nancy Lofholm, "Death of Teen in Sect Probed, Parents Belong to Church That Shuns Medical Care," *Denver Post,* February 7, 2001; Diane Carman, "A Healthy Devotion to Kids," *Denver Post,* February 8, 2001; Editorial, "Unholy Neglect," *Denver Post,* February 9, 2001; King James Bible, James 5:15.

16. Nancy Lofholm, "Faith-healing Case Ruled Homicide, Parents Kept Treatment from Mesa County Girl," *Denver Post,* February 13, 2001.

17. Lofholm, "Faith Healing vs. Kids' Rights."

18. Ibid. Owens served two terms as governor, 1999–2007.

19. Editorial, "Unholy Neglect."

20. Chuck Green, "No Penalty for Deadly Prayers," *Denver Post,* February 11, 2001.

21. Open Forum, "Faith Healing Bill," *Denver Post,* March 1, 2001.

22. Carman, "A Healthy Devotion to Kids"; Julia C. Martinez, "Faith Healing Bill Wins in House, Emotions Run High as Parental Limits Pass," *Denver Post,* February 23, 2001. Robert Lewis, a Christian Scientist, challenged the bill's purpose: "The sponsor of this bill has said it is not an attack on Christian Science. However, if that were the case, CHILD would not be represented here today. Rita Swan would not be here." Swan, *Children's Healthcare Is a Legal Duty,* nos. 1, 2 (2001): 11.

23. Martinez, "Faith Healing Bill Wins in House"; Editorial, "A Law to Protect Children," *Denver Post,* February 24, 2001; Views and News, "Colorado Repeals Abuse Statute's Religious Exemption," *AAP News,* 2001, 19:210.

24. Nancy Lofholm, "Faith-healing Death Prompts Charges, Parents Face Counts in Mesa County," *Denver Post,* March 10, 2001.

25. Views and News, "Colorado Repeals Abuse Statute's Religious Exemption," *AAP News,* 2001, 19:210; Julia C. Martinez, "Christian Scientists Reverse Stance, Leaders Back Faith-Healing Ban," *Denver Post,* March 16, 19, 2001.

26. Julia C. Martinez, "OK Faith-healing Bill, Senator Pleads, Parents Who Withhold Medical Care Would Lose Legal Shield," *Denver Post,* March 28, 2001; Editorial, "Faith Gives Way to Hope," *Denver Post,* March 29, 2001; Julia C. Martinez, "Faith-healing Bill Gets Owens' Signature," *Denver Post,* April 17, 2001.

27. Nancy Lofholm, "Faith-healing Case in Court, Couple Charged in Daughter's Death," *Denver Post,* March 30, 2001; Ellen Miller, "Teen Girl Died Because Sect's Beliefs Barred Medical Care," *Rocky Mountain News,* August 23, 2001; *Associated Press,* "Colo. Couple Sentenced to Probation," www.rickross.com, November 9, 2001.

28. Hamilton, *God vs. the Gavel,* 5, 35.

29. www.constitution.org. John Locke, *A Letter Concerning Toleration* (1689). Thomas Jefferson to James Madison, July 31, 1788, in Julian P. Boyd et al., *The Papers of Thomas Jefferson* (Princeton: Princeton University Press, 1956), 13:442–43. Hamilton, *God vs. the Gavel,* 260–79.

30. *Boerne v. Flores,* 521 U.S. 507, 539–40. Speaker of the House Dennis Hastert branded the courts "radical." Diana Henriques, "Religion Trumps Regulation as Legal Exemptions Grow," *New York Times,* October 8, 2006.

Index

Abrams, Ruth, 173–74
Ackerman, Beth, 23
Ahern, June, 31
Alabama, 189
Alpert, Norma, 53
American Academy of Pediatrics, 12, 65–66, 76, 136, 139, 156, 159, 163, 193
American Civil Liberties Union, 111
American Diabetes Association, 30
American Jewish Congress, 136
American Medical Association, 1, 159
Anderson, Madeline, 102
Andrews, John, 194
Aponte, Ruth, 193
Arizona, 19, 100–126, 155, 203n55
Arizona Attorneys for Criminal Justice, 113
Arizona Real Estate Bulletin, 124
Arizona Republic, 123
Arizona Supreme Court, 115–16, 121, 125
Arkansas, 219n1
Askew, Reuben, 45

bacterial meningitis, 6–7, 18–19, 31, 47, 53, 58, 65, 203n1
Bailey, Amanda, 194
Ball, William, 133
Baranco, Paul, 104–7, 117
Barnhart, Justin, 116
Barton, Dave, 102–3, 105–8, 123
Barton, Laura, 108
Bates, Amanda, 190, 192, 194
Bates, Gerald, 190
Bates, Randy and Colleen, 190, 194
"The Battered Child Syndrome" (JAMA article), 12
battered women, 168–69
Beard, William, 140
Beddow, Jean, 156, 158
Belatti, Richard, 156
Bellotti, Francis, 128–29, 176, 216n17
Benbow, Donald, 28–29

Bernier, Jetta, 19, 135–36, 162, 166–67, 175, 178, 180
Berry, Gayle, 192–93
Bessler, Max, 123–24
Biaggi, Mario, 26
Bird, Rose, 62
Blair, Russell, 160
Blaisdell, Linda, 130–32, 148
Blickman, Johan G., 218n44
Blood, Margaret, 163
blood transfusions, 164
Boehm, Edwin A., 101–3, 107–8, 212n9
Booth, Edward M., 29, 35–36
Boston Globe, 89, 129–30, 132, 149, 153, 163, 169, 178–79, 181
Boston Herald, 133, 141, 153, 162
Boston TAB, 169
Bowersock, Donald, 92
Brennan, Edward J., Jr., 136, 163, 167–69
Brennan, William, 14, 42, 185
Brenneman, Richard J., 204n17
Brett, James, 166
Brown, Edmund G. "Pat," 66
Brown, Jerry, 61–62, 203n2
Brown v. Laitner, 198n9
Budzyn, Lindsey Ellis, 111
Burger, Warren, 43, 213n26
Burton, John L., 75

Caine, Jonathan, 162–63
California: child abuse and neglect laws of, 47–48, 50–51, 53–54, 59–65, 67–73, 204n9, 205n44; religious exemptions and, 3, 18–19, 54, 56, 59–63, 65, 73–75, 118, 203n2; repeal efforts in, 155–56, 189; Supreme Court of, 16, 52, 59–60, 62–70, 74–75, 78, 140, 205n35, 206n61
California Department of Health Services, 53
California District Attorneys Association, 76
California Medical Association, 76
California Welfare and Institution Code, 51–52

ALAN ROGERS is a professor of history at Boston College, where he teaches American legal and constitutional history. He is author of several books, including *Murder and the Death Penalty in Massachusetts* (2008) and *Murder on Trial* (2005). Rogers is a Fellow and Overseer of the Massachusetts Historical Society.